Strangers in Paradise

Strangers in Paradise
Academics form the Working Class

Jake Ryan and Charles Sackrey

South End Press

Ryan, Jake.
Sackrey, Charles.
    Strangers in paradise.

    Includes bibliographies.
    1. College teachers--United States--Biography.   2. Social Mobility--United States.   3. Labor and laboring classes--United States.   4. College Teachers' socio-economic status--United States.
I. Title.
LA2311.R93   1984   305'.9372   84-14007
ISBN 0-89608-232-6
ISBN 0-89608-231-8 (pbk.)

Cover design by Bonnie Acker
Production at South End Press
Printed in Great Britain

SOUTH END PRESS/302 COLUMBUS AVE/BOSTON MA 02116

Acknowledgements

First and quite foremost, we acknowledge the contributors whose autobiographical essays comprise what is most important in this book. As we explain in our Preface, we received sixty-five such essays from our solicitation of them, and we used twenty-four here. Most, but not all, of the essays were written by the following people (listed in alphabetical order):

Mark Aldrich, Robert Ascher, Meb Bolin, Richard Brockhaus, Richard Butsch, Louis Casimer, Norris Clement, Jim Cornehls, Jim Dorris, Stephanie Grill, Jack Hamilton, Bob Hinckley, Davis Joyce, James Petras, Cadwell Ray, Lynn Rittenoure, Barbara Singer, Steve Stamos, Rick Tillman, and Charles Walker.

(A small number of our contributors, whose essays are used in the book, preferred not to have their names included here.)

Our contributors, were a mobile lot during their work lives, and they have taught at, among other campuses, the following ones (listed randomly):

Universidad Astonme (Guadalujara, Mexico), Universidad Agraria del Norte (Peru), Cornell University, Keele University (England), Rutgers University, Rider College, Ithaca College, State University of New York (Binghamton and Stony Brook), University of Texas (Arlington, Austin, Dallas, and El Paso), Oklahoma University, Bucknell University, University of Wisconsin (Madison), Smith College, Hampshire College, Massachusetts University (Amherst), Brown University, Bridgewater State University (Mass.), Southeastern University (Mass.), Central State College (Oklahoma), Catholic University (Puerto Rico), Eastern New Mexico University, Columbia University Teachers College, University of Pittsburg, University of Nevada (Reno and Las Vegas), California State College (San Bernadino and Bakersfield), University of Southwestern Louisiana, Sterling University (Scotland), Tulsa University, University of Idaho, University of San Francisco, University of Colorado, Union Graduate School, Wisconsin State College (Whitewater and Superior), Eastern Illinois University, Southern Illinois University, Washington University

(St. Louis), and University of Missouri (Columbus).

To all these people, and for all their work and their travels, we say, thanks, for quite literally the book could not have come to be had they not written most of it.

We would also like to acknowledge John Schall, our editor at South End Press, and Dan Clawson, the principal reader of the manuscript. John's early interest and ongoing advocacy and support of our project have kept us on the road to finishing it; and, without those we wouldn't have made it. Dan Clawson, a sociologist, gave our first real draft a reading some eighteen months ago, and his suggestions to us for a rewrite were utterly crucial in transforming our manuscript into a book. Carl Conetta at South End, our production coordinator, oversaw the various stages of forging the manuscript into galleys, page proofs, a book. He also gave our manuscript a reading at an important time, and we thank him for all his good work.

Other people have been helpful, too, either in typing or editing our work, in granting us travel money to traverse the one hundred thirty miles from Ithaca to Lewisburg, and so on. Such people are Bob Chambers, Ray Davis, Lillian Minnich, Sharon Seymour, Wendell Smith, Alice Van Buskirk, Ann Witkowski, and Mike Yarrow.

Lastly, we thanks our partners, Karen Adams and D. Toni Byrd. They work hard, fight the good fight against the various devils of our time, and we are better people because we know and love them.

Dedication

He said his name was
Horatio Alger
and we just said
'good luck.'

Table of Contents

Introduction

Primarily, this book is concerned with the issue of
social class mobility in the United States. It is also
concerned with the role and location of the community of higher education in class relationships. More
specifically, we hope to shed light on what happens to
people who are socially mobile when they choose academia
as their path to higher social station. In the United Staes, if
you are not "somebody," you might, of course, be "nobody,"
in the sense that you have the strong chance of suffering
endless indignities of powerlessness and the denial of your
very worth by others (and, often, even by yourself). Hence
class mobility questions are of great importance to people of
this and other modern capitalist societies.

In our times, the problem of claiming dignity for oneself
is particularly acute as ethnic sub-communities lose their
vitality, family farm life recedes further from memory and
the family itself loses much of its form, function and stability. Additionally, as community life disintegrates, occupational structure bears an increasingly greater burden as the
critical institutional arrangement providing reference points
for one's social status. Therein lies a serious contradiction,
indeed, since the opportunity for upward movement in the
class system has, for the most part, never been an individual
"right" except as it is celebrated in our national social
mythology. For every rags-to-riches story in the United
States, there are several jammed blocks of dilapidated

1

tenements filled with low income people, in the same desperate place where they started.

The myth of upward mobility asserts that in this land,
unfettered by a feudal past, though burdened by slavery
and genocide, all are free to rise to the highest level that
"their talents permit." No "artificial" obstacles stand in the
way. A complex ideological apparatus has evolved to etch
this message indelibly on the consciousness of us all. The
myth's function, of course, first and foremost, is to justify
the huge inequalities of income and political power that are
integral to a capitalist social order. It has the secondary
purpose of keeping the "no-bodies" in a state of political
impotence and frozen by self-contempt for their own failure,
rather than fired by righteous anger at their victimization.
No less importantly, the myth functions to make it appear
as though one's position in life were a consequence of a fair
game with all participants playing by the same rules, all
with the same starting points. Hence, it is the individual's
efforts and talent that are determinative, not the class into
which one is born.

In other words, the myth about upward mobility has,
among all its effects, one of central importance to us: it quite
simply denies the relevance of class as an arbiter of life's
chances. As we argue in detail later in this book, the bulk of
the evidence on social mobility that has been gathered over
the years refutes the typical belief about the mobility
mythology in two separate regards. To begin with, most
mobility occurs between strata within classes, or at the
"buffer zone," as Frank Parkin aptly puts it,[1] between
skilled blue collar workers, and low level nonmanual workers. Significant mobility in one life time, from blue collar to
professional/managerial realms, or from the working class
to the charmed circle of the powerful owning class, happens
rarely. Moreover, and not surprisingly, it is exceedingly rare
that the sons or daughters of the owning class end up down
at the bottom of the social heap.

Further, the *quality* of a human life is, we believe, largely formed by the chain of human need for autonomy,
creative opportunity and security in work, adequate diet,
decent housing, availability of sustaining health care,
meaningful education at all the several stages of one's life.

In fact, access to these constituent parts of life's quality is largely a funciton of inherited class position. And, obviously, since we do not get to choose a class to be born into—and since significant mobility is blocked to most people—our life experiences are importantly the outcome of a spin on the wheel of fortune. What is most striking to us is the durability of the justifying myth in the face of all the facts. And, one of our principal purposes is to challenge and thus to weaken a convenient but false claim about capitalist society, a claim which helps stabilize a system which promises so much and delivers so little to those without respectable standing.

In the larger framework of the book, we also seek to understand better the location and function of universities and colleges in class society. What is the academic ideal? What is the reality? For us, in our salad days, the ideal campus was a pretty little world set apart from the crass pursuits of the marketplace. Indeed, we assumed even as late as our graduate years the university or college to be a place where the concern for truth, justice and beauty came first; a world dedicated to teaching and to the intellectual growth of young people. Once there, however, we found much of college life a part of the very real capitalist world, a life where institutional aggrandizement, careerism, and denigration or miscomprehension of the teaching function were as often the rule as the exception. Further, we found the university to be a part of the ideological apparatus that sustains the myth of meritocratic placement, and in fact provides crucial certification of who is "somebody" and who is "nobody" in the order of things.

Nevertheless, we *also* found at universities key elements of what we had imagined the ideal university might be—libraries filled with books of every shade of opinion, and open to all; faculty and students who, some of the time anyway, actually engaged in the free exchange of all sorts of ideas; the true practicing of education, an activity that seemed to justify the pretty campuses and the cost of keeping them that way. It was an environment and a process that seemed even to justify the fact that all of us there had been given release time from the ordinary work of the world, on farms, in factories and offices, a laboring we depended on utterly to keep our classrooms clean, our mouths fed, our rent paid, our books printed, so that we might enjoy the great freedom to seek out the truth of things in an ordered space. Moreover, we both were committed to the university because we saw it as a final bulwark against the underlying dishonesty that characterizes so much of life in capitalist culture, in the marketplace and in the various levels of government. It was that aspect of the university life, its alleged commitment to people (reading, talking, and writing about the truth), that kept our commitment to it, in spite of gathering resentment at those players in the drama who, it appeared to us, had abandoned these "noble" purposes in order to parrot the behavior of, or to serve the needs of, the corporations and the state.

ii

The plan to write this book actually began with conversations over several years about the mixed blessing of being half-committed to our work, half-resentful over the fact that our workplace in many ways was so disappointing. Both of us as young academics had considered ourselves to be exceptionally lucky to have risen from non-professional families to middle-class careers. We were the "exceptions" upon which the American social mobility myth was based, members of the success elite, with the good fortune to be a "professor," bequeathed with all that such a role implies about ideals, values, and status. Why, then, were we so often not happy with our success? Sometimes, we even wondered outloud to each other whether the trip had been worth the toll. As our thoughts crystalized in these talks, we became more aware that our inability thoroughly to enjoy our great fortune had something to do with the mobility experience itself and with our work experience in schools with which we were affiliated, with our colleagues, bosses, students. We began exchanging outlines and other preparations for a writing project on the subject.

Then, about three years ago (1981), more detailed contours of this book began to take shape in our minds. Somewhere along that line, too, the title we ultimately used for the book popped into our conversations, for if nothing else, these talks had led us to see ourselves as "strangers" in the class we had entered; and though the academy might have looked like "paradise" through the lenses of our undergraduate perceptions, on close inspection it took another form entirely. Especially, we had discovered how many functions performed by the university promoted the maintenance of a class system that had borne heavily on our families, our friends and some of our colleagues.

Thus, as we prepared to write the book, we proceeded with the grim suspicion that the social mobility game as it is played in capitalist America makes losers of many of the winners. Others, in their own work, had pointed out this aspect of upward mobility, and Richard Sennett and Johnathan Cobb (in *The Hidden Injuries of Class*, 1970) had articulated the problem especially well in their analysis of working class life in and around Boston. Indeed, for our purposes, one small part of their book became a large and valuable idea for our own. Among the interviews with working class people used in their book, Sennett and Cobb talked at length with "Frank Rissarro," a middle-aged man who had experienced a measure of social mobility when he was made a bank loan officer after a long career as a meat cutter. Rissarro reported unambiguously that an important part of this experience in his new, higher, station was malaise and discomfort, that his success had been altogether different than his anticipation about it. Referring to Rissarro's situation, after his promotion, Sennett and Cobb wrote that:

> The real impact of class is that a man can play out *both* sides of the power situation in his own life, become alternatively judge and judged, alternatively individual and member of the mass. This represents the "internalizing" of class conflict, the process by which struggle between each man leads to struggle within each man.[2]

Sennett and Cobb's insightful rendering of this idea gave good form and meaning to vague notions that resided always in our discussion about the book taking shape. It became clear for us that to grow up working class, then to take on the full trappings of the life of the college professor, *internalizes the conflicts in the hierarchy of the class system within the individual, upwardly mobile person*. With this idea in mind, and with a yet undefined structure for our book, we began to wonder if other upwardly mobile academics had experienced similar feelings of displacement or dissatisfaction, and perhaps most importantly, internalized conflict.

In order to answer this question, we wrote over one hundred and fifty fellow academics, all of them at four year colleges and universities, all whom we knew, or had been told, had been raised in working class families. We started by contacting people whom we knew personally. From that group, we got other names, and we branched out in many directions, to their friends, to their associates, then to the friends of their friends, and so on. On a few occasions, we received calls or letters from people who had heard of our study at a professional meeting or elsewhere. To each member of this expanding group who were candidates for participation in our book, we sent a letter of invitation along with a sixteen page autobiographical essay written by one of our contributors which contained the kind of information we sought. (The letter is included in Appendix A.) We received about sixty-five written or taped responses, and from these we have selected twenty four for inclusion, either wholly or in edited form.

The essays have been selected for inclusion because each illuminates with clarity and thoughtfulness a theme or themes on which we have focused. Indeed, all the essays have different points of emphasis, strengths and weaknesses, and we have distributed them throughout the book according to their thematic relevance. Some autobiographies speak eloquently about mobility paths; some about internalized class conflict; others about disillusionment with the academy; still others about modes of accommodation or bitter struggles to maintain integrity in an institutionalized structure that appears often committed to the wrong values. In our view, these essays are perceptively keen and honest. Several are moving as they offer us a glimpse of the experience of class mobility and life in the academy.

iii

But, for all our broad reaching to invite one and all to write essays for us—an effort that spanned over two years—we must provide certain disclaimers concerning the results of our technique for gathering our pool of participants. To begin with, we make no pretense here that we have, in any scientific sense, a representative or random sample of academics who hail from working class backgrounds. Our respondents are predominantly social scientists, and a few are from the humanities. Of these twenty four contributors, over two thirds finished their graduate work *before* 1975 (most finished in the 1960s or before); of those remaining, all but one finished graduate school before 1980. Our contributors, then, are a specialized subset historically, as well as in other ways. And in Chapters One and Two, we shall provide the setting and details of the various paths this subset took to the campus. Other disclaimers need making, too. There are no engineers in the book (though remarkably, several began on that career path), nor are there natural scientists or mathematicians among our contributors. More of a problem, it might appear, we have no autobiographies from black people, and only two from women. The question of the lack of representativeness of our group, in both these cases, deserves attention.

First, concerning black academics, we are certain that it does not come as news that there are comparatively few blacks teaching at the predominantly white colleges and universities from which it happened we solicited our responses. Indeed, in 1980, less than five percent (about one of every twenty three) college or university professors were black people. The obvious reasons for the exclusion of blacks from our own sample do not derive principally from our technique, however informal; rather, they can in large measure be understood in terms of the racialist exclusionary traditions of the culture, as well as the essential workings of U.S. capitalism and the role that it casts for black working class people. For example, Manning Marable,[3] in a powerful manner, sufficiently explains the tendency for capitalist dynamics to contain the vast majority of blacks at a level of menial work in the social division of labor. Marable shows that this tendency has often been reinforced by traditional black institutions such as those churches and colleges that have urged accommodation to the structural hierarchy of U.S. capitalism. And when one adds other structural obstacles to black social mobility, which in large measure are contingent upon high levels of academic accomplishment and many years of formal, expensive professional training, the prospects become yet more limited and grim. Disorganized, underfunded schools reflecting the public policy biases against the poor, especially the black poor, early tracking into non-academic curricular concentrations, racially and culturally "stacked" standardized testing, the burden of the cost of higher education, even public higher education, the racist attitudes which impose negative stereotypes on black students—all combine to create huge barriers to entrance into the academic community at the professorial level.*

In a word, what actually happens to a black academic from the working class, though tangential in important places to what happens to an academic from the white working class, is obviously a *vastly* different human experience. Moreover, and to everyone's fortune, black writers themselves have often chronicled the trials of mobility into the U.S. upper classes, including university life, and to start with we would point our readers especially to the three recent books by Monte Piliawski, Roger Wilkins, and George Davis and Glegg Watson; and to Stacy Palmer's article, "In the Fishbowl: When Blacks work in Predominantly White Colleges."[4]

We have used only two essays in our book by women and that fact, too, bears explanation. By 1980, only one-third of all U.S. professors were women, and probably all our readers can cite the principal reasons why women are underrepresented in the academy as faculty members.

---

*Some quantitative details on these matters are available—for the 1973-1974 period. See Institute for The Study of Educational Policy, *Equal Educational Opportunity for Blacks in U.S. Higher Education: An Assessment* (Washington, D.C.: Howard University Press, 1976).

Readers know, too, that such reasons in some ways parallel those for black underrepresentation.

Certainly *working class* women are much more rigidly cast by class traditions in subordinate and menial roles, and by the workings of current capitalist labor markets, than are their counterparts in the higher reaches. First, of course, the *common* role of women is the reproductive one, and this holds an *especially* central position in working class families, along with the family goal for its girls of a good marriage, good reputation and all the rest. As a consequence, in working class homes, female children are less likely to be identified as the source of deliverance for a family to a higher social level, unless of course they marry upward. They are less likely to be the object of financial sacrifice essential to support many years of schooling beyond the high school level. Finally, in working class families, options to housewifery are more likely perceived as a job in the burgeoning service sectors of the work force than going through all the struggles involved in the acquisition of a Ph.D.

As we have said, everyone knows these and other reasons why more women, from all classes, are not in the academy in proportionate numbers, and, even more so, why such barriers would be particularly great for working class women. Yet, in our own gathering of autobiographical essays, we ended up with two exceptionally good ones from women. Had the two women, whose essays we have used, focused on matters of *gender*, rather than on *class* issues, we might have considered not using them, for in such a case they could not have been anything remotely representative of the opinion of academic women on that dimension of their experience. However, as our readers eventually will see, our two women contributors mostly concentrated on experiences and feelings that we believe are common to the academic from the working class *as an outsider* rather than *as a woman*. And, for those wanting greater detail about the experience of women in the world of professional occupations, where the focus *is* gender, they might well start with Susan Easton, Joan Mills, and Diane Winocur[5] and go from there to a quick expanding literature.

In other words, our study is limited to the experience of twenty four white people (almost all of them males), all of whom write about being professors at four year colleges or universities. We, therefore, do not pretend that we speak for black or female academics from *any* class backgrounds. Nor, do we pretend to speak, except indirectly, to the experiences of teachers at two year colleges, black, white, woman, or male. Of course, we are confident that our book, with all its voices, will speak clearly to many academics from the working class; we are confident, too, that studies such as this one could well be beneficial for *all* working class people who have left the old neighborhoods for other, more high-toned ones. That, of course, remains to be seen.

iv.

As well as being unrepresentative racially and sexually, we have a disproportionate number of social scientists among our autobiographers, and that is further reason why our book is not representative ideologically or methodologically. Scientists might want more precision, artists more imagery, engineers more computer runs, and *everyone* would prefer, it is our guess, fewer prose offerings by social scientists. Yet despite all these limitations we've mentioned, we are quite confident that this book fills an important need. The myriad *details* of the lives of those internally conflicted by social promotion from the working class have not often been told. For example, two especially well-known books which do deal with class experience, ones by Sennett and Cobb (mentioned above) and Lillian Rubin[6] do not deal extensively (and, in the case of Rubin, not at all) with the particular problems attached with upward class mobility.

In fact, almost all the literature on class mobility is in the form of aggregated data. And, in such aggregation, it is perhaps easier to define with some workable precision the actual boundaries of the class divisions. Indeed, such data collection can not be done *unless* neat boundaries are erected to separate one class from those above and beneath it. In our own work, however, since we dealt with several *individual* stories, in some cases the class background of our contributors was somewhat ambiguous. A word here about how we engaged the issue is merited.

In most cases, to be sure, the class positions were clear, and neatly so: parents both educated at grade twelve or below, wage earners, blue collar occupations, modest income, etc. Yet, for others the boundary was not as simply discerned. Let us cite two examples. One respondent is from a New England family that has been all over the sociological map: factory owners, bankers, respected citizens. Bankruptcy wipes out the property base of family wealth. Our respondent's father fails several times to secure a comfortable middle class position and ends up eking out a living in a small grocery store which he owns. His mother is a college graduate but only on occasion works outside the home in a professional capacity.

Some of our respondents are from farm families. One in particular is from a small farm within the Pennsylvania Dutch cultural tradition. There is family ownership of land, a decent level of sustenance and income. Yet, the work involved in maintaining the family farm is backbreaking, dawn to dusk. The parents are not highly educated. They do not participate meaningfully in the life style one might associate with the middle class: that is, they are removed from all the more prominent feature of middle or upper class life in the U.S.

Our resolution of these ambiguities with class location was to accept as valid our respondents' own sense of their distance from the middle classes, their own sense of identification with something they called the "working class," and their powerful sense of being an "outsider" in their professional lives. These criteria seemed to us quite sufficient for inclusion, given the often ambiguous nature of the circumstances of their parents' socio-economic situation, and the complexity of contemporary class structure. For certain, all our respondents have not travelled the same social distance. Yet those who have moved upward from the slippery terrain between the upper ranges of the working class and the lower realms of the middle class, have stories to tell that have the same resonances as those from the lower depths. Some see themselves as interlopers, others as traitors or miscast members in someone else's play. They too have endured the discumbobulations of the class mobility experience.

v.

Yet, another side of the question of class definition gave us pause: the issue of the *place* of intellectuals and the academy itself in the U.S. class structure. We recognize, of course, that there are a wide variety of institutions that comprise academia and that there is much variability in the quality of work life, and in the relationship of different institutions to power and privilege. Our decision was to see all academics at different levels or strata as within the same class, the *professional/managerial class*, since their most common *vital* function is one of reproducing capitalist cultural relations. In Chapters Three and Four we develop the basis and implications of these determinations more fully, and give credit to those who gave definition to some of the basic conceptual language of our analysis.

vi.

Lastly, in somewhat formal terms, our procedure for recruiting participants was a method of social inquiry that Lindblom and Cohen have called "systematic social commentary and criticism," rather than "systematic data gathering and reporting."[7] Their bifurcation makes sense to us, and we believe that what gives *systematic* quality to our social commentary and criticism is the use of "class analysis" to illuminate or explain the conflicts experienced by upwardly mobile people. By such an analysis, we mean to suggest that given the reality of capitalist societies, certain generalizations can reasonably be made about the class orderings that inevitably characterize those societies. For example, our study is rooted in the assumptions that relations between classes are antagonistic; that classes are discernible entities, even if where people fit is not always clear; that the relations between classes will in crucial form shape the life of the academic profession; and that the experience of class mobility can best be understood seen through perspectives derived from these and other consequences. In sum, there are sets of common problems mandated by the foundational structure of society, class relationships that shape and influence, to varying degrees, *all* experiences of mobility from the realms of working class life to the professional-managerial class. The framework for this analysis is developed in Chapter Four, and it is an essential point of departure in our assessment of the essays.

These, then, are our introductory definitions and disclaimers. We write from a shadowy position, off to the side and down a path which has never been trod by our footsteps. But, even with the several caveats offered for consideration by our readers, we write also from what we believe is a rock-solid position, the view that when people write honestly about things they know well—such as about their own life experience—they very often write something worth attention. And when we focus the lenses of class analysis on the stories a richer understanding emerges.

Whatever it *is*, life in our society is not simply "good," or "bad;" neither is it simply "alienated" or "free." Life, singly and collectively, is an infinity of details that are shaped in society by things and ideas, among the most important of the latter the myth that there is an escape from the influence of social class on a person's life experience. We do not believe that such an escape mechanism exists in U.S. society, nor for those in any other society that coheres around a discernible system of social classes. And, we believe that the truth of this contention is contained with some force in what follows.

Notes

1. Frank Parkin, *Class Inequality and Political Order*, (New York: Preager, 1971), p. 56.

2. Sennett and Cobb, *The Hidden Injuries of Class*, (New York: Random House, 1973), pp. 97-98.

3. Manning Marable, *How Capitalism Underdeveloped Black America*, (Boston: South End Press, 1982).

4. Monte Piliawski, *Exit 13*, (Boston: South End Press, 1983); Roger Wilkins, *A Man's Life: An Autobiography*, (New York: Simon and Schuster, 1982); George Davis and Glegg Watson, *Black Life in Corporate America*, (New York: Anchor Press, 1982); Stacey E. Palmer, "In the Fishbowl: When Blacks Work in Predominantly Black Colleges," *Chronicle of Higher Education*, September 14, 1983, p. 19.

5. Susan Easton, et.al., *Equal to the Task: How Working Women Are Managing in Corporate America*, (New York: Seaview Press, 1982).

6. Lillian Rubin, *Worlds of Pain: Life in the Working Class Family*, (New York: Basic Books, 1977).

7. Charles Lindblom and David K. Cohen, *Usable Knowledge*, (New Haven: Yale, 1979), pp. 10-39.

Part I

Part 1:
Introduction

I n Chapter One, "Social Change and Higher Education After World War II," we present our thoughts about the factors that have spawned and shaped class mobility experience into the academy. Initially, we offer an assessment of particularly relevant historical circumstances since the end of World War II. While we do not wish to deny the talents and dedication of the traveler across class lines, we do insist that the individualistic, meritocratic explanation of success that is integral to both official dogma and popular belief falls considerably short of explaining the reasons why people "get ahead" during that time period. The historical period we examine is unique in several respects, as we shall point out. Without the combination of factors friendly to mobility into the academy, most of our respondents simply would not have made the trip. The crucial significance of military experience, G.I. bills, federal loans, the so-called post-war "baby-boom," and the subsequent expansion and transformation of higher education, to mention a few, were all powerful contributors to the social ascent of our respondents.

After sketching these circumstances and their implications, we present in Chapter Two, "Upward Bound," an initial set of autobiographical essays which focus on the origins, family lives and ultimately on the mobility paths of selected respondents. We will see here the expanse of social distance covered in a short period of one lifetime and the

rich interplay of talent, excited discovery of the world of
ideas, the role of public support, expanded personal horizons, luck, and even misfortune that blazed the mobility
path, leading, often circuitously, to the gates of academia.
These essays vividly capture the complex texture of the
experience and they come much closer to the essential truth
of this kind of story than any hackneyed dogma of individualistic striving and simple meritocratic social promotion.

We then return in Chapter Three, "The Academic Work
Process," to the analysis of what we think is crucial to the
understanding of the career and of the class mobile person
who becomes an academic. Though we write from the
assumption that the American capitalist social order importantly shapes the conditions of work life within the university, we do not mean to deny there are elements unique to
universities that are shaping influences, such as the tenure
system. Yet, the increased dependency on hierarchy, epi-
tomized by the rise of "managerialism," with its narrow
efficiency measures—faculty careerism, narrow specialization of function, worship of prestige and academic status
ranking—all derive their particular form in our view from
the culture of capitlaism in which the university is embed-
ded. As a consequence, we will argue that these problems have special consequences for the class mobile person
within the academy. In this third chapter we will examine
the ways in which capitalist social realtions *mandate* circumstances that an academic must address by constructing
a strategy of accommodation and/or resistance which can
minimize distress.

In Chapter Four, "The Class Structure and Internalized
Conflict," we extend and make more particular the argument that the ordinary workings of the capitalist social
structure present a series of dilemmas for the class mobile
academic. These dilemmas are inevitable and unavoidable.
We claim that they are inherent in the class mobility experience and that they must be recognized and engaged if the
traveler across class lines is to rest with some degree of
comfort in his or her new found social niche. Specifically, we
investigate the location and function of the university in
capitalist social and cultural relations and the problem of
internalized class conflict, two intimately related concepts

which greatly and sometimes insidiously pervade the lives of the class mobile person. All of this analysis is intended principally to offer a useful context for reading the autobiographical essays which follow in Part II.

CHAPTER 1

U.S. Higher Education After World War II

Significant social change unfolded in the United States in the period immediately after World War II, changes which all but transformed the social landscape. We do not wish to engage the entire list of transforming factors, for most are well-known developments. Yet, to set our context, we must at least note some of the more significant ones. It is a period heralded as the "Age of Affluence," in which the Gross National Product underwent an unprecedented, sustained expansion; the pace of technological change accelerated and with it the increasing replacement of labor power by machines in the fabrication process; the automobile culture burgeoned; the movement of population from rural to urban and suburban concentrations changed the "small-town," rural face of the nation. The modernization of southern agriculture propelled segments of the population north, changing the geographic distribution of racial minorities within the society. Interventionist domestic policies of the state, initiated under the "New Deal," became a more permanent part of the political consensus than some may have suspected. Nuclear weapons created a new dimension to gobal politics, and the "Cold War" dominated much of U.S. political and social policy and thinking. There were also rumblings in the social order initiated by claims by racial minorities, women and others for greater social equality. And significantly, for our purposes, it was a period in which Americans went to college in greater numbers and in greater proportions than ever before.

In this chapter and in Chapter 3, we will sketch the great expansion in college attendance and place its development in the context of other dramatic events which shape this period in American life. Most of the autobiographies in later chapters were written by people who managed to leave the lower regions of the social order for higher realms in this period of change. Thus, to understand their mobility experience, it is important to note these historic circumstances, the context of public policies, changing trends in the demand for labor, demographic and economic patterns that defined that setting. The fact of our concern with this structure also intends to emphasize that personal straining for social promotion, no matter how bright and enterprising the aspirants, is in most cases fruitless without attendant friendly circumstances. One's "life chances," as Ralf Dahrendorf has called them, are "opportunities for individual growth, for the realization of talents, wishes and hopes, and these opportunities are provided by social conditions."[1] Without doubt, this book was written because a friendly context existed in the socio-historical mix of things, thirty odd years ago. And, sadly, it is worth noting that bright and starry-eyed young men and women from the working class, and other classes as well, might better think again if they wish to make their mark in academic life, for now the context for such a choice is a good bit less friendly. We will return to this matter later in the chapter.

We also wish to note that the changes that have taken place in higher education over roughly the past thirty five years have altered substantially the conditions affecting career entrance, and that the career itself is changing. In part, at least, this change is in response to the various changes in the larger society; and, in part, it results from the inexorable tendency of a highly developed capitalist society to penetrate every social institution. For example, today the values of the marketplace mesmerize students and faculty alike, more than ever before, and the blithering chatter of the new academic managers about "systems efficiencies" contend with the more traditional musing about ideals and transcendence. Hence, we need also to talk about these changes *within* universities to understand some of our respondents' reactions to their chosen work.*

i.

We can start our brief inquiry with a question: What does the old guard—*any* old guard—think when the new-comers enter the camp? Here's one example. At a 1981 conference in Lisbon, Portugal, of the International Council on the Future of the University, John A. Passmore, philosophy professor at the Australian National University, remarked that the rapid expansion of the university, because of pressures for greater democratization has led to:

> ...the appointment of second-rate individuals to university posts, persons attracted by the charms of a profitable and, as they lived it, not too arduous career, but contributing little or nothing to academic life, preferring, indeed, either complete stagnation or the delights of political agitation.[2]

Philip G. Altbach, from the United States, makes the point differently, more calmly and with less apparent disdain than Passmore, when he argues that the expansion of the U.S. system of higher education:

> ...had wide ranging implications. The social class base of both the student population and profes-

_____

*To be sure, we construct this historical framework *quickly*, for others—many of them—have already told the story well. For much of the detailed information, analysis, and adequate bibliography, the following works are representative ones: David Riesman and Christopher Jencks, *The Academic Revolution* (Garden City: Doubleday, 1968); Everett Ladd and Seymour Lipset, *The Divided Academy: Professors and Politics* (New York: McGraw-Hill, 1975); *The Annals of the American Academy of Social Sciences*, March, 1980 (a special issue on "The Academic Profession").

soriate broadened and changed. Substantial segments of the student body were no longer recruited
from elite and professional classes. This shift
meant that members of the academic community
were less and less likely to share a common understanding of the university and the way it tradi-
tionally related to the wider world. Sheer increase
in numbers fragmented the academic profession
and vitiated the base for shared action and perspectives.[3]

That is, trouble.

Without knowing they were doing so but nevertheless, Professors Passmore and Altbach were speaking
about *us* and our contributors, for both as students and
professors we all have been beneficiaries of this presumed
"insatiable egalitarian impulse," as Passmore put it in a
rhetorical flourish later in his comments. And, in Passmore's case, anyway, it is clear that he longs for what, in his
eyes, were "the good old days" of higher education in
capitalist nations, days which (as we shall see) might well
be on the way back. Let us briefly sketch the old days and
the new ones that emerged after WWII. We do this overview
in order better to understand the circumstances which
opened the university to our respondents.* We will also take
the trouble to examine the claims of Passmore that these
developments are best understood as a consequence of
"insatiable egalitarian impulses," and that the expansion
of the university resulted in its disruption.

When upper class people first established universities
in this country, such as Harvard, Yale and Princeton, they were
intended for the tutelage of elite young men, preparing them
to "take over" from their fathers the control of the major
social institutions of the nation (such as the productive
firms, the government, and the churches). The curriculum in
these early colleges was largely regimented training in the

---

*We use "university" and "college" interchangably in
this book, to avoid being cumbersome, as they share essential social functions. Where we want to distinguish between
varying kinds of schools in U.S. higher education, we will
indicate so in the text.

classical disciplines: language, mathematics, literature, history and some science. The history of higher education in the United States, however, has been a movement away from this early model of the university. The evolution gained momentum with the adoption by some universities of a European model of higher education and with the construction of land grant colleges in the mid-19th century, both types of institutions with an increasing emphasis on professional and vocational training. This movement has continued with fits and starts to this day. Indeed, the egalitarian impulse, particularly in the emergence of land grant colleges, seems to come early in the history of U.S. higher education. But does it?

Growth in the number of universities teaching professional subjects, rather than the classics only, has been regarded as an important democratizing factor in higher education in the United States. Nonetheless, until very recent times, the university experience was one confined to a very small part of the population. In 1900, of a population of 76 million, only 238,000, or less than one-half of one percent, were attending college; and, by 1930, of a population of 123 million, only a million were in college, still less than one percent. (As we shall see below, by 1981 there were over *twelve million* college students in the U.S., more than 5 *percent* of the total population.) Thus, little democratization had occurred by WWII, and even though there was continuing encroachment almost everywhere on the traditional curriculum, university enrollments were confined primarily to middle and upper-class children following the footsteps of their parents (usually their fathers) to campus. This gradual evolution away from the practice of harboring traditional students and traditional education became a revolution in the 1940s, both in the democratization and the professionalization of universities, a result primarily of the massive intervention of the federal government into higher education.

In 1944, the first GI bill was passed, and it was followed by two others in 1952 and 1966. These three bills subsidized the education of almost 20,000,000 people, providing opportunities to working class and lower middle class students in unprecedented numbers. Another great infusion of federal funds occurred after the 1957 Sputnik flight, when a new trend began in higher education in the U.S. The National Defense Education Act, other kinds of government loans with long payback periods and at subsidized interest rates, and direct grants to deserving individuals, extended the opportunity to attend college to those whose families had long been denied the experience.

Importantly, there is some doubt by informed observers whether the gates of the campus were opened to working class ex-GI's, then later to bright potential scientists, because of "egalitarian impulses," or for other reasons. For example, David Nasaw, in his study of educational reforms since the early 19th century, surveys the evidence in detail and concludes that the first GI Bill was enacted more to combat expected postwar unemployment than to improve access to higher education. He also contends that federal funding for university research and development has been motivated mostly by profit-hungry major corporations that needed science-based technologies developed as rapidly as possible.[4]

In other words, the fact that subsidy was provided for graduate education for those without other means of support was not the principal aim of financial aid programs. The growth of the economy and the tide of the Cold War simply demanded more trained human labor power in science, technology, management, human services, and also, of course, in education. It was in this period that the federal government recognized a primary national priority and assumed a major responsibility for the development of comprehensive "manpower" training and development. It was also a time when what Samuel Bowles and Herbert Gintis* have called the "meritocratic ideology" took hold

————————————————————

*Schooling In Capitalist America (1976). The principal argument in this book—a major one, indeed, regarding the historical purpose of education in the U.S.—is that the school system has served principally to reproduce the class system from one generation to the next one; that the hierarchy in U.S. education exists at every level to accomplish this purpose, from elite universities for mostly upper class people down to the tracking system in public

among many prominent social scientists and gradually became an assumed characteristic of the society by the practitioners down below. The meritocratic ideology was by no means egalitarian either in impulse or consequence, but it did contribute positively to the mix of things which opened the door a bit, both to the university and to other high status professions. Yet, this element in the context affecting mobility possibilities must be seen as a function of economic growth, changing techno-structures and a perceived national need to mobilize human resources for international economical, political and technological competition. We will argue later that, in no real sense, does the class structure of society collapse or even weaken.

ii.

Another major consequence of WW II and its aftermath was its effect on the size of the U.S. population. Beginning in 1946, and continuing to 1964, there was an increase in population growth known now to everyone as the "baby boom." From 1964, until 1982, the bulge in the population growth in the U.S. influenced every part of our national life. This "baby boom," especially from the early 1960s on, sent unprecedented numbers of youngsters off to college at the same time that there was occurring the great increase in government subsidization of higher education. The combined effect was an expansion of enrollment that may now be called the "Golden Age of Higher Education," approximately the years 1960-1980.

Table I shows enrollment figures for resident students in colleges and universities (including two-year colleges) since 1963, as well as data of related importance. The enormous expansion in the 1960s was caused by all the factors mentioned above, and it was also facilitated greatly by a booming economy. The longest recorded, sustained eco-

———————————————————

schools, directing some children up and others down before their puberty. We agree generally with these arguments by Bowles and Gintis, and we view our work as complementing and extending their's, particularly their chapter 8.

Figure 1

Total Enrollment in institutions of higher education compared with
population aged 18-24: United States, fall 1963 to fall 1981

Year	Instructional Staff[1] (000)	Population 18-24 years of age[2] (000)	Enrollment (000)	# Enrolled per 100 persons 18-24 years old
1963	281	18,268	4,766	26.1
1964	307	18,783	5,280	28.1
1965	340	20,293	5,921	29.2
1966	362	21,376	6,390	29.9
1967	390	22,327	6,912	31.0
1968	428	22,883	7,513	32.8
1969	450	23,723	8,005	33.7
1970	474	24,687	8,581	34.8
1971	492	25,779	8,949	34.7
1972	500	25,913	9,215	35.6
1973	527	26,397	9,602	36.4
1974	567	26,916	10,224	38.0
1975	628	27,605	11,185	40.5
1976	633	28,163	11,012	39.1
1977	650	28,605	11,286	39.5
1978	647	28,971	11,260	38.9
1979	657	29,285	11,570	39.5
1980	678	29,462	12,097	41.1
1981	690	29,512	12,300[3]	41.7

[1]Instructor rank, or above, full **and** part time.
[2]Bureau of census estimates as of July 1 preceding the opening of the academic year. Includes Armed Forces overseas.
[3]Estimated

Note: While 18 to 24 is frequently considered to be the usual age for college attendance, an increasing number of students in recent years have been outside this age group. According to a sample survey conducted by the Bureau of Census in October 1980, 2.2 perent of the students were under 18; 47.0 percent, 18-21; 16.4 percent, 22 to 24; and 34.3 percent, 25 or over.

Sources: 1.) U.S. Department of Education, National Center for Education Statistics. **Fall Enrollment in Higher Education**; 2.) U.S. Department of Commerce, Bureau of the Census. **Current Population Reports**, Series P-25, Nos. 519, 704, 721, and 870; and, 3.) NCES, **Digest of Educational Statistics**, 1982.

nomic expansion in U.S. history occurred in the 1960s, and it made state governments with filled coffers more willing each year to supplement federal funds already pouring into campus treasuries. It also allowed more families to finance at least part of college expenses from their own income. Another way to look at the growth in university enrollments during those times concerns proportion of college age students (18-24 years) who actually attended college. This ratio was 14 percent in 1940 and had risen to 22 percent by 1960. Table I shows its dramatic increase after 1960. It should also be noted from Table I that the expansion of this 18-24 year cohort in college is still occurring, though there has been no *sustained* growth in it since 1975.

For our purposes, a potential shortage of college teachers was the major consequence of the fact that the invisible walls to the academy crumbled from 1945 throughout the 1960s, trampled first by wave after wave of ex-service people and others, then cohort after cohort of their children after 1964. Because all these students themselves needed teachers, there occurred an enormous expansion in the demand for graduate-trained faculty at a much greater rate than they could be prepared by the traditional suppliers, the major research institutions. There emerged, in response, new programs at "lesser" schools, and the system, with all the help from the federal government, expanded to create the needed new faculty.

In fact, both of us (as well as many of our contributors) received our own Ph.Ds in the mid-60s, in programs at large state universities which, before and after we were doing our graduate work, experienced rapid growth. At the time, as we recall it, we both thought what was happening to us was a "good" thing. We did not know in those days that, in the minds of some, such as Professors Passmore and Altbach, mentioned above, the events were perceived as trouble making. Another critic of the result is Jacques Barzun, often a sensible commentator about higher education. Recently (1981), in a retrospective view on the postwar expansion of U.S. education, he stated the following:

> The once proud and *efficient* public school system
> of the United States—especially its unique free
> high school for all—has turned into a wasteland

where violence and vice share the time with ignorance and idleness, besides serving as a battleground for vested interests, social, political, and economic.

And, he stated further:

...The great postwar rush to college for a share in upward mobility and professional success was soon encouraged and enlarged by public money... Under this pressure higher education changed in *quality* and *tone*...State university systems threw out branches in cities already well provided with private, municipal, or denominational institutions... The *purpose* and *manner* of higher education was left behind.[5] (Our emphasis)

It is worthwhile to linger with Barzun momentarily, for he has been for sometime an exceedingly prolific and strong critic of the postwar university in the U.S. Barzun's *particular* perspective, however, differentiates him from many other critics of the transformation of higher education, especially his spirited championing of the "teacher" at the expense of the "scholars in orbit," the designation he once gave to ambitious academics who have used publications and consulting to gain status that eclipses that of other teachers. Nevertheless, Barzun shares with most of the commentators writing during the last decade about U.S. higher education the habit of explaining its problems, its ups and mostly downs, without seeming to recognize that the university campus is an integral part of the social class system in the U.S. These commentators seem especially to ignore the fact that its services are provided (quantatively and qualitatively) more or less proportionally to its customers' family income.

For example, what Barzun suggests (in the quote above) as the "once proud" public school system has been seen by others (Bowles and Gintis, and David Nasaw, for instance), and more clearly we think, as an important agent whereby social class orderings are replicated from one generation to the next one. And, what Barzun sees as the "efficiency" of that system is, to someone with a less romantic eye for the old ways, an ongoing success in keeping generations of young people in their places in the status system. Further, when he complains ambiguously that the "manners" of higher education have been abandoned (it is not clear in the context what he means precisely), we imagine that he is referring to the politization of university life in the 1960s and afterwards. Barzun shares a deep hurt with many academics (but not all of them) about the assault on university form, content and process during those rambunctious years of approximately 1960-1973.*

What Barzun means by the "abandoned *purpose*" of higher education is much clearer, since one of his major works on higher education (*The American University*, 1968), is concerned fundamentally with this issue. As he puts it in that book, changes between the early 1950s and 1968 caused the university to take on new functions which have

> ...torn apart the fabric of the former single-minded, easily defined American University. A big corporation has replaced the once self-centered company of scholars and has thereby put itself at the mercy of many publics, unknown to one another and contradictory in their demands.[6]

In other words, the "purpose" of the university that has been forsaken centered its attention on a "company" of scholars (and presumably their students). And, to maintain the "high-tone" and "quality," and the "good manners" of such campuses, Barzun makes clear his judgement that we need to restructure the university in order to replicate to the extent possible the same environment that prevailed in higher learning before the onslaught and its demands.

————————————————————————

*The assault on the old habits of the university by (ironically) mostly privileged students has been described, from a variety of views in the following two books: Daniel Bell and Irving Kristol, *Confrontation: The Student Rebellion and the Universities* (New York: Basic Books, 1969); and Edward J. Bander, *Turmoil on the Campus* (New York: H.W. Wilson, 1970).

Admirably, in the final chapter of *The American University* and in other articles, Barzun has put forth a good number of sensible suggestions about how to restore the crucial elements of that environment; there are *sixty-eight* such suggestions in the 1968 book alone. Yet taken together, these proposals, from our reading, demonstrate without question that his idea of the "great university" swamped by too many of everything—programs,courses, connections to government, bureaucracies of all kinds—he approves generally that they came to be. As he puts it in his "Wasteland" essay:

> No doubt some of the novelties [created by the postwar transformation of higher education] were beneficial. The junior and community college, with their self-regarding concern for good teaching, often awakened talent in students overlooked in the scramble for admission to better known places.

This view of the growth of community colleges is common to many U.S. educators. To our mind, though, it is a view taken only by those who choose to ignore entirely the location of these two year schools in the hierarchical structure of higher education. For, no matter how significant is the contribution of the two year college to the life of the working class kid (or his/her adult counterpart), *the great majority of those enrolled are there because they can't go to institutions with better reputations, better facilities, more prestige in the eyes of employers in the job market.* And, the principal reason why they are where they are in school and in the job market, is because of their parents' income and background.

These community colleges typically minimize instruction in the liberal arts and, for example, will train someone to be an engineer's "aide," rather than to be an engineer.[7] That is, they are designed explicitly in consonance with the acceptance of a multi-tiered or what some have called "dual" labor market (to be discussed further in Chapter 4). In such a market, the future managers of the Chase Manhattan Bank are trained at Harvard, Yale and Princeton undergraduate school, not at Area Community College. The students at "ACC" are being prepared for lesser stations. And, it is important to put in perspective the community college expansion in the increase in enrollments in this period. In 1960, when there were 521 two year colleges in the U.S., they enrolled about 15 percent of all post-secondary students; by 1975, this proportion had risen to about one-fourth; by 1980, approximately one thousand two-year colleges enrolled 4.5 million students, very close to *one-third* of all students enrolled in higher education, and about *forty percent* of the freshman class for that year.

There are many critics of the results of this most recent growth area in higher education besides ourselves. Some authors contend that these two year colleges have been established foremost to produce what Stanley Aronowitz[8] has called "false promises" to the working classes. One such critic of two year colleges, Steven Zwerling, (in his book, *Second Best*, 1982) extends the argument that community colleges "slot their students into the lower ranks." He states that by this process, "The community college[4] is in fact a social defense mechanism that resists basic changes in the social structure."[9] Further, the compelling empirical study by Samuel Bowles and Herb Gintis (cited earlier) has demonstrated to all but a few detractors that the existence of these two year schools—in fact all efforts made to democratize higher education in the U.S.—have failed to change the reality that one's socioeconomic class more than anything else, is predominant in determining the relative income earned and status attained by individuals in our society.

We need also to point out here that after enrollment figures in U.S. higher education take an enormous leap from 1960 to 1970, the rate of increase declines significantly in the 1970s, and has slowed further in the early 1980s, with the expectation of declining college enrollments through 1990, as the impact of new demographic patterns takes effect. In fact, and we think creating false expectations, college and university enrollments actually *increased* in the fall of 1983 by slightly more than one percent. However, the growth is "due primarily to an increase in the number of part-time students in public and private two year colleges," according to the source of the data.[10] More systematic and long run estimates make for considerably less sanguine probabilities. For example, the principal gatherer of educational data in the U.S., the National Center for Educational Statistics, produced a report in 1982 predicting: (1) a decline in full-time enrollments in U.S. higher education from 8.7 million in 1980 to 8.4 million in 1990; and (2) a decline in total expenditures on higher education (in real terms during the period) from $70.4 billion in 1980 to $66.6 billion in 1990-91. These data led to the further prediction that the full time equivalent instructional staff in U.S. higher education would *decline* from 624,000 to 589,000 by 1990.[11] That is, shrinking possibilities for any hillbillies and meanstreeters who are, this moment, growing up with fantasies about being college teachers.

Paul Blumberg assesses the effects already being experienced from this tightening of academic job markets, and he writes that:

> ...the resentment of younger faculty who feel their qualifications match or exceed those of their entrenched elders and who feel cheated by the sheer accident of the date of their birth, and the defensiveness of the tenured faculty, has created a potentially divisive conflict of generations within the academy...[12]

Indeed, the context shaping life chances in the U.S. is changing for everyone, and certainly for working class people aspiring to academia. For example, most of our respondents in this study are tenured, but for that half dozen who are not, the picture is at best uncertain. During the past year, in fact, two of those six have been dismissed, and one of them was denied tenure, even though his scholarly attainments exceeded those of most of the tenured members of his department. A second of our contributors was dismissed from his job merely as a consequence of retrenchment of an academic department; his job was simply eliminated.

Consider, further, some details here about the case of a Professor Henry Giroux.[13] An academic from a working class family in Providence, R.I., Giroux has just (1983) been denied tenure at Boston University, even though he is, by all accounts, a gifted teacher, and has published four books, edited two others, and has written more than fifty scholarly articles. However, his politics are left-wing, his intellectual dedication is to the affirmation of working class values and culture, and his academic degrees are *not* from elite undergraduate or graduate schools. Giroux's assessment of his situation is that the combination of his politics, academic interests and style, and, perhaps, ultimately, his lack of pedigree, put him under. Professor Giroux's situation is, in a central regard, like that of *all* untenured academics—as well as those with Ph.D.'s who cannot find academic jobs—in the sense that the age in which they aspire is no longer golden.

To sum up to this point: the historical and the socio-economic factors that democratized higher education after World War II have run their course, and it appears virtually to everyone now that the long, glorious, expansion of higher education in the U.S. is over. Therefore, we and most other contributors to this book were born at a propitious time, given the fact of our path to the academy, and those following us from similar backgrounds, in the 1980s, will not find it nearly so accessible a route. And, finally, there are many observers of this process who believe that when we got to the campus, we helped to ruin it.

iv.

What the future will provide in higher education to working class kids is, of course, impossible to determine now; but, it is clear that the product will be greatly influenced by the course of public policy over the next ten or fifteen years, and a host of other changes within U.S. society. For example, while the enrollments in *private* institutions actually increased from 1979-1982 by 2 percent, those same institutions recorded a remarkable fall of *39 percent* in the enrollment of students from families with annual incomes of between $6,000-24,000.[14] This collapse reflects, of course, the deep recession in the economy, and attacks by the Reagan Administration on a whole range of public programs, among them those for higher education.

A related fact is that at public institutions, the trend has been away from "open admissions" programs, started in the 1960s. At colleges and universities all over the country, a determined attempt is being made to "improve quality" in the "output." This improvement is to be achieved by toughening admissions standards and by excluding the "least preferred." Thus, the victims are once more being blamed for the failure of educational policy, which treasures consumption goods and military hardware more than schooling for its least defended citizens, low income children.

Lawrence Biermiller, in a 1983 *Chronicle of Higher Education* article entitled "Questionable Admission Practices Seen Limiting Education of Poor," reports that:

> More and more colleges, worried about keeping their enrollment up, are using admissions and financial aid practices that are ethically suspect and may limit the access of needy students to higher education. This warning came from administrators attending the annual meeting of the College Board last week.
>
> Many of the admission and financial directors at the meeting here spoke—some of them bitterly— about the pressures that the well-advertised demographic trends of the 1980s have put on admissions programs.
>
> Especially worrisome, many participants said, is an increase in the number of scholarship awards based on merit rather than on need.[15]

Biermiller states that in discussing the problem, one Financial Aid Officer (using imagery that brings to mind a feeding trough) said that the bidding for talented students, regardless of family income has "gotten frenzied in the last few years." And, implementing metaphor after hyperbole, this aid officer said that "some schools have just rolled the vaults out onto the sidewalk." Importantly, many young people from working class backgrounds with solid academic potential neither test well nor perform well. They are not motivated or are too busy hating school or enjoying the usual range of non-academic pursuits. It is our impression that many of those young folks find their intellectual curiosity and their potentiality *after* they leave home and get out into the world beyond their immediate environments. Often discovery occurs in college or in the military. As colleges cut back on the "least well-prepared," and the

Figure 2

High School Seniors
Planned Concentration in College

	1972	1980
Professional Training Subjects		
Business	13%	22%
Engineering	5	10
Education*	12	6
Health Services	12	8
Preprofessional	—	8
Other (Computers, Agriculture, Home Economics, Communications, Architecture)	14	18
	56%	72%
Liberal Arts		
Art	3%	4%
English	3	2
Music	3	2
Math	2	1
Philosophy/Religion	1	1
Language	1	1
Physical Science	3	2
Biological Science	10	3
Social Science	17	8
	43%	24%
Other (not specified)	2%	4%
	100%	100%

Source: THE CHRONICLE OF HIGHER EDUCATION, April 13, 1981

*Education might reasonably be included with the liberal arts given that the training is more in the tradition of liberal learning than professional preparation. This shift would indicate an even greater trend away from liberal learning and toward the professions.

military becomes a less honorable alternative to staying home and getting a job than it once was, the opportunities for self-discovery narrow. Many of the respondents in this study did not have the high school attainments to make themselves interesting to anyone other than community college admissions officers. And, these officers are usually close to home, geographically and culturally, from the students' starting point.

Whatever *does* happen in this coming "post" golden age of higher education, lamented so by so many, it will *not* change the fact that there was never any educational epoch in our history when substantial proportions of low income kids have had the chance to go to college. Figure 3 below places the issue into a proper perspective by looking at these proportions over the decade of 1967-1977. The chart is clear enough. During the decade, the "best" one in the postwar expansion of U.S. higher education, *less than one-fourth* of the poorest kids went to college, and most of them went to two year colleges, or four year state colleges. It is, therefore, their family's lack of resources that keeps most such kids out of college entirely, and most of the rest out of the more prestigious schools. American society continues to offer hackneyed and cruel advice to the bulk of its low income children: if you want to go to a fancy college, your best bet is to get reborn into a richer family. In short, the chart suggests that, as we move to a less egalitarian system of higher education in the United States, we should not, by that fact alone, convince ourselves that at its height the democratization was in any way remarkable. *It is only in relation to its own history that a wealthy and powerful society can boast that almost one-fourth of its poor kids got a chance to go to college in the year in which that proportion was at its historical apex.*

v.

As we have said, another part of the transformation of U.S. higher education in recent times is the decline of the liberal arts. Since this decline has been concommitant with the working lives of almost all of our contributors, we will give the matter some brief additional attention here. As we

Figure 3
**College-Going Rates
College Enrollment Rates of Dependent Family
Members 18-24 Years Old by Family Income:
(In 1983 Dollars)**

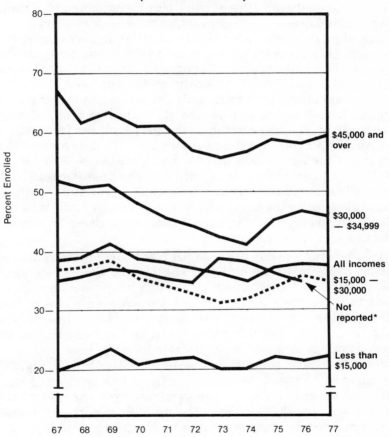

Note: Dependent family members are relatives of the family head,
excluding wife.
*Data not available for 1977.

*Source: See note 11 above and reference to the study by Carol
Francis. We have inflated the income levels into 1983 dollars.*

have pointed out, our sampling techniques, described in the introduction, produced one quite *unintentional* bias in the resulting collection of contributed essays: all of them were written by academics from the social sciences or humanities.

We are certain that had we, for example, produced a sample of essays from engineers, our book would have been different, greatly so. In all likelihood, most engineers would not bemoan the decline of the liberal arts, since it is their own income, power, and prestige which is relatively enhanced as the university allows attrition in its offerings of poetry, philosophy, and history. In fact, as we write this, a young chemical engineer, freshly graduated, can demand a salary of about $25,000 annually on the first job. However, his or her counterpart from a liberal arts discipline is either unemployed, underemployed, or, if he/she has a job, is being paid about $14,000 on the average. (And, an interesting irony, the $25,000 for the engineer is about the same as the average faculty salary in the United States—$26,000 in 1982-83.) In any case, the "decline" in the liberal arts, which actually started as early as the last half of the 19th century, has taken on a new energy in recent years. In Table 2 on the following page, we demonstrate some evidence of this rapid decline as it has occurred in the 1970s.

The study plans of these high school seniors reflect at least three basic changes in the United States economy during the 1970s, two of which already have been mentioned but bear additional emphasis. First, economic stagnation has made most everyone who works, or who will work for a living, considerably more job-conscious. Conversations with any random group of college students will show that most want to study something "which will enhance my job prospects." Indeed, one commentator has suggested that the job prospects for college graduates *for the rest of the 1980s are "bleak."*[15] Second, the managers of the economic system, in and out of government, have decreasing needs for liberally educated students. An engineer, an accountant, a graduate of a prestigious business school, all neat and clean, will be more appealing to the modern manager than a dreamy, star-gazing, lad or lass, one perhaps who is reflective about or critical of things as they are. Furthermore, as scientific management finds its way further into the heart and the viscera of the economy, we can expect more and more college students to *prepare* themselves—this is the correct word, we fear—to be the willing minions of corporation managers, or to be managers themselves, who, primarily with computer technology, every day are learning more about how to separate hand from brain at all levels of the productive system.

Third, the abandonment of the liberal arts by college students reflects the continuing influence of government expenditures for higher education. The Pentagon is a major employer of college graduates, and its income will double during the next five years, a result of the new (Reagan) wave of fear about communism. The Pentagon, which now hires directly or indirectly one-third of all U.S. scientists, above all else wants engineers, computer programmers, and other vocationally trained people, most of whose high school and college years have yet to introduce them sufficiently to ways of thinking differently from those of the applied sciences. Therefore, as the Pentagon gets the funds that, in the 1960s and 1970s were spent for community projects (staffed often by liberal arts graduates), we will likely see yet a greater deterioration in the popularity of liberal arts at universities. It could well be that the universities have entered what David Riesman[16] has chosen to describe as the age of "student hegemony." In this era, high school students and their parents, using the increasing competition of universities for their tuition money, will dictate to the academy an even greater emphasis on preprofessional and vocational training as a condition of their childrens' enrollment. These parental concerns also reflect anxiety about maintaining class standing or enjoying heightened status through the attainments of their children.

We have seen already *how* these students plan to protect their options by forsaking poetry and philosophy. A parting word here underlining *why* they do so is informative. A recent survey[17] reports that 65-70 percent of the Freshman Class of 1982-83 (in higher education in the U.S.) listed "being able to make more money" as the prime motivator in their college plans. This figure does not surprise us; in fact, we think, were students from any recent generation in the

U.S. entirely honest in answering such a question, the figure would be higher. Yet, these first-year students did distinguish themselves and their values in answer to other queries. For instance, only 46.7 percent listed "developing a meaningful philosophy of life" as a prime motivator. Presumably half, or slightly more, have never heard of the idea, or have given up on it, by age eighteen. And, only 30.7 percent listed "promoting racial understanding" as a prime motivator in their college plans. All this can no doubt be interpreted in several ways, one being that it bodes better times for accounting professors than it does for academic philosophers.

vi.

All in all, then, after World War II the system of higher education got big enough to let *us* inside. It has been transformed as it has grown into a system with ever greater similarity to, and dependence on , the federal government and the great corporations: events from 1945-1980, for all the sound and fury of some of them (especially in the 1960s), did not work to alter this growing symbiosis between campuses and other social institutions. Moreover, in response to democratizing legislation, and some of it importantly affecting access to universities by working class people, the U.S. electorate ended the 1970s by putting into power its most right-wing government in recent times. This Republican victory in 1980 attested strongly, among other things, to the narrow confines into which imaginable social change must be squeezed in our society. It seems clear that the mild elements of democratization at home, plus a losing grip on foreign resources, strained the limits of these confines, and people from all classes brought to power a president whose one great success so far is that he extended unparalleled government concern for wealthy Americans.

But, to this point, we have more or less *stated* our claim; we now need to provide more detailed evidence. We have shown clearly enough how access to the university was transformed by larger events, such as wars, hot and cold, population explosions, and related factors. Yet, when rapid social change does occur, and forces changes in the myriad institutions by which society itself is comprised, these institutions *also* place a limit on the larger forces. That limit is maintained from one instance to the next, shifting as they do, by the *people* of a culture, by their rules, their habits, their politics, their dreams, their hatreds, by all the things that make them human beings. And, so as society "swept up" higher education, lower education, industry, and everything else along its own huge tides, it was sweeping a *specific* topography of different terrains, a tremendous host of individual human actions, and each of them had its own effect on what became known as "postwar history in the U.S."

Embodying a tiny fraction of such actions, in our next chapter we offer a set of autobiographies which speak dramatically to the journey of class mobility to the academy within this historical setting. For the most part, the essays show the intricate interplay of individual striving, historical circumstances, and the dynamics of the class system in operation. These autobiographies have been tailored to convey the essential drama of discovering and moving down the pathway to the academy. In every case, they describe how our travelers got to the gates of the academy. What happens for folks once inside, we reserve for Part II.

Notes

1. Ralf Dardendorf, *Life Chances* (Chicago: University of Chicago Press, 1979), p. 30.

2. Malcolm Scully, "'Doctrinaire Egalitarianism' of the 1960s Has Weakened Academia, Scholars Warn," *The Chronicle of Higher Education (CHE)*, March, 1980, pp.2,3.

3. Philip G. Altbach, "The Crisis of the Professorate," *The Annals of the American Academy of Political and Social Sciences,* March, 1980, pp.2,3.

4. David Nasaw, *Schooled To Order: A Social History of Public Schooling in the U.S.* (New York: Oxford, 1976.

5. Jacques Barzun, "The Wasteland of American Education," *The New York Review of Books,* Nov., 1981.

6. Jacques Barzun, *The American University* (New York: Harper and Row, 1968), p. 3.

7. Arthur Cohen and Florence Brawer, "The Community College as College: Should the Liberal Arts Survive in Community Colleges?", *Change*, March, 1982, pp. 39-42.

8. Stanley Aronowitz, *False Promises: The Shaping of American Working Class Consciousness* (New York: McGraw Hill, 1973).

9. Stephen Zwerling, *Second Best: The Crisis of the Community College* (New York: McGraw Hill, 1976), p. xix.

10. *CHE,* Nov. 23, 1983, p. 2.

11. Martin Frankel and Deborah Gerard, *Projections of Educational Statistics: 1990-91,* Vol. 1 of *Analytical Report*, March 1982. Also see Carol Francis, *College Enrollment Trends* (Wash. D.C.: American Council on Education, 1980).

12. Paul Blumberg, *Inequality in an Age of Decline* (New York: Oxford, 1981), p. 221.

13. Bill Reynolds, "Henry Giroux, Ph.D., Has the Working Class Blues," *Providence Sunday Journal Magazine,* May 15, 1983, p. 4.

14. *CHE,* Sept. 1 1982, pp. 1, 18.

15. Jack Magarrell, "Job Market for College Graduates Called 'Bleak' for Rest of 1980s," *CHE,* June 15, 1983, p. 1.

16. David Riesman, *On Higher Learning* (San Francisco: Jossey-Bass, 1980).

17. "Freshman Aim to Make Money But Shift Slightly to Left Politically," *CHE,* Jan. 26, 1983, p. 10.

CHAPTER 2

Upward Bound

Wherein, our five
young heroes,
barefoot boys
with cheek
them all,
trod,
plod,
jump,
dance, and
trip
their way
toward heaven.

Bob Cole

Neither my father nor my mother wanted me to be a miner. They both absolutely did not want me to work in a factory. They, like most people in my home town, wanted their children to "have it better" than they did, which meant to them I should work in a clean job or be a school teacher, preferably the former, and preferably in my home town. They were vaguely proud of the fact, but could not comprehend my going to college.

My father was a coal miner for 40 years. My mother worked in factories during WWII and during my childhood and adolescence. They both graduated from the eighth grade and were rather intelligent, though not well-read. Around 1955 my home town, a boom and bust mining town for decades,went bust again. My father was over 50 and unemployable. It was the beginning of a bitter, degenerative period for him which lasted until his death twenty years later. My mother ran a small laundry for a while, then went back to the factory, making about $25 a week. I was ten years old.

I loved school and can still remember the smells and feelings of being in the first grade—oiled wooden floors, chalk, crayons, books. I was shy and a model student, properly respectful (or fearful as the occasion demanded), in awe of learning.

At about the same time I started school I began to go to church, and, in fact, school and church experiences sort of blend together in my memory at times. My parents were non-practicing Primitive Baptists. I chose to be a Methodist because I was invited to the church by my first grade teacher. I went alone. This, coupled with my love of school and my propensity to sit alone a lot, not fight and not raise hell, kept my parents from knowing how to deal with me.

Class differences in my town were pronounced, but not spoken of. Those with money and power got it primarily through the mining operations. Those without money were generally careful not to look the part; there was a cross-class norm that one ought not "put on." Everyone had a stake in being "common folk," but there still were differences. Since I was a clean-cut, church-going, patriotic (I won a VFW Voice of Democracy award in high school), poor, good student, there were many well-intentioned acts of paternalism. I was given money to go to church camp. The banker lent me money to buy a car, even though I was a junior in college and had no collateral. I appreciated such acts, and, upon reflection, still do. They did, however, serve to reinforce my feeling of difference, my apartness from what appeared to be an "in-group."

Money was a problem for me when I was young. I once thought, in the seventh grade, I'd play baseball, until I found that I'd need to buy shoes and equipment. My father said, "Why do you want to do that?" I didn't. I also wanted to be in the band. My father said, "Why do you want to do that?" I really wanted it. My mother, the only breadwinner at that time, thought I should. They fought a bit, and I felt guilty. We only had $20 to $30 per week income, for four people—my niece was also living in our house. My mother arranged $5 a month payment plan and I joined the band, playing a cornet.

I was big, 5'7"and 160, in the eighth grade. The band needed a sousaphone player. I was appointed. I taught myself to play and, being the only bass horn player, began to develop some confidence. I still loved school and was still a loner, preferring to sit by myself and read or think, rather than socialize. I had no close friends. I never spent the night in a friend's house. No one visited me, perhaps because of my home—there was no place for anyone else to sleep.

I remember shame attached to living in a shack, though many people in my town lived in the same conditions. My mother was a lousy housekeeper, and the house was basically uncleanable anyway. There was a sense of futility and cynicism, fostered by my father. When my mother or I attempted to clean house, he would encourage us to stop: "Why do you want to do that now?" He would clean and cook, and was pretty good at it, but the house was filthy most of the time.

Life at home seemed futile in many ways. I could not study after dark when I was in high school. My father went to bed at 8:30 at the latest, and in a four room house, if there was a light on, or noise, even walking, he would raise hell. I learned quickly to acquiesce. There was nowhere else to go, so I did my reading and work at school or before dark. At bedtime I either went to bed, or went and stood at the four-way stop in town and watched the cars go by.

I had no bedroom; my bed was in the kitchen. I had no privacy. Even the outhouse was only semi-private since there were holes between the boards.

Although I was encouraged to do my "homework," it was more for propriety's sake than for learning. Learning was important to a point; one should do well in school (meaning not fail) and become able to handle the practical aspects of living. Other than newspapers, *Grit*, and Western novels, we had no literature in the house. It wasn't that my home life was unhappy—I was very happy—it just wasn't conducive to planning for the future or for transcending class. To some measure school and community filled the gap.

I was absolutely naive about higher education. I was the first in my family to graduate from high school. Only recently was I reminded that I took SAT exams; I had no idea about such things at the time. I did very well, as it turned out. I was also something of a music "star," singing solos at school and church, winning awards with my tuba, and being the highly visible only bass player in a 100 piece band which was winning many awards.

One day a representative from a nearby college came to school and offered me a grant-in-aid, if I would major in music. The mines were still not running, so, being flattered, I accepted the offer and found myself in college. My father said, "Are you sure you want to do that?"

My first semester was awful. I was lonely, insecure, threatened,and broke, competing with people not only from Louisville, but from New York and Pennsylvania! The grant, coupled with an NDEA loan, gave me enough money to live on at a subsistence level, but I was still so concerned with money that I gauged the papers I wrote on their length; they had to be short. I couldn't afford the paper. I learned in the first semester that I couldn't read music. I also learned I could survive. Second semester, I changed my major to English (I could read), got a job, and connected with the Methodist Student Center.

My parents seemed not to want me to be a miner (although I believe my father would not have minded too much—he loved the mines). They both absolutely did not want me to work in a factory. They, like most people in my home town, wanted their children to " have it better" than they did, which meant to them I should work in a clean job or be a school teacher, preferably the former, and preferably in my home town. They were vaguely proud that I went to college, but could not comprehend why. When I decided to go to graduate school, in another state, they were agreeable, but totally uncomprehending. Here I was again, doing something weird. Why didn't I just come back home and teach?

In graduate school I was struck again by how much I didn't know, how much I hadn't read, how truly ignorant I was. The realization was more profound this time, and I reacted by beginning an anti-social, cynical period, closed socially, uncommunicative about my background, constructing a new self as I went along. The "good old boy" act still worked, but I began to see places and times when it was artificial, contrived, deceitful, even counterproductive. It also didn't fit me anymore. I did not want to be either a good old boy, or an arrogant know-it-all intellectual.

I was a good student, though my papers were still gauged on how many sheets of paper I'd need to buy. My background began to haunt me. My major professor wrote a recommendation for me that said, "given his background, he has done amazingly well." Though meant as a compliment, it hurt.

It was 1968, and I was burnt with academia. I decided to drop out, in a socially acceptable way, of course. There was a teaching job open in a Black school in middle Georgia. I took it. By this time, I had consciously destroyed my native Kentucky dialect. The job I took called for me to help the students, faculty and staff in this rural town to get rid of theirs. The reasoning behind the Program went: a major reason Blacks are raising hell and not fitting in is because they're different—they think, talk, and act differently than whites. It was thought, then, that if they changed the way they talked they could change the way they thought and acted.

The county was ninety per cent black, but it was run by whites. Blacks had, until 1962, gone to school in churches, taught by whomever was available, for about three months a year, all the time they could take away from farming. There was massive illiteracy and poverty. The students were just beginning to develop a sense of awareness of any pride in blackness. The last thing the students needed was a poor-white-trash man trying to get them to talk white. I didn't try.

What I tried to do was to teach them how to organize messages—written and oral—to channel their blossoming hostility into an effective method for dealing with the white world, using and appreciating their own dialect. It was basically a failure. There were good moments, but they didn't trust me and had no reason to. I was, incidently, making twice as much money as black teachers who had been teaching there five years or more. I learned some lessons about class and racial differences and power. I'm not sure the students learned anything. I felt like a white do-gooder who had raped the community.

I couldn't stay in Georgia. The draft was breathing down my neck, and in 1969 I ran north, taking a college teaching job. I was an outspoken liberal, for the most part. I had enough money finally to relax a bit and try to plan. Did I want a Ph.D.? What did I want to do? What could I do? How big was my bootstrap? I was teaching, mildly protesting, and fitting in rather well with university life. My friends were unassuming academics, from working class families. I shied away from the "big time" crowd and felt vaguely uncomfortable around them. I got married, fat, and comfortable.

Then, in August, 1970, at age 26, I was drafted. In ten days I went from a comfortable existence as a liberal "intellectual" college professor back to my roots—a nobody who, under threat, would shuffle for his superiors, ROTC lieutenants and working class sergeants trying to overcome their fears. My confidence was shaken to the core, and my fears, rooted in class and father fear came into focus again. My cynicism was made more solid; my romantic optimism faltered.

I survived basic training by relearning what my experience in factory work had taught me: learn the rules, do the work, keep your mouth shut, put your body on automatic pilot, and let your mind roam. It was more difficult to do since I was supposed to be learning to kill and was treated as a part of a distinctive young subculture: working-class, killing machines.

After the army I decided to go back to school. I was cynical, arrogantly class conscious and somewhat more politically radical. I could not work in industry. I didn't feel smart enough, nor the right "sort" to become a lawyer. The profession for which I seemed best suited was the academy. For that I needed a Ph.D. I wanted no part of hurdle jumping, so I chose a college close to my home town, which had a reputation as a degree mill.

It was at that college that I first began to feel I could actually become a scholar. It turned out not to be a degree mill. I was challenged, personally and academically. Again, I went into a new discipline, for which I had no preparation, and found myself doing well, achieving respect from peers and professors alike. I opened up to others. My confidence soared. Then my major professor decided to say "fuck it" to academia, and, mid-way through my dissertation pulled up stakes and left. My cynicism about what "doing well" means in academic institutions and in the world generally, grew. My introspection into my background relative to my future as a "scholar" began.

In 1978, I moved to the East Coast and was confronted again, this time more strongly than ever with class differences.

Steve Sanger

> By far the greatest influence on my academic orientation was my fundamentalist background. Hell-fire and Brimstone drove me to rational thought out of pure fear.

I was born in 1931 in a three room clapboard house on a share-cropper farm in East Texas. About the time I was born, my father "took to preachin'" in Southern Baptist churches on a part-time basis, and then when I was about five years old we moved off the farm as he responded to the calling full time. During the remainder of my childhood and adolescence, we moved from town to town at about two year intervals. Such credentials would appear to place me firmly in the "working class" of the rural South. Problems arise.

From the earliest memory I was class conscious. There were three distinct classes. At the bottom were niggers; only slightly elevated was white trash; then there were the good, honest, hard-working God-fearing folk such as we. I guess there was an awareness of the existence of rich folks somewhere, but they were not part of our world. Also, within the classes there were ill-defined gradations.

Many of the share-croppers were sons and daughters of fairly prosperous parents, and would eventually buy land of their own. My parents had bought and lost a farm during the early part of the Depression. Both sets of grandparents owned farms and fairly ostentatious homes. My family thought of itself as among the "better" families in the communities in which we lived. My father's calling resulted in an additional measure of prestige for the family.

One question has long interested me. What happened to the slave holding class after the Civil War? To what extent did they retain their identity and their status after the War?

When I was growing up, a scant 70-80 years after the War, there was little awareness of a "southern heritage." There did not seem to be an awareness of "southernness" until the Civil Rights Movement. Interest in my southern roots developed in the 1960s and led me to probe my family background. One discovery was that all of my ancestors were southerners at the time of the war, and most of them were slave-holders. It now strikes me as remarkable that such information had not been passed down. It was as if slavery had disappeared from the memory of the white community, though I suspect not from the black. It does seem probable, however, that there was continuity in class awareness. In any event, the class structure of the rural South does not neatly break down into "working class" and "bourgeoisie."

So far as can be determined, my parents had no specific career ambitions for me, but they, especially my father, had a great deal of ambition in general for me. In other words, I was always aware that I was expected to "get ahead" with "ahead" being only vaguely defined. My father completed nine or ten grades of public school, which was all that was available in his community. He was always keenly aware of his lack of education, especially after entering the ministry. In his late thirties, he commuted to the Baptist Seminary in Fort Worth in an attempt to remedy his perceived educational deficiency. He saw education as a way to "get ahead."

Interestingly, my delving into family history revealed a surprising level of education in the ante bellum period. There were lawyers, doctors, and an engineer. Apparently the poverty and exigencies of Reconstruction focused attention and energies on matters closer at hand, namely survival. My paternal grandfather succeeded in wresting a farm and a large colonial home out of the niggardly rural economy only by extreme exploitation of his nine children, and a single minded pursuit of success. He had little use for education, which was perceived as irrelevant to the task at hand. Thus, I think part of my father's concern for education stemmed from a strong urge to escape the cotton patch.

My mother also valued education. There were lots of teachers and a smattering of lawyers and judges in her family background. She taught in the small rural grade school of Indian Gap, Texas, for two years after completing high school. I think my mother vaguely wanted me to be a teacher.

From a very early age it was understood that I was going to college. My sister had gone to college briefly when I was about ten years old. Then she married my brother-in-law who had just graduated from college. In my later years of high school I began to think about college, mainly because there did not seem to be other acceptable alternatives. I vaguely assumed I someday probably would teach something or the other. I was not happy in college and left after one and a half years for a stint in the navy, during which time I got married. I returned to college with driving ambition. Because I had to specify a career objective in my application for the G.I. Bill, and because I was eligible for four full years of school which would carry me beyond a Master's degree, I specified as a career objective a doctorate in economics.

Any account of my formative educational background would be incomplete without mentioning three extraordinarily traumatic developments which have shaped my attitudes, thought processes, and experience in academia.

First, I flunked first grade! God almighty, I flunked first grade! Any one who has not flunked first grade cannot possibly understand the trauma. The budding self image is totally demolished. Talk about shame! In fact it has only been in recent years that I talk openly about it. And when I think about it now, I sometimes still, after forty-four years, catch myself hating Miss Feeney, my beautiful red-haired first grade teacher, my first love, who betrayed me. I have often puzzled over the effect of that experience on my life. I know that there was, and perhaps still is, a deep seated need to prove that I was not stupid. Undoubtedly those feelings have been a motivating force in my educational experience. (I should note one other interesting thing by way of an excuse for flunking first grade. At least one of my children has dyslexia, an inherited brain dysfunction. This was not even recognized when I was a child, but I strongly suspect that I too was dyslexic.)

By far the greatest influence on my academic orientation was my fundamentalist background. Hell-fire and Brimstone drove me to rational thought out of pure fear. I was first made aware of my moral depravity and impending (eternal) doom at age six by a cowboy preacher at a revival meeting. At age nine my degeneracy was further affirmed at a Baptist summer camp by Brother Haygood (for real). There was only one hope for my wicked soul, only one hope to avoid burning for *ETERNITY*. I accepted the Lord! The experience was mortifying. Worse, it had to be publicly repeated back in my home church in Prosper, Texas, prior to baptism. But at least I had repented and escaped that most horrible of fates. Or had I? I heard my Dad and other preachers saying that it was possible to join the church without being saved. Again I was panic stricken. Was I really saved? At that point, at the tender age of about twelve, I launched headlong into the world of rationalism and empiricism. In desperation I began to dissect and analyze what it meant "to be saved" and "accept the Lord" in hopes that I could ensure my salvation. The result of that line of inquiry was that I was a confirmed agnostic-atheist by fifteen years of age. The analytic thought process developed quietly and independently. I knew no agnostics nor atheists, nor infidelism and I did not discuss such matters with my parents, peers, or anyone else. I did take some pleasure, though, in my newly discovered powers by tormenting college students and others who would stay in our home while helping conduct a revival. They would depart considerably less secure in their salvation.

I have long been curious what in my situation caused me to respond differently from most people exposed to fundamentalism. I have discovered, however, that my reaction was by no means unique, and that numerous academics have had similar experiences.

No doubt these early religious experiences had a great deal to do with shaping my mentality and contributed to an independent and critical curiosity about social arrangements, not to mention a good measure of hostility toward authority and toward orthodoxy in whatever form. I became attuned sensitively to fraud and witchcraft in all their manifestations.

The third trauma (shades of first grade) was when I flunked written comprehensive examinations for my doctoral degree, twice, the consequence of which was that I was relegated to the dung-hills in the academic vineyards for life. I suspect that I still have not gained sufficient detachment from that experience to objectively assess causes and effects, because my attempts at dispassionate analysis still lead to the inevitable conclusion that I ought to lure a couple of motherfuckers down a dark alley.

Nathan Green

Going to college in my home town, even under the family pressure, was enormously liberating. My friends tended to be other townies drawn to the local university by the then low tuition and/or GI Bill. They were Italian, German, Irish and black working class boys and I visited homes where no Jew had ever set foot. It was heady and liberating. They liked me and it was mutual. It provided comradeship I had not experienced among rising middle-class Jewish and non-Jewish people.

Nothing in my background pointed me in the direction of academia. It resulted from a combination of accidents. I come from authentically-minted nineteenth century immigrant stock. My grandfathers came to the USA in 1905 and 1881. One was a carpenter and the other a tailor and so they remained their entire lives. Neither ever earned very much: neither ever penetrated the substance of America. Both had been soldiers in European armies and new wars and reconscription along with pogroms and anti-Jewish riots brought them here. My maternal grandmother never learned to read English. In my puckish boyhood I used to hand her the local newspaper upsidedown and she never knew the difference. Deeply religious, she was also superstitious and would mutter in Yiddish, "Not my fate" three times when she saw a "shooting star." Her marriage was arranged and endured through 50 years of unending conflict with a man whose stubborn will matched her own. My carpenter grandfather somehow ended up in a small upstate New York city and built his house there on University Avenue. His neighbors were professors whose children in those 1930s depression years were more ragged than I ever was. The university area to me meant student high jinks, football games and a few book bag hauling faculty members who walked slowly up the street. I noticed them only in passing and we never once visited the campus only three blocks away.

Five children of my mother's family survived childhood. Two sons climbed into professions, earning their own way through college. Neither was comfortable being Jewish and both nearly make it out of the immigrant status but were, despite their achievements, basically "Willie Lomans."

The older of my mother's two brothers went to Columbia Law School and built a lucrative practice before running afoul of the authorities. He was disbarred in 1934 and sent to Attica Prison. This event burdened the family for years. The older brother became an optometrist, married an "English" Jewish woman of great beauty who would never have been taken for Jewish by even the most obstinate anti-semite. She died in childbirth along with her baby and my uncle's hopes for a successor focused on me, which turned out to be unfortunate for both of us.

None of the daughters in this family went beyond high school, and one dropped out after only a few years. None married a man judged to be a success. My mother's education ended with vocational high school. She was a talented pianist but music school for which she yearned was out of the question. She went to work as a secretary and would continue to pursue that into her sixties. As I played with my tootsie toys in the 1932 living room, she would play Beethoven, Chopin and Mozart, her favorites. She pronounced Beethoven, "Bee-thoven" and Mozart with the "z" as in English. She was pretty, sensitive and poetic but her strong mind was never honed by liberal education. She read widely and indiscriminately and as a young boy I adored her and got in touch with some of the experiences with art she was going through alone.

My father's family was a different story. From the tales I have been told about his tailor father who died in 1913 he loved to talk; he loved playing cards; he never finished a garment on time; he loved his children (by their testimony) and he failed miserably to make a living. My father was born on New York's "teeming lower East Side" in 1896, one of six children, four of whom lived to adulthood. They were orphaned early when my grandfather, a fervent socialist, died at a party meeting.

My father's boyhood was one of extreme go-to-bed-hungry poverty. Among my paternal grandfather's nephews and cousins were factory workers, barbers, cobblers, house painters, tailors and handicappers. My father's sisters worked as candy dippers while young girls. His brother had virtually no schooling and spent a life founded by unskilled labor, horse rooms, crap tables and a place called "Choco-lates." He ran the "oldest established permanent floating crap game" in upstate New York, inhabited by such charac-ters as Utica George and "Pope" Rosenbloom. I saw him in a suit only once, and that was at a wedding. His coat was buttoned in the wrong hole as he turned his gape-toothed smile on one and all.

My father was the only one in the family to go beyond elementary school. A gifted mathematics student, he even attended engineering school under the sponsorship of the US Army in 1917-18. After this stint (I don't think he was serious about engineering), he worked as a shipping clerk in a pants factory where he met my secretary mother. Eventu-ally he went "on the road" for them plying his wares in small out of the way towns in New York, Pennsylvania, and Ohio. During the depression thirties he was often away for two weeks at a time and I missed him sorely. He made very little. In 1935, unable to maintain mortgage payments, we were dispossessed of our house and put out on the lawn with our belongings. I remember the desperation with which he sought a new flat. We moved to a shabby working class neighborhood where several of my playmates later served terms in the penitentiary.

My father knew very little Yiddish and almost nothing about reciting prayers in a synagogue. I never saw him read a book and he never attended a concert or a religious service. He loved sports and followed the local teams avidly. So did I. However, he had been a fine basketballer as a boy and my athletic accomplishments could be inscribed on the head of a pin. He never let on that this bothered him and retained all his life one of the most peaceful natures I have ever known. Felled by heart trouble he would die at 63. One of the few self-conscious moments in our relationship still makes me feel good: several years before he died, I wrote him a letter of appreciation.

My parents did not have deep affection for each other, but they treated each other with respect, especially in later years. Most of my youth comes back as an overwhelming feeling of uncertainty and instability, highlighted by the Depression, and my parents constant reference to being "poor, working people." The sense of never being able to breathe easily is still with me. At any moment the bottom can drop out...of course.

I can't honestly say that I was a bookish boy, at least I don't think I was or that people remember me that way, although I did go often to my branch library. I even took books with me to Boy Scout camp to which I was driven (over my protests) by my optometrist uncle who played an increasingly important and even sadistic role in my young life. "It will make a man of him" was the claim. Here, luckily I met a boy I would not under ordinary circumstances have met since he came from a higher social class. A rich Jewish doctor's son, he was more inept than I was at boy scouting and already at 14 wanted to be a professor. This began a profound and enduring friendship between the two boys, each of whom was an outsider and misfit. I learned a lot from him and we both used intellectual concerns as a defense against the Jewish bourgeois (and non-Jewish). It was our mark of self-worth and we clung to it with some arrogance. We were together almost constantly until he went off to graduate school at Harvard in 1948.

Being Jewish has occupied a contradictory place in my life. Neither zionist or observant, I feel Jewish. Yet, I have never in my life belonged to a synagogue and have, in fact, been put off by most of my experiences there. For some years during my first marriage I was a barely comfortable Unitarian but that too has worn out, perhaps because there are too many academics professing the one true non-faith.

I hated high school. I was a poor student, in contrast to elementary school. I found high school bewildering in a sense. None of the subject matter engaged me and for that I blamed myself. I found myself unable to study in any systematic way and high school experience taught me that I was dumb. Only the world of work was positive. With men away in the service, 1944-45, I found myself able to occupy adult positions. I was a machine operator, warehouser, shoe salesperson, and store wrapper. I liked my fellow employees and they seemed to like me and for the most part my bosses were okay about my performance. School told me I was lousy and even irrelevant but the world of work said I was OK.

Despite their own backgrounds both my parents were convinced that college was a great idea. Still my father harbored doubts and was more in touch with my own predelictions. Long before all the decisions had been made about my future I had told him of my interest in journalism and he thought it was a great idea, but his lack of power before my mother and her brother left me unable to be assertive or even recognize my own preferences which lay in the direction of history, the social sciences and humanities. To them it looked like too good a thing to pass up, insurance against disaster.

Going to college in my home town, even under the family pressure was enormously liberating. My friends tended to be other townies drawn to the local university by the then low tuition and/or GI Bill. They were Italian, German, Irish and black working class boys and I visited homes where no Jew had ever set foot. It was heady and liberating. They liked me and it was mutual. It provided comradeship I had not experienced among rising middle-class Jewish and non-Jewish people. Going to college meant merely walking a couple of miles in a different direction from high school but I entered a wholly different world. Freshman courses in politics and English were particularly eye opening to me.

By chance I heard a chamber music concert (I had been studying one evening in the chapel room where they set up). A traveling show of French impressionism hung in a building where I had a class and a Pissaro painting of a Paris street captivated me. I began to buy phonograph records almost without control. I can't recall how I fell in love with jazz but I remember buying a Commodore record of Muggsy Spanier and it churned lovely passions at first hearing. For years much of my energy was given to collecting records of Bix Beiderbecke, Bessie Smith, the *real* Louis Armstrong, Fats Waller, James P. Johnson. The college jazz club and its largely gadfly membership figured largely in my life. Once I sat next to the piano and listened to James P. Johnson play until five in the morning.

My reasons for choosing academe were based on a mixture of notions infused by popular culture and post-war idealism. It was a way to lead a life of some use, so I thought. And at that (1950), intimidated by the idea of working for a Ph.D., I chose secondary teaching.

Jobs were hard to find. Had I been able I probably would have stayed in my home town to teach. Such was not the case and I spent five years in rural America. The film "The Last Picture Show" was autobiography for me; I recognized everything in it even though that was Texas and I was in New York.

My first teaching job was in a depressed area and the sad and broken lives of my pupils were all too apparent. Everything stood out in sharp relief. The superintendent looked like Calvin Coolidge in the role of a Methodist Deacon. I worked on farms, however, and came to know that life to a certain degree and in some ways to relish it. I had never stood in a field before where all the land I could see belonged to one man. In college, one of my working class pals had once accused me of having a "Hebraic urge for the land" and I guess there was something to that. In those days the work was back breaking and I remember hoisting bales of hay onto the wagon with my under-developed city muscles aching.

My first teaching job was a disaster and reinforced my self-image of incompetence. I "lost control" of the kids by Thanksgiving because of my ill conceived view of Deweyan Progressivism which led me to shrink from even giving assignments. They had to want to do it. Can you imagine what resulted? I recall that the day after commencement I slept 'round the clock.

I was rightfully canned at the end of the term, returned to my father's house, worked in a factory that summer (at $20. per week more than teaching yielded) and thought of moving to New York to try to become the London correspondent of *Time*. Late in August I was informed of a teaching opening in yet another rural school and smarting at my failure decided to have another go at it. I met the superintendent, a rasp-voiced Pennsylvania German who had it as his mission to set the world straight. He told me that when he read my credentials he decided to send for me since "everyone needed a second chance." He treated me like a son and I came through.

This turned out to be one of the happiest years of my life. I was a SUCCESS. The kids liked me, the principal liked me, my colleagues favored me; even I had to accept the idea that I had done very well. Of course, I resigned and next fall went off to the Columbia School of Optometry which proved to be a disaster the very first week of classes. I yearned to be back teaching and the next year I did, eventually returning to that country school for three more years.

In 1962 I was awarded a National Defense Education Act Fellowship and went off to graduate school at age thirty-four. I would like to have done the study in history; instead I did the Foundations of Education, that being the only subject then designated as "defense" other than science and mathematics. I have often been struck by the sheer imbecility of this idea. I maximized my study of liberal arts history, philosophy and sociology and did the minimum in education. It is striking that the three graduate faculty members I felt at ease with were all from working class backgrounds.

I did my dissertation research in Great Britain. My topic seems to me typical and appropriate: "The Education Policy of the British Labour Party." My education professors barely approved; one wanted me to study room usage in British universities! However, my history mentor who had been a first mate in the merchant service heartily approved and his standing outweighed that of the *Ed boys*, thank God. Never having been out of the country before, the 1965 trek to Britain was a fairy tale. The family went and we stayed a semester and most of the summer with my kids attending local schools. I interviewed retired cabinet ministers, members of the House of Lords (all Labour), writers, socialist agitators and left wing educationists. My research took me to Labour Party headquarters and the Trades Union Congress. It was a heady and constantly exciting time for me and I would have gladly stayed in Britain had there been a way. But I didn't! I returned to the U.S. and have since undertaken a career as an academic that has been fraught with frustration and disappointment, though periodically punctuated with moments of great excitement and satisfaction. It was only in those moments that the past seemed distant. The rest of the time it has not.

Alonzo Bastian

The real breaking point in my life probably was my entry into military service following a year in college. The U.S. delivered me, green and full of eagerness, to no less an oasis than Paris, France ...The friends I made in the army...were mainly college graduates, many from such schools as Princeton, Columbia and Harvard.

I did not "choose" my academic career but more or less chanced upon it. I certainly did not seem a likely candidate to myself. Having been raised in a working class family that placed little or no emphasis on academic achievement, I had no early great interest in an academic career *or* intellectual accomplishment. And, having learned early on that I could get by adequately in most learning situations by simply staying awake, I failed to compile a distinguished high school or first year college academic record.

My father, though possessed of good business acumen, had very scant formal education. I believe he never completed more than six years of elementary education. An orphan at age 13, he worked to support himself and a younger brother. He worked at manual labor, becoming an electrician and a staunch union man. Through my father, I learned loyal Democratic politics and unbridled empathy for the working class.

My mother had more formal education than my father, having completed high school. There was evidence of more emphasis on book learning from her side of the family. One of her uncles had given her a complete set of the works of Shakespeare and she possessed another gilt-edged set of historical novels. I always admired these as a child and thought they somehow made my mother special, though I never saw her read them very often.

My family was traditional. My father earned the salary and my mother kept house and tended the children. She never gave any indication that she was dissatisfied with this role. My father never gave any indication that he would have tolerated any other role for her or himself. Even in the Depression years, when he was months without work, my mother never worked outside the home.

Her own mother had died at the birth of her and her twin sister. My mother and father traveled a good deal, so she was raised by an older half sister who ran a boarding house in a small east Texas town. She worked long hours in the kitchen and did farm chores.

I don't recall any real strong emphasis on class differences as a child, although on occasion, my father referred to "high falutin" people, a term I understood to mean the rich. But there was no animosity expressed and my father associated with his own bosses at social functions, apparently on intimate and good terms. He prided himself on hard, well-done work and became a well-respected craftsman in his trade. There was in my family, of course, the usual racist attitude of Southern families in the 1940s, and both my parents (and everyone else we knew) spoke disparagingly of blacks.

I believe I might have drifted into some trade or craft. However, already at age 14 or 15 I had become restive. I had discarded religion and had strong feelings about the treatment accorded black people. I would not speak out at the time, however. I only harbored within my own misgivings. I did enroll in junior college for an experimental year.

The real turning point in my life, however, was my entry into military service following the year in college. The U.S. Army delivered me, green and full of eagerness, to no less a cultural oasis than Paris, France. I was, quite literally, overwhelmed by the sophistication and culture of Europe, and by France in particular—additionally, the friends I made in the army, because of my job placement, were mainly college graduates. Many were from such schools as Princeton, Columbia and Harvard. I felt a little out of place with them, yet somehow fascinated at the same time. I threw myself into learning about gourmet foods and wines and about travel, architecture and language. I developed an appreciation for books and began to read: Tolstoy, Dostoyevsky, Thomas Mann, Voltaire, Henry Miller, Albert Camus and many others. These were writers I had never heard of before.

In France I also fell in love and lived for more than a year with a French woman seven years my senior. She was my tutor in the arts of love, cuisine and travel and assisted in my transformation from a green Texas kid into a more mature, self-assured young man.

Europe, and my experience there with the army, convinced me there was much more to life than I had ever imagined back in Texas. My own reasoning suggested to me that education was perhaps the way to get that extra dimension out of life. But having discovered so much of such interest outside the U.S., I wasn't ready to return. Unable to remain in France for financial reasons, I decided to attend college in Mexico, where I could live inexpensively and remain outside the U.S.

This basic dissatisfaction with the quality of life in the U.S. has persisted throughout my life. It is what sharpened and kept alive my critical attitude towards U.S. culture and values, with one lone exception. I continued to admire the U.S. for its greater opportunities afforded the common person. But I was dissatisfied that my country could obliterate so many other cultural, social, environmental and aesthetic values at the same time. It seemed to be a schizophrenic society.

I received a lot of impetus and encouragement to pursue my education while in Mexico. Now instilled with an interest in learning, I excelled academically, graduating first in my class. My teachers constantly encouraged me to continue in graduate education.

My wife, whom I met and married in Mexico, added another important source for this impetus. She came from a distinguished intellectual family. There were concert pianists, professors, medical doctors, artists, symphonic directors and attorneys. Though my wife did not directly try to influence me (she was probably more suspicious of academic intellectuals than I, and with more cause), the overall influence of her background and family definitely had something to do with my mounting drive to "get a Ph.D."

Whatever the precise combination of motivating factors, I did well academically and, upon graduation, I received several excellent offers to attend graduate schools in the United States.

Dick Brandt

...I had wanted to be an architect. My parents were not willing or able to pay for my college education. It was understood that I could live at home and they would pay my room and board, but I would have to pay for all my college expenses, my transportation and all of my own entertainment. So I became an engineer basically by default.

I'm the youngest of seven children from a working class family, and I grew up in a midwestern city, and I'm the only one to have completed high school. I'm 37 years old. My parents are in their mid to late 70s. My father was a machinist in a steel plant most of his life and grew up on a farm. He was a member of the United Steel Workers Union. He remembers and was involved in the organizing strikes of the '30s in the steel plants. My mother always has been a mother and housewife. She's not held a job for many years. When my parents were first married she worked as a seamstress in a sweatshop; and she had worked as a seamstress in a sweatshop before she was married from the time she was about 15 years old. Her father was a foreman in the steel plant where my father worked. I have an older brother who is about 16 years older than me who also worked in the steel plant as a brick layer. I had two uncles who were brick layers in the steel plant and another uncle who worked there as a laborer. My other brother, who is about ten years older than me, is an electric lineman for an electric company in the metropolitan area. My older sister is married to a printer. My next oldest sister is married to a man who went to college and eventually became an executive for a large corporation. And my next sister, eight years older than me, married a dentist.

Most of my family grew up in a working class neighborhood, but when I was fairly young my family began to move around. I was not part of a very identifiable working class

71

community. To any extent that there is any ethnic background in my family it was German although we did not identify strongly as being German.

My entry into academia was a long and circuitous one. My entry into sociology was an even longer one. I suspect that his kind of indirect route to academia is more common among working class people than middle class people. I have a feeling that this roundaboutness is why you find more academics from working class backgrounds in less prestigious schools than in more prestigious schools.

Let me describe the route of my education. As the youngest child in the family I was described as a somewhat bright child and I had opportunities that my older brothers and sisters didn't. I had an opportunity to go to a special Catholic preparatory high school. This high school had almost exclusively middle class students and I felt rather out of place there. I didn't know how to dress. I felt funny. My clothes were always baggy and the other kids were well dressed. Other kids had money to do things, to buy lunch, to do things at lunch time, etc. and I didn't. But more importantly there was a distinct difference between their cultural outlook and mine. I was a very shy kid and I never really said anything. This high school environment had a significant effect on me in some ways. I was interested in academics, I was interested in knowing things. But I experienced the snobbishness of many of these middle class kids.

I suppose I did a little anticipatory socialization of myself by beginning to read; by for example subscribing to magazines. Magazines were things that were not available to me in my home. In fact, the only kinds of magazines we ever had in the home were "hand-me-down" magazines from my aunt's family. And those were religious. Occasionally we would get a *Reader's Digest* but that was about it.

I received very little guidance although I got good grades. I knew little about loans, scholarships, or anything else. As a consequence, I would go to college assuming that I really didn't have any choice other than a local college in the city. Also, I had to choose the engineering program because, by doing so, I would be able to pay my own way. In fact, I had wanted to be an architect. My parents were not willing or able to pay for my college education. It was understood that I could live at home and they would pay my room and board, but I would have to pay for all my college expenses, my transportation and all of my own entertainment. So I became an engineer basically by default.

It wasn't that I disliked engineering. I certainly enjoyed the academic parts of it as I enjoyed most academic studies. I enjoyed learning, I enjoyed finding out things, I enjoyed learning how to do things, and engineering satisfied these needs quite well. I was proud of being an engineer because it was hard work and it implied a certain amount of intelligence on my part. On the other hand, I disliked the negative image of engineers. It wasn't until I finished getting a bachelors and a masters degree in engineering, and then working for a couple of years in a large corporation as an engineer, that I decided that I did not want to continue the rest of my life in this kind of environment. But rather than knowing what I wanted to do and knowing what choices were available, once again I entered graduate school, this time in Social Psychology, with relatively little knowledge of that field. I chose a school which was in the general vicinity and where I could receive a sufficient teaching fellowship to support myself. My basic goal was to get a Ph.D. so that I could teach in a college or university. I saw such a plan as being the least of evils, as it would give me job security. As it turned out, the job security was not really there for many years to come. I was admitted to a very good program in the field of social psychology.

While I was in graduate school I gradually came to realize that I was dissatisfied with that field. But, again I was unaware of desirable alternatives. Eventually, after two or three years searching on my own I decided on being a sociologist. I nevertheless got my degree in psychology and began looking for a job in sociology. All of this resulted in a rather haphazard development of my career. The consequence is that I was a late starter, not only in getting my degree, but also in developing my research and my scholarship, since I did not study within an existing traditional framework. Basically I followed my concerns. There were answers that I was trying to find and I searched anywhere I could.

Basically, also, I was on my own, with little guidance from any mentors, masters, or major professors to find answers to these questions. I took something from here and something from there and constructed something myself. There is probably nothing wrong with what I came up with and many people, even well known people, have given me high praise for some of the things I have written. Yet the consequence of that style of scholarship has been that my work does not fall neatly into any little niche, any little pattern. It doesn't fit easily in any tradition and therefore into any journals. Often things that I submit for publication will get a wide range of reviews from different reviewers from very good to very bad. The problem with publishing them is that I simply don't fit into a niche.

The reason that I mention all of this is because I think that, in some ways at least, it is traceable to my working class background. I did not know what I was doing, I was merely following my concerns, my interests, my nose. There was no guidance there for me. There was no guidance from high school; neither of my parents were knowledgeable enough to know how to guide me. So, basically I had to find out on my own.

CHAPTER 3

The Academic
Work Process

I n the *next* chapter we will consider the contradiction
and tension associated with the movement from the
working class to a middle-zone between that class and
the upper classes. We will also examine the problem of
alienation in its several dimensions, that is, in the sense of
separateness from the academic community, of being a
stranger, distanced from an authentic sense of self, and also
from one's past, the cultural network of earlier life. However,
it will add depth to that exploration in the next chapter—
and to the rest of the book—if we look more directly and in
greater detail here at the manifestation of capitalist social
relations within the worklife of the academy. We thereby
extend our discussion, begun in Chapter 1, of the process of
higher learning in the U.S.

i.

In the socialization of the academic aspirant, particularly through the channel of graduate education, the candidate for professorship is made acutely aware of the role
played by prestige and standing in the realm of professional
academics and academic administrators. Indeed, such concern competes powerfully with truth, justice, beauty, and
the autonomy of the university to pursue inquiry in a free
and unencumbered manner. The preoccupation with standing can be understood in a variety of terms. With high
standing comes reputation, which attracts good students

and faculty, which in turn attracts sponsors and donors, which creates the financial base to attract more good students and "productive" faculty. For the individual there is the need to stand out above the crowd of ordinary plodders. For the institution or department, there is the need to secure position in the first rank.

It had not been obvious to us that this scramble for standing always represents hunger for knowledge, or the noble impulses to release the human race from the bonds of ignorance or superstition. It *has* appeared to us as a rather predictable result of capitalist social relations. Such implications, for certain, can be drawn when we elevate this struggle to the level of institutional competition. In the opinion of Robert Blackburn, Professor of Higher Education, Center for the Study of Higher Education, University of Michigan:

> The factor which dominates all other professional concerns is attention to status. Professors wish to be number one - if not for themselves then for their department, as teachers, and certainly, for their institutions as a whole and its ranking with other colleges and universities. A concern for excellence in this regard reveals their highly competitive nature.[1]

What Blackburn does not state here but implies is the range of significance attached to standing in a class society. The competition is fierce, for the stakes are great. The psychological survival of ego, whether it be the ego of professional individualism or administrative careerism, is determined by how you emerge from the melee. It might be supposed that the competitive mill can be attributed to the pursuit of excellence or some other high-minded notion. Yet, we can see this phenomenon as reflecting capitalist culture, where, in this case, prestige replaces wealth as the mediating value.

Where might we locate academics from working class backgrounds in this competition? One study, a 1977 survey of about 4,200 faculty, made by Everett Ladd and Seymour Lipset,[2] showed that academics from working class backgrounds constitute about *one quarter* of the total academy. Of course the number alone means little, other than that we are a "sizable" minority. What can we, or others, say about this minority worth noting? Peter Blau, in his analysis of academic work, offers some noteworthy inferences with respect to the question of "who gets where in the academy?" He finds that a highly disproportionate number of faculty whose fathers have a college degree are members of the more prestigious Ph.D., granting institutions. He concludes in his study that the reputation of an institution has a profound connection to the social origins of the faculty.[3] And D.W. Light and Associates, in an extremely useful study of the academy, confirm others' findings that class background has much to do with access to the doctorate and success in completion and quality graduate school admission. Concerning the prestige of graduate school, they point out that "training at a top graduate school is important throughout an academic career, because academic life tends to be ascriptive."[4] Moreover, they found that *a full 83% of the faculty at the top twelve graduate schools held their highest degrees from the same institution.*[5] In sum, access to these institutions is, not at all surprisingly, largely a function of social class background which formulates direction of a career, determining in large measure where one stands in the academic ranks. Further, Robert Presthus has noted that an Ivy League school on occasion will hire faculty who have been denied tenure at other Ivy League schools before they will take a person who has put together a highly successful career outside the rarified confines of the Ivy League.[6]

The upshot of all these analyses is that the late arrivers on the professional scene, for the most part, end up somewhere towards the bottom of the prestige scale of the profession, if for no other reason, they are affiliated with second rank institutions. Assuming working class academics are to some degree assimilated into the cultural ethos of the professional, they may subjectively experience their social reality as back down on the bottom of the heap, as mass, indistinguishable and undistinguished. The 1979 Richard Coleman and Lee Rainwater study of social class standing gives some credence to this suggestion. In their study of status groups, they found that most commonly the reference group that people used to ascertain their individual standing was the one they toiled in rather than the one they started in. Further, the criteria of that reference group was used to assign self-location. This result is particularly likely for higher status groups who use the relative prestige of social club membership, size of houses, neighborhoods, associations as basic markers by which they differentiate themselves.[7]

For academics, criteria such as publication record, prestige of the institution of association, how little or how much one teaches, one's pattern of collegial association (cosmopolitan or local), are the conventional symbols of status. Consider the opportunities for self-loathing to discover that it matters little that one one has climbed out of the depths of the social order to make "something" of oneself, only to find that again one can end up at the bottom of a much approved heap, but nonetheless a heap and there is a bottom. Also, these new opportunities emerge ironically in the midst of uncommon personal success.

To put the matter more broadly, capitalist social relations *always* have a few at the top and the many at the bottom. Access to the top is masked as simply a matter of meritocratic selection rather than as inherited advantage. Those who hold sway in the academy are invited to be self-congratulatory, even pompous, and the folks at the bottom are encouraged, if not by persons by circumstances, to be envious, self-abnegating, or invisible. Although sometimes underfoot, they ultimately are useful in doing the academic dirty work, namely teaching students who often have little use for ideas or even for their own minds. And,of course, as it is in the larger society, those who control the real and symbolic stations of power get to call the tune while the rest hope that they hear it and dance to it well. Importantly, all these kinds of behavior have been encouraged especially by the imposition of a particular model of professionalism, perhaps appropriate at elite, Ph.D. granting institutions, on the entire professoriate. This remarkable piece of mischief needs some attention here.

ii.

A dominant result of the so-called academic revolution after WW II is the enshrining of the *research oriented university* and the *research oriented professor* as the model for the profession as a whole.[8] The consequences of this development are numerous and have vast implications for the internal life of the profession and the careers of academics. The establishment of the research university and the scholar research model of an academic career as the "ideal" establishes hierarchy where none need exist. Academia is complex and diverse and is comprised of vastly different institutions with respect to size, financial resources, student quality and faculty abilities and interests. All academic institutions *could* be respected for what and who they are and regarded as integral components in an enterprise dedicated to the weakening of the "irreducible philistinism and anti-intellectualism of the American population," as Norman Birnbaum has put it.[9] The levels of this huge undertaking *could* be mutually regarding and mutually respectful, and mindful of the different missions that must be addressed by the profession as a whole. Instead, we have what Everett Ladd has called, "the tyranny of the research model," engulfing, if not devouring the entire profession, a model which is inherently hierarchical and attractive to academic administration at large.[10]

In this framework, the language of academic administration takes on that of the manager in the factory setting. And, we find college administrators pontificating about productivity measures that are easily quantifiable in the assessment of the worth of the faculty member and the "progress" of the institution, measured by the number of published pages-per-full-time faculty equivalent. The logic of such a policy can hardly be denied, given several key assumptions. First, it must be assumed that good teaching depends upon active and continuous scholarship; second, that there is no inherent conflict between "publish and/or perish"; and third, that the reputation of the institution is based on the scholarly output of its faculty, which in turn, influences its ability to attract good students and more good faculty. Hence, scholarly output improves the institution and sustains professional development. We do not wish to engage the questions raised by these claims for the purpose of putting them to eternal rest, but certain aspects of the issue are reasonably clear. For example, Ladd's work has shown that a considerable majority of academics—perhaps as many as *seventy percent*—think of themselves as "teachers," as opposed to "scholars" or "scientists."[11] This self designation is, as one might suspect, more common among those attached to two-year, liberal arts, or non-elite comprehensive colleges and universities. Yet, Ladd points out in his commentary on the matter that most faculty feel professional self-identification as "college teachers" is deficient or inappropriate, and they are thus invited into the pit of self-deception, some the victims of "research model tyranny."

For most academics, their normal duties, indeed the bulk of their responsibilities, are teaching and some participation in the operations of maintaining their educational institutions. Caplow and McGee point out in their work on academics that in *most* occupations people are judged by how well they perform their *normal* duties. But, quite differently, academics at schools where the research model dominates are judged most importantly by the performance of the part-time, voluntary job they create for themselves. These authors argue that in such institutions "it is only a slight exaggeration to say that academic success is likely to come to the man who has learned to neglect his assigned duties in order to have more time and energy to pursue his private professional interests."[12] While we agree with the claim that active scholarship and good teaching are sometimes positively related, clearly the possibility of this result is greater at elite institutions where student loads, teaching schedules and support for research are more suited to allow professors to pursue *both* activities. At lesser institutions, particularly middle rank institutions (where most of our contributors reside), the tensions are greater, given the weight of the "normal duties" and the human limits on time and energy. Light remarks that "A teacher at Eastgate College, by neglecting students to research, write, publish," can secure his position or be recognized within the institution and the profession. The conflict, according to Irving Goffman, makes "the moral career of the academic man, perhaps as complex and troubled as the moral career of the mental patient."[13]

The adoption of this research model at "lesser" institutions is best understood, in large measure, as a consequence of the rise of managerialism in U.S. Higher Education. The two developments go hand in glove. Since the bureaucratic institutions thrive on a clearly defined hierarchical order, the maintenance of such an ordering of status depends fundamentally upon some simple set of evaluative criteria that are readily quantifiable. What better device could one hope for than the published article, a discrete unit of evidence which can be offered as proof of productivity and quality? Other preferred measures of faculty worth are similar in their "concrete" quality, such as numbers of grants obtained, the dollars attracted to the campus, consultantships, and also quantified student evaluations of teaching effectiveness.

The rise of systematic, often quantitative, evaluations of teaching has come from demands by students for a say in their assessment of their professors' performance as teachers. It is our observation that these assessments have become grist for bureaucrats to be interpreted as they choose. Student evaluations of teaching often can be predicted on the basis of the professor's personal style, and while a strong case can be made for the reliability of these evaluations, a strong one can be made against them, too. Put simply, students might make common judgements about who is, and who is not a good teacher, but usually there is little in such evaluations which offers a solid sense of who, in fact, is effective in the facilitation of students' intellectual and moral development. The upshot is an unresolved quarrel about what are the characteristics of good college teaching, and this more than anything else, in the managerial era, has led to deemphasizing of teaching as a basis for faculty retention and promotion. Teaching evaluations, of any kind, tend to be, in the mind of the modern administrator, of second order of relevance, and in some cases, of no concern at all. The bureaucratic conscience too often suffers not at all from the exclusion of unmeasureable criteria; that is, what is not quantifiable to such a mind, *is not real*. Further, the "litigious society" has encompassed the university as it has most of our institutions, and this has given further impetus to the use of "hard" data in evaluation procedures on campus—such as the *number* of things (pages, dollars, students, conferences, lectures, etc.).

There is, of course, the annual tip of the mortar board to teaching, ordinarily in the form of "Teaching Awards." Jacque Barzun has fittingly described the probable psychological matrix into which these awards are ceremoniously thrust. He writes that:

> Some effort, it is true, is made to recognize the stay-at-homes who do the most consecutive teaching and thereby ballast the balloon. Money and honor are bestowed on such men in the form of Distinguished Teacher Awards. The students...turn out...to applaud. The trustees are sincere in their congratulations. But the aroma of the consolation prize clings to these distinctions. Even on his own campus the "great teacher" can be explained away as a lovable man of average competence—"not enough for a great university." His counterpart, the average man of research, lovable or unloveable, is still felt to be worth more. The difference tells us what society, in its loving dependence on the new university, instinctively seeks and willingly pays for.[14]

Mr. Chips, now among the most pathetic creatures on the campus!

Another way in which universities try to measure their own success is how many of their graduates go to the "better" graduate schools, medical schools, law schools or climb on the "best" career ladders. That is another numbers game. But, there is a terrible blinded side to this index of success. For example, when a prized student graduates, becomes a crack lawyer, then writes elegant foreclosure notices for the local bank, it is *not* ordinarily a matter of public importance to the administrators back on the campus that the young lawyer has trampled people in trouble, and has done so without a noticeable flutter of internal conflict. Nor would the Dean of the Engineering School be likely to find reason for a public and personal renunciation because his or her most brilliant student sells his or her services to a chemical company to make nerve gas for the Pentagon.

Perhaps, in light of recent revelations[15] the ultimate example here is Henry Kissinger and Harvard University. Much has been made of the fact that the Great Kissinger left the Great Harvard, to offer his services to the Great Nixon. Yet, as the historical record is uncovered, Kissinger is described more with each episode unearthed quite often to be a liar, always a manipulator, and, perhaps, on more than one occasion, a party to mass murder. However, Kissinger is "Kissinger," and Harvard is "Harvard" because the public which evaluates the performances of both has become infatuated with "brilliant conceptual thinking," and other forms of "hardball intellectualizing." One wonders, when one thinks of Harvard University, and its many luminaries—including such brilliant ones as McGeorge Bundy, Robert McNamara, and Kissinger—how many defenseless people in the world have been blasted to smithereens because the awesome "intelligence" of these three men was warped by dehumanization of the faceless thousands they ordered to be murdered by others. One wonders, too, whether the research model, with its particular emphasis on "objective" scholarship, has not been a silent partner to these proceedings where the line between "intellectual hardball" and barbarism is often hard to distinguish.

Whatever pretense remains that the academy is a repository of virtue, or has the special responsibility to the moral conduct of the larger society and to make known its view, or prepares students to march through life in quest of the truth, is increasingly relegated to bursts of rhetoric reserved for commencement day speeches. Given the crass reality of the educational experience and the overwhelming evidence that the academy increasingly is dedicated to a narrow bureaucratic conception of success, it is not surprising how that fewer listen to its whining justifications for what it does on behalf of bankers, politicians and generals.

iii.

How does one actually account for the rise and triumph of the bureaucrat at universities in the U.S.? To this question, Norman Birnbaum answers that the division of academic labor expresses, more or less with some lag time, the division of labor in the larger society. Thus, if the production system is experiencing a managerial revolution, characterized by bureaucratic decision styles, these styles will ultimately touch, if not overwhelm, the substructures of society, such as the academy.[16]

Harry Braverman, in his groundbreaking work, *Labor and Monopoly Capital: The Degradation of Work in the Twentieth Century* (1974), has described in great detail the rise of managerialism in the modern capitalist firm. And, we can see in the following passage from his book that he is describing succinctly the process Birnbaum claims to have been mimicked on the campus. As Braverman puts it:

> ...Corresponding to the managing functions of the capitalist of the past, there is now a complex of departments, each of which has taken over in greatly expanded form a single duty which it exercised with very little assistance in the past. Corresponding to each of these duties there is not just a single manager, but an entire operating department which imitates in its organization and its functioning the factory out of which it grew...Management has become *administration, which is a labor process conducted for the purpose of control within the corporation*, and conducted moreover as a labor process exactly analogous to the process of production although it produces no product other than the operation and coordination of the corporation.[17] (Braverman's emphasis)

Birnbaum describes persuasively the parallel development that has occurred at the university.* In the medieval university, he suggests, the faculties exercised a collective mastership over learning. But, as industrial society evolved

———————————————————————

*The evidence here is compelling to say the least. Logan Wilson reports that in 1942 for every *100* professors in U.S. higher education, there were about *16* administrators. By 1976-1977, in public universities the ratio was 19/100; in private institutions, the ratio, apparently verging on being out of control, was 35.7/100! (Wilson, op.cit., 1979, pp. 81-82)

in the 19th century, the old order came under stress because bourgeois individualism asserted itself with the emergence of what Birnbaum calls "scholarly virtuosi." These events were followed closely by the development of disciplines which rigidly compartmentalized knowledge, that reflected further the division of labor as it evolved in the larger society. The rise of the managers to control, long ago heralded by Thorstein Veblen,[18] Upton Sinclair, [19] and others, completes the transformation of the university from the archaic, medieval community of scholars to the production-oriented, efficiency-conscious educational system of today, a reflection of the "organizational society" of which it is part. It would perhaps be more appropriate that today's academic regalia be comprised of expensive business suits and that the marshall of academic procession carry an attache case rather than a mace.

As all know, there is a continuum here, from the major universities, where the research model dominates; to the private college devoted, if not in waiting, to undergraduate students, where teaching is at a premium; to the two-year schools, where heavy teaching loads absorb all the time of the faculty. However, predominant in U.S. higher learning is an ambiance dominated by the ideal of the research model. The overriding presence explains why it is possible for the exceptionally fine teacher at the community college, spending fifteen hours per week in the classroom, to feel inferior, or subordinate, to his/her counterparts at an elite university, who are most intensively producing publications—often of no social use whatsoever—that will make them academic stars. As we have argued, the major problem here is that it would take a thorough reconstruction of society to produce higher education which made heroes of fine teachers, rather then research scholars, most of the latter of whom do not communicate in a language understandable for the larger public, and who avoid students when possible, particularly undergraduates. It is a measure of the state of things—especially the status of teaching in universities— that an academic at a research university can be expected to take great pride in wrangling a contract for the following year, perhaps buttressed by outside research funds, which will allow him or her to abandon students and, with luck, the campus, too.

The acceleration of the trend toward managerialism might best be understood in its specifics as importantly the outcome of the requirement of accountability established by outside funding agencies, such as federal and state governments and large foundations. These institutions play a significant role in the fiscal life of a good many universities, great and not-so-great, alike. Consider this example of that influence and the moral grounding of the university that it implies. In April, 1981, the leading academic officers of several large, research oriented universities appeared before the House Armed Services Committee to beg for defense funds for their schools. As Will Lepkowski tells the story, the lead witness was Richard C. Atkinson, Chancellor of the University of California at San Diego. Atkinson argued that:

> Given the immense security needs that face the nation, Department of Defense's underinvestment in basic research is alarming and cannot help but have a devastating effect on our national defense capabilities.

Then, Atkinson was followed by high officers from the University of Rochester, the University of Alabama at Huntsville, Rutgers University and the University of Utah. Said Vice-President for Research Brophy from Utah University:

> In defense, our current superiorities in the technologies of missile guidance, advanced aircraft, submarines, and space defense systems rest on a foundation of research built up over the last decade or more. If we are to retain our lead in critical areas and remain competitive in the world market place, additional work is needed in fields such as computer sciences, materials, advanced electronics.[20]

Specifically, according to Anne C. Roark, in another account of this same story, these university officials wanted $4 billion in Pentagon funds for all U.S. campuses for basic research, in addition to what they were already to receive, during the next fifteen years.[21]

Other examples of such university feeding habits abound. For instance, the President and Provost at Princeton, and 160 others, hold security clearances enabling them to traffic in classified information that relates to military research done there. Indeed, Seymour Bogdonoff, head of Princeton's Mechanical and Aerospace Engineering Department, which is, according to Steve Burkholder, "close to being an extension of the Pentagon," told Burkholder that:

> We don't work on applications [of military research]. But what we do has a lot of applications...We don't do anything unless we think there are important applications...I like working for the Department of Defense—and you can write that if you like. They've supported us in basic research for years.[22]

At the University of Michigan, in response to student and faculty protests in the early 70s, the University banned research that might "destroy human life or incapacitate human beings." Yet, alongside the Ann Arbor campus exists a private think tank (once a part of the university) called "Environment Research Institute of Michigan," which, in 1981, did $5 million in Pentagon business. Two thirds of this research was secret military work and much was done by University of Michigan faculty members. All in all, in 1980 the Pentagon spent over $500,000,000 for military research at U.S. universities. About *one third* of this went to Johns Hopkins, *one-fourth* went to M.I.T., and the bulk of the remainder was spread out over most of the rest of America's most prestigious research universities.*

The symbiosis thus gets tighter between the generals and the scholars, and that is why Dr. George Gamota, the Defense Department's research director in 1981, said that "That's a new population out there. The universities participate because of their interest, not ours. We don't solicit."[23]

As the Pentagon and other federal agencies have become more and more enmeshed in higher education, complex procedures for grant applications, administration and

---

*After John Hopkins and M.I.T., the top twenty recipients of military research funds in 1980 were: University of California (system), Illinois Institute of Technology, Stanford, University of Texas, University of Rochester, Georgia

evaluation require more management technique and, consequently, more personnel. State legislatures demand more and more evidence of "productivity" before they approve huge state higher education budgets, pressing university administrators to urge the faculty to "produce" more of what could be offered as evidence that the public's money was spent well and that professors weren't idling about, teaching or thinking unpublishable thoughts. Of course, much the same can be said of foundations and their granting procedures about the level of scholarly productivity that is necessary to be eligible for support. More bureaucratization became essential and, of course, more measurable faculty productivity. And as this process unfolds, the faculty member whose services are now in demand beyond the campus and whose status often depends upon that demand, begins to see the "teaching profession" as a vehicle to other kinds of career goals. Coupled with the demands of academic managers for higher productivity to enhance the universities' eligibility for funding, one has the circumstances which produce the neglect and desertion of students and the increasing reluctance of faculty to spend time and energy on the requirements of the normal operation of the university, setting the stage for student unrest and their bid for greater attention and responsiveness from their institutions.

All these trends and developments culminate in the need for more management personnel (as have affirmative action rules and the budgetary crisis of the 1970s caused by protracted stagnation). As Jacques Barzun describes them, U.S. universities:

> ...have become bureaucracies like business and government. To defend its life against envious neighbors, against city hall, the state, and Washington, as well as against militant groups and individuals within, the academy obviously needs officials of the bureaucratic type; and their attitude

---

Tech Research Institute, University of Dayton, Penn State University, University of Southern California, University of Washington, University of Alaska, Carnegie Mellon, University of Illinois, University of New Mexico, California Institute of Technology, Harvard, University of Pennsylvania, Columbia University.

inevitably spreads throughout the campus by contagion.[24]

Thus, under these circumstances, the university is transformed, and along with it so is the academic career. A hallmark, and indeed one of the significant benefits of the academic work life, was once the strong possibility that intrinsic motivation, or inner directedness, could produce certain psychic rewards. Today, the type of organization that academics find themselves in is described by Robert Millikan as a "semi-military form of organization with lines of authority and responsibility clearly marked." He continues by asking:

Let me call it the Pentagon philosophy of organization, and let me recognize the fact that wherever *action* is more important than *wisdom*, as in military operations and to a lesser extent in American business, it represents at any rate a natural, if not necessary, mode of organization.[25]

We believe that Millikan's characterization accurately describes the transformation of the academic institution to the present day. Increasingly, the faculty member must function within action-oriented organizations. As Logan Wilson expresses these matters, the academics' dilemma is as follows:

Those who dispense largesse are certain to make dependents, if not create disciples: for much of the academician's immediate welfare, irrespective of his technical competence, depends on administrative policy and how he fits into the scheme of things.[26]

Calculations about where one fits in the administrative scheme of things surely call to question the survivability of intrinsic motivation, autonomy, and any other factors that have made up the reward package that once attracted people to the career.

iv

Today the academic career game is played on the administration's turf, and it surely does not lack for players.

A theme which runs through many—but surely not all—of our autobiographies is dismay at the prevalence of careerist calculation among colleagues. Career consciousness and its careful nurturance, we assume, is a skill much more easily learned in a middle or upper class family. No doubt, talk of "getting that promotion," or moving laterally within the field, are common topics of dinner conversation and, indeed, a preoccupation, of those "getting ahead." Alternatively, *having* a job and *keeping* it, is more a working class perspective on the world of work. To the academic from a working class background, the preoccupation of colleagues with career advancement *may* appear puzzling. It may also appear as behavior worth mimicking, or as a unenviable cave-in to the bosses' manipulations. If there are differences *between* the classes* on this matter, and we believe there are, they may be best understood as reflections of the differences in socialization. Sizing up the organization and what it takes to succeed is a skill more available we think to the person with a background where such concerns are commonplace in his/her family. Again, we have a neat fit between the academic manager's need to structure the career path of the faculty, and a majority of faculty members dying to follow it. The concept of intrinsic motivation or autonomy, sufficient for the real self to be present in work life, go into the dust bin of academic history. And for the working class person, disenchanted by the realization and poorly trained as a careerist, the possibility of that wonderful combination of impotent fury, rooted in confusion.

As is widely known in the academy, the tradition of tenure is the only thing that keeps the frolicking dreams and clever manipulations of academic managers somewhat at bay. It is the only protection available to someone who resists the prevailing values in the academy, either by such un-academic behavior as engaging in spirited political

---

*As we shall see, there are most certainly differences *within* classes as well: our autobiographical essays make that point clear enough. Our point here is only that the careerism that dominates middle class life is *habitual* to its members, but it must be newly learned by many, but not all, working class people who enter the world of work.

activity off-campus, or loudly and aggressively resisting the latest effort by trustees to turn the campus into a replica of a department store or a chemical plant, in its personnel policies. No doubt, each evening upon retiring, some university and college administrators actually confronted with such misfits, pray for a bolt from the blue or the courage to cashier the 1940 AAUP statement on tenure and to assign it, also, to the bin of academic history. Like academic regalia, Mr. Chips, in *loco parentis*, or the idea of a unified faculty in control of its work-life and dedicated to admirable values, the dust bin beckons "tenure."

What is "tenure," and where does it come from? For many readers—perhaps the great majority who are not academics—this question needs answering. Concerning, first, how does a tenure policy *work*, we describe a *typical* one briefly. (And, among universities, the details will vary, but what follows is the essence.) Approximately three quarters of all academics at four year colleges and universities have what is called a "continuing contract." This means that a person (who in the *great* majority of cases must hold a Ph.D. from an accredited institution) is hired for an initial two year period as an "assistant professor," working under the tutelage (if not the thumb) of "associate" and "full" professors. At the end of that two year probationary period, then again after four years (if rehired), the "candidate for tenure" will be subject to a full review of his/her work.

The basis of that review will be three general areas: scholarship (the ideal of which means publication in prestigious academic journals, or book writing); teaching the students; and "service to the community," off and/or on campus (which can be serving on university committees, in organizations of the local community, and so forth.) Then, if the candidate is still at the institution after *six* years, another review is done, this one the most extensive of them all, and again it is a review of scholarship, teaching competence, and community service. On the basis of this "tenure review," the candidate is either sent "upward," usually as an associate professor, or "outward," onto the street as an outcast (the latter route after a grace year is given to find another job.)

Typically, the participants in the review process, who truly count, and in the order in which they participate, are 1) the candidate's department members who themselves have tenure, and sometimes with counsel from representative students about the candidate's teaching prowess; 2) the Dean of the candidate's college, such as the College of Arts and Sciences; 3) the President, or some other academic officer, or both; and 4) the Board of Trustees. Almost always, once an appointment is approved by the President, the Board will go along, though there are occasional exciting exceptions to this rule.

Of course, to describe the review process is also to give signal that there is often cause for struggle in tenure decision making, for it is a process involving several people with differing ideologies, different niches in the social and institutional hierarchy, with differing amounts of power, vying with each other over a complex, often contradictory, number of factors. Consider a hypothetical (but common) example of such a "tenure struggle." Let's assume a university where the chief academic officers (president, dean, provost, vice-president) believe faculty should, in order to get tenure, publish widely in prestigious journals, or write scholarly books, particularly ones that bring favorable attention to the university and, of course, to themselves as its officers. Let's assume, further, that both the candidate and the members of her department consider fine teaching most important in such "retention" decisions. The outcome of the struggle that will likely ensue (unless the assumed faculty adopts a subordinate function in personnel matters) is always difficult to predict in advance, as one can imagine. But, whatever the outcome, it will be a result almost always of the relative power within the institution that the contestants can bring to the affair, most especially the extent to which each camp can usher to its side support from the rest of the faculty.

We recognize the difficulty our readers might have in appreciating this hypothetical example, particularly if they have never been exposed to tenure politics on a campus. Fortunately, many specific details, at the level of both fact and feeling, of real struggles between faculty and administrators are contained in the autobiographies, in Part II, as we shall see. For such readers, we beg patience until we get to these autobiographies.

Given its nature, and as we might imagine, the conflict between the teacher/scholars and their would-be bosses over the power of appointment and retention is an old one.

So let's look briefly at the history of tenure, that slender legal reed on which this policy hangs in higher education. Actually, it is an exceedingly interesting history, featuring princes, popes, other powerful people, often pitted in harsh combat with academics, academic administrators, sometimes both. Also, fortunately, it has been concisely summarized by Howard Metzger,[27] and we will follow his facts and interpretation in our brief comments here. According to Metzger, as recently as 1913 a professor of economics at Wesleyan University named Willard C. Fisher was forced to resign his post for public remarks in which he urged less rigid observation of the Sabbath and the subordination of church-going to good works. Prior even to Fisher's travail, in 1900, had been the celebrated "Ross" case, involving a professor of economics who was openly critical of laissez-faire doctrine and the practice of the Southern Pacific Railroad. His remarks made Jane Lathrop Stanford, widow of a California rail baron and sole trustee of Stanford University, very unhappy. Stanford's president at the time, David Starr Jordan, after some soul searching, induced Ross to resign for the good of the organization, meaning, in this case, to avoid having his head delivered to the university's sole benefactress. When pressed by the professional community, Jordan insisted that Ross was not pressured to resign for what he said, but rather for his slangy and scurrilous way of speaking. Academic freedom was not the issue, Jordan argued, it was more a matter of inappropriate conduct.

It was cases such as these that led members of the academic profession to band together to form the AAUP and to secure for professional academics protection from abuses to their assumed freedom. The culmination of this movement was the 1940 AAUP statement on tenure, which became widely accepted as the governing document in U.S. higher education. The 1940 statement established a clear distinction between a probationary period of seven years at the maximum, and a tenured appointment. In this probationary period, faculty could not claim entitlement to a continuing position. If they were not recommended for tenure by their peers and so annointed by the administration and trustees, they were expected to pack up and move on with little or no fuss. However, the circumstances of dismissal were vastly different for the academic, once tenured. Here,

the rule was emphatic: "Except in the case of financial
exigency, all dismissals were to be for cause and were to be
judicially determined."[28] Hence, the burden fell onto the
university to show that financial exigency did in fact exist,
or that Professor Doe was in fact, grossly incompetent, or
immoral, or dangerous. What is carved virtually in stone at
this point is the policy of "up or out," and, "if up, then in."

While the policy was never without complications or
critics,* it survived the period of post-war growth and
expansion mostly unscathed. Yet, the question arises whether it will withstand the circumstances that come with the
"post golden age" and the deeper establishment of managerialism, in academic administration. The frontal attack on
the system has come through a possible modification of the
"financial exigency" provision of the 1940 AAUP statement. In short, that modification holds that if an administration deems that a certain instructional program no
longer warrants support by the institution, it *might* now be
the law that the program can be discontinued and the
faculty attached to it dismissed, regardless of their rank.
This interpretation of tenure law was upheld by the U.S.
Court of Appeals for the First Circuit in 1981, in a suit
involving Humacoo University College of the University of
Puerto Rico. The school had dismissed two tenured professors of physical education because its administration had
judged their services no longer necessary because of declining enrollments.

The possible gravity of this issue, certainly for a faculty
member, can be measured by events that have followed the
case. One such event involved David F. Figuli, an attorney,
who has appeared for the American Council of Education at

---

*One such critic, Sheila Slaughter,[29] argues that the 1940
Statement was a tradeoff by faculty of civil liberties for job
security. Slaughter's view is consistent with our own to the
extent that we all consider present tenure policy as tenu-
ously floating about a "danger zone," in which the civil
liberty/job security tradeoff is ever likely to be made. And
for another perspective, see Bertell Ollman, "Academic
Freedom in America Today," *Monthly Review*, March, 1984,
pp. 24-46.

assemblies and told various high officers from U.S. universities that the Puerto Rican case had modified substantially the "financial exigency" provision of the 1940 Constitution. In fact, Robert Jacobson reports that at one of these assemblies, Figuli told the administrators present that if they needed to lay off faculty, they should "...sit down and make some programmatic decision and [not] get into the muddy water of financial exigency." Figuli's busy work created a storm, and certain officials of AAUP contested his interpretation of the case. However, according to Jacobson:

> ...the AAUP's general counsel Julius G. Getman, professor of law at Yale University, said his main concern in reading about Mr. Figuli's analysis was that some institutions apparently were adopting the philosophy behind it and "trying to whittle down the rights of the faculty members."
>
> Calling such attempts "shortsighted," Mr. Getman never-the-less acknowledged that they represented a "problem."
>
> "Universities are increasingly resorting to labor relations lawyers in dealing with faculties," he said.[30]

Apparently, all parties are now waiting for more case law, more specific instances brought before the various courts; and, in the meantime, the battle heats up as the Great Contraction occurs.

It is our judgement—shared by others, particularly faculty members—that this growing discretionary latitude gives administrators impetus to unleash the monster called the "numbers game," a game in which departments, programs and individual faculty enter into the no-holds-barred competition for students in the rollicking spirit of free market competition, with student bodies the coin of the realm. We have already described, in Chapter One, how the competition for talented high school students threatens the still meager proportion of minority students on U.S. campuses. Managers sit back and watch the scramble and, when the spectacle gets boring, invent faculty "merit pay systems" or other measures of efficiency or productivity which give new life to the gladiator's struggle in the pits of academia in the post-golden age. Indeed, times of adversity can be happy ones for the efficiency experts and a grand opening of the academy to the play of market forces and ultimately full-blown capitalist social relations.

We do not mean to claim here that there are no inherently very difficult management problems in an area of anticipated decline and shifting student interests. We do assert, however, that the narrowness of faculty training and the rigidity of the institutional structure, designed as it is around disciplines and narrow compartmentalization of knowledge and training, is in some measure responsible for the apparent crisis. We are already witness to the process whereby, when confronted with a declining number of students, academic managers go immediately to market system mechanisms in order to inspire a Darwinian scramble, and to a weakening of a tenure system which, when intact, limits the ability of the managers to play their games at full throttle.

This "power shift" that has occurred between faculty and administrators can be measured in a number of ways, some quantitative, some qualitative. Exemplifying the former, data recently published indicate that during the 1981-82 academic year top officials at universities on the average made *more than twice* the average salary of their faculty members.* Other data from this source shows that recent years have continued the decline started in the late 1960s and between 1975 and 1982, for example, the real income of

––––––––––––––––––––––––––––––

*The data here are from *The Chronicle of Higher Education*, oft quoted in this book. In fact, ongoing accounting of what happens at U.S. campuses is literally chronicled in *The Chronicle*, a weekly publication read by most college administrators and many faculty members. There is a frequent "Fact File" which, among other things, keeps the readers posted on the basic data of higher education, including: the salary schedule for administrators and faculty, mentioned here; kinds of and amounts of aid to universities from government and from private sources; the status of minorities on campus; student enrollments, past, present and projected, and so on.

U.S. professors declined by about twenty five percent. No wonder the gathering storm around issues of status, privilege, and rank.

As *their* income has risen, academic executives have taken on even more of the trappings of their managerial counterparts in the corporation, the Pentagon, and in high public office. Most academic leaders eschew the simple style once thought becoming to the scholar, and often prefer to live in regal splendor. For example, David P. Gardner, the new president of the University of California in Berkeley will be paid $150,000 a year as a salary, and the pot for the first year was sweetened by a $295,000 low interest loan to buy a $480,000 home. (He was, because it was neither safe nor private enough, not satisfied with the "Blake House," ordinarily the home of U.C. presidents.) Perhaps, as much as any part of this story, it is a sign of the times that, according to one account, the student lobby dropped its support of the resolution (against the compensation package) because a spokesman said, "We need good relations with the president." This account also described faculty protest against Gardner's salary, but not enough to have it lowered (a salary, by the way, about three times that of the governor of the state.)[31]

Qualitatively, the evidence about the faculty loss of power to administrators abounds: we have cited the new environment likely to emerge after the case concerning professors at a Puerto Rican university. Other examples are more flamboyant, and we should consider an administrator's dream come true in a college in Charleston, West Virginia. There, when the college went bankrupt, the trustees saw fit to hire Thomas J. Voss, a bright young man, in his mid-thirties at the time, as the new president. Voss was given almost complete powers to restructure the institution, and he did just that: he abolished tenure, laid off forty percent of the college's faculty and staff, that number including seven faculty members with tenure. He also changed the institution's name from Morris Harvey College to the University of Charleston, thus giving what he called "new name recognition." Concerning his firing of the personnel, including tenured faculty, Voss stated that "it was nasty...because we had to let some people go who would have been there a long time."[32] There is, by the way, a mixed opinion at the University of Charleston whether Voss has been a "success." That conclusion would depend, among other things, on whether you were part of the 40% of the personnel fired there, or part of the sixty percent who weren't.*

Finally, in this lineup, there is a related trend in higher education, the effect of which has been to further weaken the relative power of faculty members. This factor is the growing use of non-tenure track appointments, part-time appointments, or visiting instructorships. In recent years, some institutions have projected that up to 25% of their instructional staff would be appointed in this manner.[33] This policy tends to ameliorate the problem of having a faculty which is almost all tenured (thus leaving no spots for newcomers), at least from the viewpoint of the administrator. However, it is a practice that develops a cadre of second-rate citizens who typically do not enjoy any sense of real membership in the faculty where they work. And, this lack of community adds to the grim fact that, while the part-time person is as likely as not to work as hard and as diligently as the others, he or she is denied less of all benefits to be had.

Additionally, these part-timers, along with their beleaguered and badgered colleagues at two year colleges, are the latest evolving evidence that the inclination to divided labor is an unending feature on the road to organizational efficiency. As we have said earlier, though universities were more elitist institutions prior to WW II, they more nearly approximated a "community of scholars," where the status differences were less than they are now, and where, compared to now, they were yet still more likely to share basic values with administrators and more likely to unite against administrative encroachments. Thus, as the academic managers have emerged, doubly paid and full of vigor, so has a further division of academic labor. Or said another way, it is

_____

*Recently (April, 1984) we noted an ad in the *New York Times* seeking applications to the University of Charleston, for its presidency. The ad led us to wonder if Voss had left the campus for higher reaches, or was tarred and feathered, or both.

a principle of the development of organizations that bosses and hierarchical line organizations come together, and at the same time. Since World War II, we have seen the verification of the principle in the academic world with overwhelming clarity.

It is now time to summarize our main points. First, we have examined the context of academic work in general and in particular its impact for those with working class backgrounds. We did so mainly to provide a basis for understanding the autobiographical essays which make up the second part of this book. We found the academic profession to be a hierarchy where one's place is determined by institutional affiliation and professional performance consistent with the research model of an academic career. The evidence suggests that class mobile academics are less likely to be affiliated with the most prestigious institutions, and consequently, to some degree, less likely to be a "research model" professor. Hence, many can be found clustered towards the middle or the bottom of the academic heap and this is their reference point for status, rather than their point of departure. As the academy becomes more bureaucratic in structure and its leadership more managerial in style, the research model becomes more oppressive to those at middle-level institutions not well suited for its full manifestation. As managerialism progresses and the post-golden age becomes entrenched, tenure weakens, administrative power expands, and with it a further opening of the campus to market system mayhem and the influence of nonacademic institutions with money to spend (particularly the Pentagon).

To conclude, the essential dynamics of capitalist social relations have crept in, taken hold and shaped the conditions of work life in the university. And these conditions, while they impress upon all, might be expected to impose a particular strain on those least well situated and prepared for the game. Yet, we have merely touched upon one aspect of the course of difficulties our travelers might confront. The context of their work lives are more fully comprehensible when we examine the deeper workings of the social class system, the crowning embodiment of the capitalist order. We now turn to this point to grasp more fully the problems confronting the class mobile person trying to make life work inside the ivy walls.

Notes

1. Robert Blackburn, "The Meaning of Academic Work," in James I. Doi, Editor, *Assessing Faculty Efforts* (Jossey-Bass, 1974), p. 80.

2. Everett Ladd and Seymour Lipset, 1977 *Survey of the American Professoriate: Selected Tabulations* (Storrs: Social Science Data Center, 1978).

3. Peter Blau, *The Organization of Academic Work* (New York: Wiley, 1973), pp.92-94.

4. D. W. Light, et. al., *The Impact of the Academic Revolution on Faculty Careers* (Washington D. C.: American Association for Higher Education, Feb., 1973), p. 27

5. *Ibid.*

6. Robert Presthus, *The Organizational Society*, Rev. Ed. (New York: St. Martins, 1978), p. 72.

7. Richard Coleman and Lee Rainwater, *Social Standing in the United States: New Dimensions of Class* (New York: Basic Books, 1978), pp. 144-54.

8. For a description of this process, see Christopher Jencks and David Riesman, *The Academic Revolution* (Garden City: Doubleday, 1968), pp. 510-523.

9. Norman Birnbaum, "The Academic Disciplines," *Change*, July/August, 1969, p. 15.

10. Everett Carl Ladd, Jr. *The Work Experience of American College Professors: Some Data and An Argument* (Storrs: Social Science Data Center, 1980).

11. *Ibid.*, p.4.

12. Theodore Caplow and Reece J. McGee, *The Academic Market Place* (New York: Basic Books, 1965), p. 189.

13. Quoted in Light, *op. cit.*, p. 14

14. Jacques Barzun, *The American University* (New York: Harper and Row, 1968), p. 62.

15. See for example, Seymour Hersch, *The Price of Power: Kissinger in the Nixon White House* (New York: Summit Books, 1983).

16. Birnbaum, *op. cit.*, p. 11 ff.

17. Harry Braverman, *Labor and Monopoly Capital: The Degradation of Work in the Twentieth Century* (New York:

Monthly Review Press, 1974), p. 267.

18. Thorstein Veblen, *The Higher Learning* (New York: Huebsch, 1918).

19. Upton Sinclair, *The Goose Step: A Study of American Education* (Pasadena, 1923).

20. Will Lepkowski, "The Chancellor Goes to Washington," *The Progressive*, June 30, 1981, p. 30.

21. "Universities ask for $1 billion from Pentagon to Revitalize Nation's Science and Technology," *The Chronicle of Higher Education*, May 13, 1981, p.1.

22. Steve Burkholder, "The Pentagon And the Ivory Tower," *The Progressive*, June 26, 1981, p. 28. (Burkholder is a free-lance writer in Madison, Wisconsin, and a former research fellow with the Foreign Affairs and National Defense Division of the Congressional Research Service in Washington, D.C.)

23. *Ibid.*, p. 31. On this matter, see also Daniel Greenberg, "The New Harmony Between Campuses and the Pentagon," *The Chronicle of Higher Education*, February 23, 1981, p. 25.

24. Jacques Barzun, "The Wasteland of American Education," *New York Review of Books*, November 5, 1981, p. 35.

25. Quoted in Robert Presthus, *op. cit.*, p. 218.

26. *Ibid.*, p. 219.

27. Howard Metzger, "Academic Tenure in America: A Historical Essay," in Commission on Academic Tenure in Higher Education, *Faculty Tenure* (San Francisco: Josey-Bass, 1973), pp. 93-159.

28. *Ibid.*, p. 153.

29. Sheila Slaughter, "The Danger Zone: Academic Freedom and Civil Liberties," *The Annals of the American Academy of Political and Social Sciences: The Academic Profession*, March, 1980.

30. Robert Jacobson, "AAUP Challenges Claim that Faculty Layoffs Need Not Be Based on 'Exigency'," *The Chronicle of Higher Education*, March 31, 1982, pp. 1, 8. See also Jacobson's article, "Colleges Advised They Need Not Declare 'Exigency' to Lay Off Tenured Professors," *The Chronicle of Higher Education*, March 17, 1982, p.1.

31. Jack McGurdy, "Cal. Regents Assailed for Loan to New President," *The Chronicle of Higher Education*, Sep-

tember 21, 1983, p.3.

32. For the story, see *The Chronicle of Higher Education,* March 17, 1982, p.5.

33. AAUP Committee, "A Report on Academic Freedom and Tenure," *Bulletin*, September, 1978, pp. 267-77.

CHAPTER 4

Class Mobility and Internalized Conflict

T he promise of class mobility underlies the ideological justification for inequalities within capitalism. In this chapter, we will examine class mobility, the frequency with which this occurs to a meaningful degree, and the inherent problems that the mobile person might encounter along his or her mobility path. Further, we will look at the meaning of class relations and the place of the academy in the social structure. We explore these concepts in order to provide for a better appreciation of the autobiographical essays which follow, ones which convey the experience of the upwardly bound person in an academic career. So, we begin this interpretation by defining the basic characteristics of the dynamics of the social system and the place of the academy in the order of things.

I.

We are certain that our readers are aware that there have been developed in recent decades two great opposing ideas among U.S. academics (and some others) about the class system in capitialist societies.* These conflicting per-

_____

*And, for those who aren't, a good place to start is with Celia Heller (1969).[1] Heller presents a concise history of the neglect of the concept of social class by U.S. social scientists until it was forced into the debate rather recently by Marxists and others. The classic text in Marxist analyses is, of course, Marx, *Capital*, Volume 1. For its originating

spectives are, generally speaking, known as "structural-functionalist," and "Marxist." The first of these two, which largely dominates modern sociological analysis in the U.S., and is implicitly accepted by most other social scientists who are not Marxists, suggests that class order represents relationships that are potentially, if not actually, a harmonious and rational social division of labor; this division serves the common good better than any other division; and, significantly, entry into all social classes is open to everyone, depending upon talent and motivation. In political theorizing, the idea of "pluralism"—suggesting that a "democracy" exists in the U.S., made that way by competing interest groups, with government as neutral artiber — is conveniently compatible to the structural-functionalist notion of a tendency toward harmony in social relations. As well, among mainstream economists, structural-functionalism (at least its basic conclusion) is nowhere revealed better than by their unending fascination with the self-regulating models of "free enterprise" and "market capitalism," in spite of the fact that long ago, free enterprise *and* markets were replaced wherever possible by huge conglomerate firms. These two notions—pluralism and free enterprise—are loaded language implying a diversity in political culture and freedom of entry into the economy that, in our judgement, exists only inside the heads of the people who use such language in their analytical work. Nonetheless, the presuppositions of structural-functionalism that capitalist social relations tend toward harmonious equilibrium is dominant in the ideology of modern U.S. social science, whether its practitioners are part of that "school" of thinking or not.*

––––––––––––––––––––––––––––––––––––––

counterpart in structural-functionalism, see Talcot Parsons (1951).[2] Other items in the debate are listed in this chapter.

*Without question, we have suggested a much greater demarcation than exists between pluralist political theories and their alternatives. Between the simple pluralism here and the considerable variety of Marxist political theories, there many hybrid versions (including one labelled "Pluralism II"). For an excellent discussion of the matter,

Alternatively, in the Marxian view, it is assumed that people exist in groups and these groups stand in a particular relationship to each other with respect to privilege, authority, and, ultimately, power; and that the relationship between these groups is antagonistic. Further refined, Marxists assert that position in class relations is determined particularly by two factors. The first is where one exists in relationship to a society's productive resources. Does one stand in the position of ownership, command or control, or among the "priests" who interpret and thereby legitimate this social order? Or, is one among those others in the relationship, the many without ownership or control, who are in fact the subjects of power held by those in positions of dominance? The second component in the relationship between classes is that each has a distinctive social existence, a culture as it were that gives a particular sense of kinship or sense of belonging to its members. The strength of this sense of bond and the richness of the texture of interrelationships will vary by person and by historical circumstance.

For our own part, we implement the Marxian perspective, as it is stated so briefly here, as the *broad conceptual framework* in which we will seek to explain what follows. We do so without arguing the case, for others have done so for a long time and successfully. In any event, the class perspective outlined is but an *analytic point of departure* which is basic to our understanding of what happens to people who live part of their lives in one social class and the rest of their lives in another. It must be recognized that moving from one class to another involves more than simply improving one's lot, which is the most obvious and indeed celebrated attribute of the mobility experience. It is also a matter of moving from one *point* in the relationship of power to another and from one cultural *network* to another. Central to this movement is not only that social promotion involves engaging new circumstances and new cultural networks, but that the old and new ones are antagonistic and conflictual. In our view, this is the key to comprehending the contradictory experience of upward mobility. It is also, therefore, the key to

---

see: John F. Manley, "Neo-Pluralism: A Class Analysis of Pluralism I and Pluralism II," *The American Political Science Review*, V. 77, 1983, pp. 368-389.

appreciating most completely the autobiographies to follow, and we will develop it further for that reason.

In Marx's conception, maturity of the social order results in the distillation of two antagonistic groups, the bourgeoisie, or capitalists, and the proletariat, or working class. The upper class remnants of the prior feudal order become absorbed into the bourgeoisie or otherwise disappear. Similarly, the independent artisans, small shopkeepers and other elements in what Marx called the petty bourgeoisie become absorbed in either of the remaining classes. Society is comprised of owners and workers are left to fight it out—one group fighting to increase its control over the labor process and thus, profits; the other fighting to improve its standard of living through higher wages, to better working conditions; and often times, battling about the capitalists' "right" to own and control society's productive resources themselves.

John and Barbara Ehrenreich[3] have argued for a modification of this perspective, and we find their views plausible and useful. They contend that the "monopoly stage of capitalism" has produced the"professional and managerial class" (PMC), that stands between owner and workers. *It is our assumption here that academics, those who serve in universities and colleges, are most reasonably placed in the PMC.* The Ehrenreichs define the PMC "as consisting of salaried mental workers who do not own the means of production and whose major function in the division of labor may be described broadly as the reproduction of capitalist culture and capitalist class relationships."[4] The outlook of the PMC emphasizes science, expertise, and knowledge as the base of legitimate power. Members share this outlook and other attributes of culture that give them sufficient cohesion to exist as a discernible class grouping. The PMC might also be seen as in conflict with owners over differences in outlook and competition for shares of the economic surplus; and it might be seen also to share with workers the vulnerability that comes with selling one's labor to the owners. Nevertheless, its members contribute, consciously or not, to the reproduction of the system itself which keeps cultural and class relationships more or less in order.

We shall not try to make the Ehrenreichs' case here concerning *non*-academics in the PMC; but, for academics it seems to us straightforward that, as a subclass they do, indeed, serve importantly "capitalist class relationships." To begin with, the university is the principal provider of certification that separates the working class from the middle class. We agree, for example, with Robert Paul Wolff when he suggests that:

> The real function of the Bachelor's degree in our society is certification, all right, but it is class certification, not professional certification. The B.A. stamps a man as a candidate in good standing for the middle class. It is the great social divider that distinquishes the working class from the middle class.[5]

Whatever else the academy does that is liberatory and laudible, it is, in a credential-conscious society, the guardian at the gate leading to the supposed good life. And, as we stated in the previous chapter, pointing to the evidence in Bowles and Gintis, it also plays a crucial role in "the production of labor power, in the reproduction of the class structure, and in the perpetuation of the dominant values of the social order."[6] The university is particularly instrumental in the propagation of the PMC outlook which emphasizes knowledge and expertise as an important source of authority. In addition, it does much to support the meritocratic ideology which claims entitlement to privilege and reward for those capable of high levels of achievement and the hindmost for the most ordinary plodder. The insidious element in meritocratic thinking is the way it contributes to a dominant ideology that is rooted in the notion that privilege is earned and, hence, deserved, rather than being significantly a result of initial social class advantage. Further, universities and university professors are part of the weeding and ranking process that reproduces hierarchy, far more often than not, based on initial class advantage.

We would argue that no matter what the politics or ideological stripe of the *individual* professor, or what the content of his or her teaching, Marxist, anarchist, or nihilist, he or she nonetheless participates in the reproduction of the cultural and class relations of capitalism. Indeed, professors may struggle against the structural constraints imposed by the location of the university in the social division of labor, find avenues for attack and escape, and even produce contradicting results. We do not deny that nonconformist intellectuals can, through research and publication, chip away with some success at the conventional orthodoxies, nurture students with comparable ideas and intentions, or find ways to bring some fraction of the resources of the university to the service of the authentic class interests of the workers and others below. In fact, if one is bent in the direction of such work, it is not impossible, we believe, to lead a principled and purposeful life within the academy and have a modest impact on the institution and profession of one's service, or even influence the tide of events in the larger society. We do not wish to throw out the baby with the bathwater; but unfortunately, all academics, everywhere, must operate within the structural constraints scripted by the role of the academy in the social division of labor.

Moreover, it is not simply a matter of subjective preference about which aspect to focus upon, the constraints or the possibilities. Clearly to our own minds, the constraints are much weightier than the dissidents' opportunities for making change on the campus. Put another way, the academy in its ordinary functioning contributes much more to keeping in place the distribution of power and privilege, and the ideas that legitimate these distributions, than it does to change or weaken them. For example, the grading process and the orchestration of competition for academic rank is central to schooling, and to the extent that such practices are commonplace in the academy, surely the university greases the wheels of the machinery of capitalism. Can there be any doubt that the *overall effect* of these functions are inimicable to the interests of the working class as a whole? Ralf Dahrendorf reminds us that "...working class children grow up a considerable distance from institutions of higher learning, a distance of information, a distance of motivation, a distance of culture."[7] Consequently, as we have noted in Chapter 1, they do not enroll in the same proportions as members of the higher classes and suffer

higher attrition rates. And, Sennett and Cobb[8] make well
the argument that those who do not qualify to gain entrance
or who fail to continue are invited to take personal responsibility for their failures and are encouraged to accept their
fate should they end up in the lower reaches of the social
order.

On another level, universities train the labor force for
the existing social order and are in major respects a "service
station" for society. We have noted this fact above, yet it
bears a second emphasis. In the words of Clark Kerr, former
Chancellor of the University of California system:

> More knowledge has resulted from and led to ser-
> vice (by the University) for government and indus-
> try and agriculture...All of this is natural. None of
> it can be reversed...the campus has evolved
> with society...the university and segments of in-
> dustry are becoming more and more alike...the two
> worlds are merging...[9]

Kerr's dream may be a bad one for many academics, yet
there can be little doubt that his "vision" moves closer to
reality with each passing year. Since the uprisings on campus in the 1960s were, in part, a reaction to the tide of
merger, the spirit of resistance might rise again. But for
now, as we have asserted earlier, the university in service to
corporate power presses forward under the twin banners of
vocationalism and national service.

Finally, the position of the academy and academics
within the PMC has a unique dimension that further
heightens the antagonism between this class and the working class. To distinguish themselves as a subgroup worthy
of membership, academics must flaunt their special credentials, their quality of knowledge, their eloquent taste, even
their hip life style. Claim to membership cannot, in many
cases, be based upon income, since nowadays paychecks are
often more in line with unionized municipal workers than
corporate managers and lawyers. In their flaunting, academics well may distinguish themselves from the "crass,
monied, success elite" in order to demonstrate, ironically,
that they belong to "another class." The point is that while
doing so, they contribute to the cultural forms and styles

that oppress working people, and contribute further to the propensity of such people to self-loathing. This assumed tendency to emphasize knowledge, cultured taste, and sophistication as credentials for membership in the PMC also limits the potential for sustained political alliance between left-leaning academics and working class rank and file, who may prefer overtly oppressive "regular" guys, like Ronald Reagan, or the local "major domo" of the Chamber of Commerce.

Academics, then, whatever their socioeconomic background, occupy some ambiguous zone in the higher reaches of the class system. As Eric Olin Wright (in response to the work of the Ehrenreichs' presented above) argues the issue, most teachers (at every level):

> ...still occupy a contradictory location within class relations at the ideological level. This generates a particularly complex set of pressures on teachers within the class struggle. On the one hand, although teachers occupy a contradictory class location between the petty bourgeoisie and the working class at the economic level, many teaching positions are unquestionably being proletarianized at the level of social relations of production. On the other hand, these same teaching positions still occupy contradictory locations between the bourgeoisie and the proletariat at the ideological level, and this location tends to tie them ideologically to the bourgeois class.[10]

It is, as Wright later states, "to be objectively torn between two classes."

It is our view on this matter that in the final analysis, colleges and universities, whether elite or non-elite, are deeply implicated in the propagation of the meritocratic ideology, a critical piece of the body of beliefs which sustains capitalist social relations. Moreover, if class is also a cultural network of shared values and meanings and interactions, academics hold much more in common with each other and with their compatriots in the PMC than with those conventionally understood as "working class." *In short, our conclusion is that the academic work process is essentially antagonistic to the working class, and academics for the most part live in a different world of culture, different ways that make it, too, antagonistic to working class life.* Though we believe that Eugene V. Debs over-dramatized the case when he stated that "Universities and the working class are separated by great walls of fire," we share his sentiment, generally.

This conclusion, it needs reminding, derives its meaning from a look at the academy *as a whole*, rather than at its several parts (elite universities compared to two-year colleges, or *all* professors, as compared to individual ones, or small groups). At the individual level, there is no question in our minds that teachers at two-year colleges, and at many state colleges, do not work to the detriment of their students, most of whom have working class origins. Nevertheless, the great majority of classroom instruction in prestigious schools in U.S. higher education is geared to the preparation of students to take effective control of the economy and the state, and the "lesser" schools are preparing their students to work at lesser stations. Indeed, as we showed in Chapter1, as the expansion of the two year colleges continues apace, ironically, all the evidence about future opportunities points to greater barriers yet between working class children and the most prestigious schools. Like their counterparts in the elite schools who have a commitment to working class Americans, teachers at the two year schools, for all their good efforts, are constrained by a social order that needs a second level work force more than it needs fairness in educational opportunities.

We have dwelled upon the relationship of academics to working class interests in order to place that relationship into a reasonable perspective. Social promotion obviously carries real advantages to the individual, with respect to opportunity for income, creative work, security, and respect. We do not deny these improvements are desirable for the individual. They are seemingly the realization of life chances, the attainment of the American Dream. Yet the tensions created by the move into the PMC must now be obvious. The academy, one way or another, serves to perpetuate a system of privilege which visits great material and psychological suffering upon one's class of origin. If one teaches at an elite

institution, the academic from a working class background
is the trainer and certifier of the sons and daughters of the
dominant class who will, for the most part, replace their
parents in stations of command. One actually helps train
those who will become the bosses of one's own friends and
relatives. If one teaches in *non*-elite public or private higher
education, one participates in a "weeding-out" process
which sifts the relatively few "worthy" members for the
rewards that come with social promotion, and in so doing
perpetuates not only the structure of capitalist class relations, but also the powerful myth of fair and equal opportunity for social mobility upward. All of this is weaponry of the
dominant classes to sustain the legitimacy of their privileges, because the actual frequency of significant social
mobility is quite different from what the myth would have
us believe. Let us briefly examine the evidence concerning
such social mobility as it bears on our argument about
internalized class conflict.

ii.

The reality and frequency and range of significant
upward mobility, while it varies slightly among capitalist
nations, stays within a tight range. It is fair to say that "few
are called and even fewer are chosen." Recently, Kenneth
Keniston, author of a comprehensive study of social mobility, sponsored by the Carnegie Council on Children, concluded that some children will move up or down the social
ladder, but not many of them, and usually not very far. For
the great majority, the rule is rags to rags and riches to
riches.[11] Other major studies over the past two decades have
produced similar conclusions, such as those by Blau and
Duncan,[12] Lipset and Bendix,[13] Lucile Duberman,[14] to mention a few most prominent ones. All these studies are largely
in concord with the findings reported by Richard Coleman
and Lee Rainwater[15] of a survey conducted in the early
1970s of about 900 people from Kansas City and Boston.
These two sociologists found an inordinate number of
respondents who believed they had experienced "significant" social mobility. However, upon closer examination,
Coleman and Rainwater discovered that these respondents
equated such mobility "solely on advances in income and

standard of living." Closer to the truth was a less glamorous picture. As Coleman and Rainwater stated it succinctly:

> Our findings from this sample, refering now only to those in the group who were ten years into adulthood when interviewed, are as follows: 42 percent had moved up at least one class from class of origin, 49 percent were in the same class as their parents had been during middle-adulthood, and nine percent had sunk to a class below the parental level. Upward mobility by two class levels — from lower-American status up to middle-class middle-American, for example, or from working class middle Americans up to professional-managerial upper-American standing - was *strongly indicated in 7 percent of the histories*. Two class downward mobility was suggested in 2 percent. (Our emphasis).[16]

Of course, during a period of prolonged economic expansion, one's real income and *absolute* standard of living will increase along with everyone else's. Yet, such a higher real income levels does not increase one's *relative* status to one's peers. It is in *this* sense that Coleman-Rainwater argue that, during the 1970s, one's chance of staying in the working class if one's parents are there, was about four in ten; from such an origin, the odds were about nine in ten that one would either stay in that class or not rise far above it. Further, the chances of eventually moving upward substantially, say from the working class to becoming a professor at a university, were about one in fourteen (7 percent). If anything, it seems clear to us, all these likelihoods are smaller now, given the decline in blue collar working opportunities and in labor union power.

The data and implications here are both straightforward and, as we have said, consistent with similar studies done before. Yet, even in the face of all this evidence, the resilience of the rags to riches myth should come as no real surprise. The ideological apparatus of this society is complex and it is unrelenting. How many times a day does the message get conveyed, on the airwaves, in the classrooms, in public celebrations of the American way? How many people, young and old, mostly poor, are injured each of these days by their sense of personal failure if they have not moved significantly beyond the social position of their parents?

Another feature of the Coleman-Rainwater study merits brief attention, for it confirms many surveys over many years that the social status of university professors is relatively very high. Coleman-Rainwater have delineated a ranking system inferred from their work in Boston and Kansas City in several ways; one of these is the form of the thirteen level system that is represented on the following page in Figure 4. There, we have, perched solidly in the upper-middle class, a (very successful) college professor. (The income of $30,000 in 1972 would be exceptionally high for the profession as a whole.) This high ranking derives from two principal factors in terms of which their respondents viewed different professions: 1) the schooling necessary to attain one's position *and* 2) the *most* important factor — how much money one makes from it. Other data by Coleman-Rainwater, as well as other surveys, attest to the fact that, even in the face of a decline in real income since the early 1970s, and perhaps, too, a decline in their relative social status, professors at four year colleges continue to be viewed by the population at large as in the "upper" classes. It is of course a position threatened by the continuing decline in real income, and it is not possible to know how long the public will allow professors to offset the fact that many of them make less money than unionized factory workers, or well situated craftspersons with considerably less education.

Most important to this discussion of mobility is that it may best be understood as a significant consequence of two basic factors. The first is the degree of economic growth; the second, the change in the market demand for the various kinds of laborers, blue collar, white collar, etc. Hence, in meritocratic terms, the talented sons and daughters of the working class are not simply displacing less talented progeny of those above them. Rather, for the most part, they are *joining* them. Basically they are *invited*[17] to join the higher social ranks because the middle and upper ranks do not

Figure 4

A Representative Status Estimate for Thirteen Subclases
(Adapted from Coleman/Rainwater, 1972 data)

	Annual Income Level*	Occupation
Upper-Class Upper Americans		
Upper-Upper	$2,000,000	Chairmen, Board of Directors of large corporation or bank
Lower-Upper	2,000,000	President of large corporation or bank
Upper-Middle Upper Americans		
Upper Middle Elite	30,000	College Professor
Upper Middle Class	29,000	Civil Engineer
Upper Middle Marginal	19,200	Accountant
Middle-Class Middle Americans		
Middle Class Elite	22,400	Store Owner
Middle Class Core	14,300	Construction Foreman
Middle Class Marginal	11,100	Bookkeeper
Working Class Middle Americans		
Working Class Specials	9,500	Machinist
Working Class Core	13,200	Dock Foreman
Working Class Marginal	10,200	Press Operator
Lower Americans		
Not the Lowest	3,000	Ditch Digger
The Bottom Layer	2,500	Hospital Attendant

*1970 dollars. The figures are clearly misleading because of the effect of inflation. However, as relative measures they present the complicated interplay in the minds of the particiapnts of the study, between the importance of intrinsic job status and job income. For example, here the dock worker has less social standing than the bookkeeper, even though he/she makes roughly 20% more income.

produce sufficient offspring to staff the desirable positions at certain junctures in economic development.* The following example of this process has been discussed already in Chapter 1: the postwar baby-boom had much to do with the expansion of higher education in the 1960s. Therefore, it explains, in part, the disparity between Ladd and Lipset's finding that 25 percent of all academics are from the working class, even though the usual rate of mobility from blue collar to higher level professions is less than 10 percent.

To sum up this point, we have argued that U.S. culture is class-dominated; that the refinement of the Marxist perspective by Barbara and John Ehrenreich, in their idea of a Professional Managerial Class, is an important development; and that, as a group academics in the U.S. are located in the PMC, thus in an antagonistic relationship to the working classes from which about one-fourth of them originated. Lastly, we have shown that working class people who do rise to the professional ranks are rare, since less than ten percent of the U.S. population of any given generation moves upward to such a degree. And, we believe that the

———————————————————

*Readers familiar with the "dual labor market thesis" and basic Keynesian macroeconomics will see both ideas implied here. To Keynes (and Marx, of course), the labor force is comprised of an "extra" segment (what Marx called the "industrial reserve army.") This "army" is absorbed into the workforce when the economy expands, is expelled when there is an economic decline. The dual labor market theorists have showed that when extra hands are brought into production, they work in the "periphery" of the economy, where wages, benefits, security — everything — is less. Thus, as working people were drawn into the academy in historically great numbers, as we pointed out in Chapter 1, they also typically joined the periphery of the profession. We don't know whether, as the Great Academic Contraction occurs, they will be the first to be expelled. It is, as graduate professors always say, an interesting topic for research. Many who are tenured will survive. Perhaps a still more interesting topic for research is the new entry into the academy from working class ranks.

combined force of all these factors makes particularly unusual and complicated the circumstances of an academic from the working class. Most especially, they might well believe that they have actually betrayed the people left behind by offering their lives as examples attainable to all of talent and industry. This notion of such an "internalized conflict," is, as we have said, a key to the autobiographical essays that follow, and thus we will probe at it a bit more deeply, in part to begin the transition from our voices to those of our respondents.

iii.

In fact, what *is* the experience of moving from the working class to the "Professional Managerial Class," and, most particularly, what does it mean to ascend to the *academy*? Because the interests of the two classes are inimicable and the cultural styles antagonistic, the mobile person is often torn between competing loyalties and adrift with respect to his or her sense of membership in class culture. It is the sense of being nowhere at home. Of course, what is also true is that the class of origin and the adopted class are hierarchically related to each other. Hence, the sense of being invested with authority based upon social rank and function as expert or priest clashes violently with a sense of being the subject of authority, menial and without respect. This in essence defines the dilemma of "internalized class conflict."

We believe that the structure of this dilemma confronts all mobile persons, to varying degrees, depending upon the particular circumstances of their family and class position. For example, individuals who begin the journey from the lowest point of working class life may be especially conflicted. Such a person might be most disposed to resolve the crisis of conflicted identity by resorting to imposture or "fronting" it. Simply, the person would assume that his/her previous identity could be overcome by learning new behaviors that would make his/her origin imperceptible. In short, he or she learns to "pass."

One of our respondents from such a background reports his experience when he had to confront his imposture, the performing self he carefully developed over the years. He had occasion to view himself on a video-replay of a program on which he was an expert panelist. The person sitting behind his name plate on the panel was a stranger to him. Worse yet, he didn't like that stranger. He talked and looked too much like people he had disliked in the past. He had, that is to say, become one of them. Perhaps working class people with stronger personal or ethnic identities would be less disposed to this degree of imposture. Yet, it is our view that to some degree, at least, everyone going through this experience is touched by the invitation to employ such a coping mechanism.

For further example, let's return to Frank Rissarro in the study by Sennett and Cobb. Rissarro, who was interviewed at length by the authors, admits that he resorted to imposture as he moved from his occupation as meat-cutter into the world of young, educated, junior bank executives. The interviewers were astounded that Rissarro believed his "front" hid his cultural roots from his fellow employees. Rissarro, on the other hand, assumed he was getting by in his new profession because he had them fooled.[18] Of course, at best, such a mechanism for coping can lead to a life divided between a "performing" self and an "actual" one. At worst, the actual self is lost totally to the imposter. This is a bitter price to pay to get some respect in the world.

Rissarro's occupational mobility was relatively short-ranged compared with the leap from working class to the PMC. To develop a good "front" for acceptability in the academic sub-stratum can take incredible energy, attention and talent, for the professional role is an especially complicated one to act out. It is not surprising that it can offer in return migraines, ulcers, hypertension, and the unrelenting fear of being "found out" and subsequently humiliated.

Imposture is not the only option. Being *better* than "they" are is a common response, as we all know. Then there is the fawning, the "good old boy" routine, getting them to like you, as long as there aren't too many of your own type around. And, of course, there is just good old diffused anger, chronic unfocused anxiety, and, we suspect, not infrequently, "the bottle." More point of fact than conjecture, Lucile Duberman, citing studies by a number of sociologists, showed their agreement, and as one of them put it:

...the mobility experience in a status-minded society is likely to have some disruptive consequences, either because of the status orientation or anxiety of the mobile individual, or because of his inability to adjust successfully to the new groups into which he moves, whether up or down.[19]

As a measure of these "disruptive consequences," one theme that resounds clearly in a majority of the essays that follow is the intense resentment of colleagues. Over and over, this theme rings loud and shrill. "My colleagues lack character, integrity, intelligence, morality, decency. They are careerists." Might these be the cries of the alienated pressed into service with their class enemies, forced into a game of which they do not know the rules with players who seem to? Is it not like the reports of women and racial minorities as they enter a part of the world strange to them, be it the locker room, or the white gentlemen's club? Are these simply other facets of internal class conflict, the separation from the self and from a sense of meaningful association?

The other side of the coin is the strain of disconnection from the past, parents, siblings, who "stayed behind," old friends, neighbors, neighborhoods. In the eyes of those left, we may not be one of them any longer.* And, of course, they are right! Ralf Dahrendorf argues that to realize "life chances" we must have options and ligatures. He defines ligatures as:

...Bonds or linkages [that] give meaning to the place which the individual occupies. Throughout, the element of ligatures signifies meaning, the anchoring of persons and their actions, whereas options emphasize the objective and horizon of action.
...Ligatures without options are oppressive, whereas options without bonds are meaningless.[20]

————————————————————————

*One of our respondents, back home for the holidays, and carrying a load of books into the house, was told by his car mechanic brother-in-law, "You read all them books, and you're going to turn into a geek." Interesting theory; perhaps true, on occasion.

We think this idea a good one, and that in the fullest sense class mobility does not offer a life chance, *only the possibility of one;* only the possibility, moreover, if one can find a way to forge the accommodation necessary to construct the crucial supportive links which, in turn, can provide a full, meaningful life. Thus, for those working class academics who are hiding behind a "front," a work table, or a bottle of gin, it is difficult for them to connect with each other, to lend support and build a sense of common bond.

There is, of course, another strategy for escaping much of the discomfort in being almost detached from one class position and not yet fully connected to another, higher one. One can, and some do, of course, quite simply "join up" with the faster crowd. As an academic, for example, one can bask in dedication to the meritocratic ideology that dominates campus life and turn to the job of ranking and grading people, shutting them out or welcoming them into the world of attainment and recognition. Yet the potential for conflict and exceedingly rough sailing abounds here. For instance, do you give an *F* to the struggling or indifferent working class kid, because he or she lacks motivation and skill, and an *A* to the doctor's child, who has been to the "best" preparatory schools and whose family is replete with successful role models?

The meritocratic ideology supports the structural-functionalist notion that all in society are best served if the most skilled and responsible of its members fill the critical occupational niches in the social order. If you come to believe this claim and see school as the testing ground and legitimate site for weeding, there hardly seems to be a choice other than being in service to a reproduction of the social situation that made you a minority in the academy in the first place. On the other hand, how *does* one counsel the aspirational working class youth bent on social promotion? Given what we think we know about the mobility experience, it seems to us that virtually any way one turns, our working class hero is confronted with the antagonism of the class system and the reality that he or she might be participating in the oppression of the folks back home.

In sum, these are the structural dimensions of internalized class conflict. The lived reality as it emerges on the following pages represents a variety of responses to the dilemma, and various degrees of awareness of it. The class mobile academic has much with which to contend. The conditions of academic work, in themselves, are difficult enough. The workings of power within the university deliver their own alienating punch, indeed to everyone, but perhaps the blow is harshest on the interloper who likely enters with a marginal sense of membership. Coupled with this problem is the confused sense of separation from the past and the realization that one's work might perpetuate oppression and without a doubt we have a set of structured dilemmas that are integral to the mobility experience. Some of our respondents have found their way through creative accommodations. Some have not. Others strike out on their own, or insulate themselves and use the autonomy offered by the career to make meaning elsewhere. Others live with it rather well. But they *all* speak clearly about the struggle to make sense of their lives. We are now, therefore, where we have wanted to get to, voices other than our own, with stories worth hearing.

Notes

1. Celia Heller, *Structured Social Inequality* (New York: McMillan, 1969).
2. Talcott Parsons, *The Social System* (Glencoe: The Free Press, 1951).
3. Barbara and John Ehrenreich, "The Professional-Managerial Class," in Pat Walker, editor, *Between Labor and Capital: The Professional-Managerial Class* (Boston: South End Press, 1979), pp. 5-45.
4. *Ibid.*, p. 12.
5. Robert Paul Wolff, *The Ideal of the University* (Boston: Beacon, 1969), p. 151.
6. *Schooling in Capitalist America,* p.202.
7. Ralf Dahrendorf, *Life Chances* (Chicago: University of Chicago, 1979), p. 127.
8. *The Hidden Injuries of Class* (New York: Random House, 1973).
9. Quoted in Bowles and Gintis, *Op. Cit.*, p. 201.
10. Erik Olin Wright, "Intellectuals and the Class Structure of Capitalist Society," in Pat Walker, *op. cit.*, p.211.
11. Kenneth Keniston, *et. al.*, *All Our Children* (New York: Harcourt, Brace, Jovanovich, 1977), pp. 39-49.
12. Peter Blau and Otis Duncan, *The American Occupational Structure* (New York: Wiley, 1967).
13. Seymour Lipset and Reinhard Bendix, *Social Mobility In Industrial Society* (Berkeley: University of California Press, 1959).
14. Lucile Duberman, *Social Inequality: Class and Caste in America* (Philidelphia: Lippincott, 1976.) Duberman reviews the literature on this matter quite well, especially pp. 101-108.
15. Richard Coleman and Lee Rainwater, *Social Standing in the United States: New Dimensions of Class* (New York: Basic Books, 1978).
16. *Ibid.*, p. 231.

17. On this point, see Frank Parkin, *Class Inequality and Political Order* (New York: Praeger, 1971), pp. 107-109.

18. *Hidden Injuries of Class*, p. 194. Also on the attitudes of working class men toward men from the higher classes, see the essay by Kate Stewart, "The Marriage of Capitalist and Patriarchal Ideologies: Meanings of Male Bonding and Male Ranking in U.S. Culture," in Lydia Sargent, Editor, *Women and Revolution* (Boston: South End Press, 1981), especially pp. 288-98.

19. Lucile Duberman, *op. cit.*, p. 109.

20. *Life Chances*, p. 31.

Part II

Part II

Part 2:
Introduction

We come now to present voices other than our own about postwar upward mobility into U.S. higher education. For the most part, we will let our autobiographers speak for themselves, for they do that well, and our comments here and before each group of essays are intentionally brief. To the extent that there are common themes in the essays, resonances that are unmistakable connecting points, such themes will be gathered and reported in our concluding chapter. For now, we need only make certain that we distinguish our voice, the perspective of the previous three analytical chapters from those about to be heard.

Let it be said, foremost, that our interpretation of the events that have transformed university life since 1945 is just that: *ours*. We have spoken without question from a position that favors faculty over administrators in the struggle for dominance in the academy; that bemoans the eclipse of scholarly teachers by scholars and administrators who avoid students as a condition of their work; that champions the liberal arts in undergraduate schools, rather than pre-professional training. We therefore leave it to others to present the defense of the new academic managers, the imposition of the research model, the growing oneness of the academy with government and business.

Let it be said, too, that, as we have noted earlier, we have much in common with our respondents: we share with them class origin, profession, and we followed our own stars roughly during the same time they did. Yet though we share with *some* of them aspects of our point of view just summarized, a few of our contributors would take issue with that view at almost every point. No one of them would find it wholly on the mark. A minority of our essayists are, in fact, academic managers who have done their work exceptionally well and, it appears, consistent with their own values. Many other contributors have accommodated to the research model and have resisted the academic managers who ushered it forth in the postwar university. We have, then, in one guise or another, representatives of all the major players in the postwar academic extravaganza.

In the following four chapters, we have arranged and organized the stories such that each group demonstrates what appear to us as common *strategies* for *accommodating* to the mobility experience and to the difference between university life and the manners and habits of the old neighborhoods. For certain, these groupings are by no means neatly consistent: some of the essays could have been put in virtually all the chapters, while others did not seem compatibly adapted to any of them. Yet, ultimately, our grouping and arranging are relatively unimportant, for our contributors speak well enough for themselves in whatever place we have allowed their voices to be heard.

CHAPTER 5

Acceptance

One way to cope as a newcomer anywhere is to learn the rules before the bumbs on your head get too large and too many. Of course, such a strategy takes a certain amount of of brassiness, smarts, determination, and self-discipline. To some, such a strategy of acceptance and achievement also demands a rising-to-the-occasion of playing at others' rules a well as, or better than, they do, particularly to keep from feeling overwhelmed, inferior, incompetent, or all three. This can be a complicated strategy, to say the least, particularly in such a setting as postwar higher education, where the rules themselves were changing drastically and rapidly. Such an environment thereby called all the more for discipline, ambition, spunks, smarts.

Two of the stories in this chapter describe actual embodiments of the American Dream! And, the folks back home may even have cheered the results (though perhaps it was not of great interest to some of them what the results actually meant). For one of our essayists here, a strategy of acceptance has resulted in a good measure of conflict, the strains of pulling and being pulled into too many directions themselves a key part of the drama; and in one case, the outcome appears to have afforded very little satisfaction in the attainment achieved: that is, in no real blessing at all.

131

Robert Brown

I would do it again without question. To be sure, there have been serious frustrations arising from my background, from attending less than first-rate colleges and universities, etc. But, I have not forgotten the frustrations of farm labor, factory work, secretarial work, civil servant and naval enlisted man. They were so boring much of the time. So dead end, it seemed; always on the bottom rung with no security, no past, no future...

A campus is not a paradise, but what is? By definition a human is structured to experience pain as well as pleasure, and any work situation will bring on both. Academic life, on its best days, provides a very high ratio of pleasure to pain, even for those of us whose class origins deviate sharply from the norm.

My mother was first generation Irish, and had an 8th grade education. She was never employed after marriage. My father was second generation Scotch-Irish with a 10th grade education; an unskilled laborer, chronically unemployed because of the seasonal nature of such work as farm laborer, textile mill, hat manufacturing; or because of poor health from age 40 on.

There are four children in the family of whom I am the eldest; two girls, two boys. The family lived in Massachusetts and New Hampshire. We moved often—nine times by the time I was thirteen—usually tenements without all the amenities, such as electricity and central heat. Chronic poverty was a way of life. Charity and welfare was the model existence for the family throughout the 30s and 40s and, periodically, thereafter.

I worked away from home as a farm laborer beginning at age thirteen. At first, for room and board only, and after two years, for the then famous room, board, and twenty-five dollars a month. But, when one's family is destitute and chronically hungry, any job will do. At sixteen, when I graduated from high school, I worked three months as a short-order cook and general "go-fer" for a rather sleazy shore resort hotel. That was followed by six months in the CCC (under the White Mountain Forest Service); three months in a hat manufacturing factory on the wool drying ovens; three months in a metal fabricating factory unloading steel; six months in a NYA camp in Maine learning office practice; four months as an apprentice machinist in another factory; then came escape in the form of a civil service appointment in 1940 as a clerk-typist in Washington, D.C.

Washington—white, segregated Washington—was a new world to me, very heady stuff for a 19 year old who just acquired his first new suit! Opportunity was everywhere, so by working two jobs (as a cab driver at night) and by being aggressive in pursuit of promotions, and by running a coop apartment, I was suddenly in a thoroughly middle class environment with aspiring power brokers everywhere. Since Washington was clearly preparing for war, there was an absolutely phenomenal expansion of agencies and jobs. As a result, I was promoted twice in the first year; then transferred to an agency as a supervisor of an IBM tabulating group. But I soon learned that who made it had more to do with formal education (and social background) than with work; without college training, there was only a dead end clerical job in which one had large responsibility but little authority and little prospect of growth.

I soon managed to "liberate" my brother from factory life and bring him to D.C. to shift for himself, which he did very nicely and then I liberated a sister who also obtained employment promptly and achieved exceptionally well. The fourth child was still in high school then and she has never been able to escape the factories of New England. I enlisted in the Navy in 1942 at age 21, as a Yoeman third class rather than as a seaman; I had learned enough about D.C. to know that one did not have to start everything at the bottom. My branch of service was intelligence work and the first assignment was convoy duty on the North Atlantic run to Murmansk, Russia—six months of nightmare. Then, to anti-submarine warfare in the Carribean for 18 months, at which point another escape, this time from the typewriter to college.

By routinely reading Navy regs, and by working as a clerk for high ranking naval officers, I was able to learn of opportunities for training in the U.S. Further, by boxing regularly, something I had begun in adolescence in hopes of using that as a way out of poverty, some visibility came to me. In 1944, a Navy Captain and a Rear Admiral sponsored me for the Naval College Training Program.

On March 1, 1944, I was assigned to the Naval unit at an Eastern Private College as a 23 year old deck engineering student. By September 1, 1946, I was out of the Navy, had a bachelor's degree, and three offers of college teaching jobs. Times had changed! But, as it turned out, only in some respects.

Let me backtrack a bit. My high school record was excellent—the top 10 percent of the class. My curriculum was "clerical," not academic—no one whom I knew ever even talked about going to college, only about finding jobs as soon as one could get working papers. High school was followed by part-time attendance at a business college when I was employed long enough to have some tuition dollars. What was available, readily so in New England, was the Public Library, a place which provided warmth, encouragement, entertainment, direction, and approval. My library card become my most valued possession. Mainly, I read escape literature, from Burroughs' *Tarzan* to Zane Grey westerns, and of course the American success stories, such as the Horatio Alger Series. By the dozens and eventually hundreds, I read books at the rate of 2-3 a week. Inevitably, I was led to some of the classics, too. Later, I worked in the library of the NYA camp and there learned of a literature of social criticism and commentary—*Studs Lonigan, Christ in Concrete, How Green Was My Valley*, and so on to Hemingway, Faulkner, and others. I continued reading, almost every day through life in Washington and life in the Navy. But, I was poorly prepared for college work, particularly for engineering. No algebra, no physics, no chemistry, 7 years out of high school, competing with 18 year olds, nearly all of whom had prepared for and expected to attend college. What a freshman year that was! Three semesters a year, 17 credit hours minimum. I made it without a D or an F but only because of a sympathetic faculty, my enormous capacity for work, and high verbal ability (from all those library books).

College was another lesson on the role of social class in governing behavior. Fraternities and sororities continued to function even in wartime. They served then as now as gateways, social sifters, and social centers. One month of Sigma Chi and I left the whole scene; it was a foreign world to me and it was evident to me that I couldn't belong. Differences in speech, manner, value, and habit separated us from the mainstream almost as effectively as race. So, we went back to type—to boxing, the local bars, and non-college women.

After a three-semester year at the first college, the Navy transferred me to an Ivy and out of engineering. Again, class differences were strong, even stronger, in fact, but in a city it was easy to confine one's school life to the classroom and laboratory. Work went well, grades were high, and they remained so thereafter. Social life was not college-centered; it was back to street life.

I left the Ivy immediately following VJ day, since my sea duty gave me enough points to be discharged with the first wave, and returned to the first college. Graduation the next August and on to teaching as noted above. I taught 15 credit hours and took two graduate courses each semester, obtaining an MA in 1948. Then in 1949, I began commuting on weekends for doctoral work, a one year leave from teaching in 1950-51, and a doctorate in hand in 1951. So, a freshman in 1944 and a Ph.D. in 1951, with four years full time experience as an instructor and assistant professor and a half a dozen publications to my credit. A short six years later, I was to be a full professor and department head. Horatio Alger, Jr. and his American dream was valid it seemed!

All that has been said to this point has been intended as background information about my experience in the academy. In the Horatio Alger stories, the hero always married "the boss' daughter"; one's social class origins were never a barrier to much of anything that one wanted to achieve. Hard work was the avenue to all. Well, not in academe as represented by the selective private Eastern colleges with which I was associated. Indeed, they were meritocratic and they recognized achievement when forced to do so. So promotions came, awards were received, salary grew, as publications piled up to 20, 30, 40. Research grants came in and so there was a certain validity to the myth.

But, was one *accepted*? Did one belong? Could one be oneself and admit to a past or was it necessary to posture, to act out the model of "the professor?" And, here it becomes very difficult to know the answers for the answers might only be self-serving. How is one to know whether he would have felt just as isolated were his background to have been more traditional? What I did know, in the sense of what I believed to be true, was that I did not fit—was no more comfortable than was the case when I was a student. One of the things that years of living in poverty had done was to condition my views of "me," views, of course, which guided my actions with others. So, no, I did not feel very positive toward practically all colleagues, their lives and mine seemed so very different. But, did I give them much of an opportunity to do anything about my feelings toward them? Of course not, it was too risky; my status was too fragile. The fear of ending up back on the streets symbolically was much too great to take any chances. The great problem was that I wanted to belong, to be like them, to be comfortable with academic life. So I tried where it was "safe" from failure (classroom, laboratory, research) and isolated myself where it wasn't (committees, coffee hours, cocktails, arts events). And, that is the way it has remained. Never comfortable, never a sense of belonging socially; yet, more than satisfactory recognition "at home" and "abroad" for my scholarly work.

My feelings about being from the working class are all tangled up with also having been very poor, so how can I come to understand what the sources are of non-belonging in the academy? My generation started childhood in a time of prosperity for many, thus, minimally adequate income for most. That changed before we reached adolescence and those on the margin were in abject poverty promptly. As children, we were a generation without hope since there was little or no prospect of regular employment and there seemed to be little stake for us in society. We lived in the midst of poverty and all that goes with it—hostility and aggression, some of it toward women and children, so that beatings were commonplace, drunkenness, as one way out; theft, bootlegging, and prostitution all around us; the eternal bickering over how to "make ends meet"; then came cynicism, bitterness, and for many despair for the future. And, of course, there are the more obvious results and signs of that life of deprivation. Malnutrition—how did I reconcile the complacency of the middle class regarding the poor with my memory of a sibling who became unconscious in school because he had not had enough to eat? Of the well-meaning people who gave us a couple of meals and told us that everything would be all right if we would "just find a job and work hard." The neglect and loss of teeth at an early age reflected in a partial plate by age 20 in order to qualify for naval service, chronic life-long health problems traceable to neglected childhood diseases and diet. And worst of all, of the second-hand, worn out clothes, patched over patches, of hated denims (the irony of the "Blue-jean culture!"), of shoes which were second hand ("the Goodwill Stores"), of wearing the badge of "different from others." The social isolation and sense of inferiority that results from such experiences quite simply cannot be separated from the perceptions which one would have arising from a working class where there indeed was work to be done, i.e., where there was regular employment.

So, I suspect that were I to have had the good fortune to have had some insight into my life in Washington, in the Navy, as a college student, and as a faculty member, it would have been rather clear to me that the sense of isolation, of not belonging, and of not fitting was much more internal than external. I was not rejected; instead, I rejected them, by being unable to accept them, to accept what they wished to give. And, I have come to see that it is more useful for me to think of myself now as being *classless* as far as belonging is concerned. Years of living a university life have isolated me from my working class origins. What do we have in common, what can we talk about? Their interests are not my interests, their values are no longer mine. So, I certainly am not middle-class in any conventional sense, certainly not in the sense of identifying with and belonging to. A recent comment from a friend that, "You could have prepped at Choate for all anyone could tell by now," only saddens me for "by now" is too late.

Concerning students I've taught, they were at first a mixture of the women who were in college at the traditional age and in the traditional manner while the men were a mixture of World War II veterans and the traditional students. Since I have always taught in a selective, elitist institution, my experiences with students from working class backgrounds have been limited to some of the GIs, a handful of scholarship athletes, school teachers seeking master's degrees, and nursing school students (moon-lighting for 5 years). In the main, I have had the good fortune not to be conscious of the social class background of my students. In sum, it simply has not been a problem for me, *where the males are concerned*. It took me many, many years to reach the point where I was comfortable with women students. Why? Well, I really cannot be certain that I know. In part, their manner, their speech habits, the opportunities and experience which they had, and their often very fine educational background. They were what I thought I could never be, in that respect. But, in part, the reason lies in the markedly different attitudes toward women which exists, in my generation, at least, between the middle and the working class. The cues, signs, "body language," and approaches were so different; it was all so much of a foreign culture to me; one that I observed early was a very dangerous one for a young, faculty member. The overtones of friendship and the easy natural manner of relating to males were simply that, not more. From the point of that discovery on, I have always enjoyed teaching the women students more than the men and many, many of them went on for doctorates and now are teaching or practicing psychology all over the U.S.

The closest relationships with students—10-12 students who became friends in a literal sense—were either from upper class or working class families. Three of the males in that group are by now very wealthy in their own right, yet, our friendship continues. I visit them, meet their friends, am accepted and am comfortable with the relationship. Those from the working class group and I have a more formal professional friendship—I do not visit them. Why has it turned out to be so? The middle class still is an alien land for me and it will always be so. The upper class is more accepting of differences. Further, they often are more interested in discussing ideas than is the middle class. And, they seem to have greater respect for competence wherever it is found than is the case for the middle class. Although I am as classless with them as with any other group, I am more at home with people of wealth and "background" and would be happy to spend much of my life with them. Alas, that is not to be.

Has my experience in the academy worked for me? By all means, and I would do it again without question. To be sure, there have been serious frustrations arising from my background, from attending less than first-rate colleges and universities, etc. But I have not forgotten the frustrations of farm labor, factory work, secretarial work, civil servant, and naval enlisted man. They were all so boring much of the time, so dead end it seemed; always on the bottom rung with no security, no past, no future. My two sojourns to other jobs in the 1960s only reinforced my deep conviction that academic life is far, far more satisfying than business or government work. Your students rarely care about your origins, where you got your degrees, who your spouse is, and so on. They are accepting if you are, thus, the initial basis of the relationship is positive. With some luck and much skill one can keep it that way. Further, the currency for the relationship is ideas and they never become dull, tiresome, or dead end. It is an absolutely marvelous way to earn one's living. It would be even nicer if students were more intellectual but that is a dream; they never were. After all, neither are many of those colleagues who lament the lack of intellectual interest in their students.

My reaction to all authority, whether academic or not, is to keep a distance from those who have it, to resist, usually lightly, those who wield it with any zest, and to live my life in a manner which minimizes the direct intrusion of authority on it. Academic authority is vested most heavily in faculties and they are so ambivalent about that fact; perhaps even a bit guilty and anxious, They devote an enormous amount of energy to displacing that anxiety and ambivalence on to other groups, particularly administrators and boards of overseers. I have found academic politics to be complex, difficult, dirty, and "played for keeps" and have not minded that even while wishing it were not so. What I have most disliked about academic life is the faculty's hypocrisy regarding its attitudes toward and practice of its authority. My usual simplistic thought is, "They wouldn't last long on the street if they behaved that way," but, of course, they are not *on* the "street"and with luck will never have that misfortune. A campus is not paradise, but what is? By definition, a human is structured both to experience pain as well as pleasure, and any work situation will bring out both. Academic life, on its best days, provides a very high ratio of pleasure to pain, even for those of us whose class origins deviate sharply form the norm.

Myron Bowen

> I think it unfortunate that some of us who were youngsters during the Great Depression and experienced poverty and deprivation as the sons and daughters of working people have been (in many cases) exercising control of higher education. We brought with us deep-seated fears that place a high premium on security and guarantees against the vicissitudes of the human experience...We have been excessively hesitant and excessively cautious. Too many of us have forgotten the intellectual excitement and commitments of our youth. To kindle that potential in our students is the central purpose of our profession.

On that dark day in October 1929, when the stock market crashed, I was seven years old. I lived with my parents and two younger sisters in an eastern seaboard city. My father was a ladies' garment worker, barely earning a living before the Crash, with a lot of unemployment to experience during the decade ahead. Both my parents were first generation Americans, having arrived from eastern Europe when they were very young, my mother a child, my father a teenager. Our family was Jewish.

Within those conditions were a variety of powerful influences that helped shape my inclination toward an academic career and my experience in it. The Great Depression brought us painful deprivation and a terrible sense of insecurity. Country folks could (under many circumstances) work the land and grow much of the food they needed. Those of us in the cities needed jobs to earn cash. The Great Depression made our generation conscious of the value of security, that is, of a steady income. We talked and thought much about the safe and secure job even if the rewards were smaller than in jobs with greater risk of lay-off. We children of the Great Depression were conditioned away from risk-taking. Ergo, the choice of a profession with something called "tenure."

My parents were not educated, my mother having left school after three months into her high school freshman class. She has never learned to spell or punctuate. My father arrived in America at the age of seventeen. He went to work immediately at the trade he was taught by his father in the little Slavic "staedtl" where he was born. He never learned to read or write English or, though he claimed otherwise, any other language. As grade school students, the elder of my two sisters (two years my junior) and I taught my father to sign his name. It was a lengthy task, consuming several months of Sunday afternoons, and producing for the rest of his life a shaky and curvacious approximation of his name in cursive English. I don't think he ever learned to identify any of the letters in his name.

And yet my parents loved and supported education with a passion. My father's eyes were aglow when he talked about the brilliant elderly men who in his staedtl gathered regularly to study the Talmud and related commentaries. He spoke with particular approval of the children (that is, male children) of friends of his who had gone or were going to college. That, in his mind, led only to becoming a professional, a doctor, a lawyer, an accountant. I never learned whether his list might include a professor. My mother claimed with pride that she was "descended from a long line of rabbis," most of whom became aged patriarchs living into their late eighties and nineties. Her father had broken the line, however. He was sent by his father to the rabbinical yeshiva, from which he departed unceremoniously some few weeks after he began, to turn up later on the African continent working as a blacksmith for the British army. He was consumed by the love of adventure rather than the niceties of Talmudic textual comment. That passion for travel and risk-taking, that insatiable curiosity and desire to experience much, clearly flowed into his grandson's (me) genes, as an influence in conflict with the desire for security.

My parents faith in education grew also out of their Jewishness, that is out of centuries of discrimination. Though they lived in Jewish ghettos in both Europe and America, they sensed the difficulties of penetrating the mainstream of the larger society. But give the young man (sic) "a good education" and you have armed him with the means to become a professional, to become a successful and secure member of the society.

The poverty, the Jewishness and especially the flight from eastern Europe supported that objective. The refugee has aspirations and is enterprising. He does not stay behind. He takes action against his woes. His fantasy life is filled with the promise of milk and honey and even gold-paved streets. What he gets for his trouble is often another ghetto in crowded tenements infested with cockroaches and rats, and more poverty, although pogroms are left behind. He continues to struggle in poverty. His aspirations are transferred to his sons. They shall be enterprising professionals, shall become financially secure and shall enjoy high social status. And the means shall be education.

It was in that setting and with that set of values that I traversed my childhood and my early youth. Interestingly, the schools I attended supported those values. When I was ready to enter junior high school, my family moved again (we had moved many times before). This time we were on the very edge of the ghetto. I attended junior high by crossing into a gentile community as poor as was our ghetto. I was the only Jew in all of my classes. In a school of perhaps two hundred, there were no more than six or seven Jewish children. Yet I had no problem with this, and got on very well with my gentile schoolmates and teachers. I was a serious and successful student. My teachers often would turn to me for the solution after a number of other youngsters had failed to come up with the answer. I can still hear the oft-repeated prelude to being called upon, in a variety of forms: "Now let's hear the answer." I rarely failed them. Yet I cannot recall that this often-replayed scenario produced resentment either from my schoolmates or my teachers. As a matter of fact, my teachers encouraged me to plan my secondary school experience in an ancient and honorable classical high school with selective admissions from across the entire city. My teachers made suggestions for special study I might do beyond regular class expectations to prepare myself for a demanding high school experience. I remember my math teacher's response in the seventh grade when I raised a question about how one determined the square root of a number when one does not have the appropriate table available. (There were no pocket calculators then.) She responded that it was too complicated to spend class time on it. But that afternoon during a study period she invited me to her desk where I got a special and private lesson in the cumbersome procedure for calculating the square root of a number.

The high school experience emphasized demanding subjects: languages, including Latin (four years), French (four years), German (two years) and English (four years), history (including a full year each of ancient and American),mathematics (four years) and science (one year each of physics and chemistry). The institution published a catalog, with a full description of all courses. Though there were few chances for electives, the curriculum being almost entirely prescribed, I relished reading about what was to come in future courses. It was a stimulating adventure. Those wonderful high school school years supported and were supported by the aspirations and expectations of my social, familial and religious environment.

By now war clouds were hovering over Europe. The drafting of American youth for war service was discussed, proposed, challenged and adopted amidst a good deal of political conflict. At my high school commencement the summer before the Japanese attack on Pearl Harbor, all of us knew, and the speaker emphasized, that we would all see war service. (Ours was an all-male high school.)

But I completed a year of college before entering the service. My goals to that point had been ambiguous: medicine? law? and another that my vigorous high school education was prompting, teaching. The war years, mostly in the Southwest Pacific Theater, opened some of the world for me, but more than that gave me insights into the rest of humanity. I was surprised to learn that people from elsewhere in the country, large numbers of them, had also experienced poverty and, shockingly, that their educational achievements had been quite low level. Somehow I had thought that most people of my age had attended demanding high schools and aspired to professional careers. Many of the men I met in the service had not only experienced the Great Depression more severely than I had, but simply had not had the opportunity to pursue education very far. The war

experience strengthened my interest in a career in education. My consciousness of the extent of poverty in the world
supported my interest in security, already grown large from
the unhappy decade of the Thirties. At the same time, the
opportunity during World War II to experience wide travel
and to undertake adventure stimulated me and my imagination.

But after the war I returned to my family and to college.
I completed my remaining undergraduate years (in two
years and two summers) in the humanities, and proceeded
to do a year of graduate study.

At that point I sensed the need to move into the big
world and away from my home town, my family and the
limited and provincial setting in which I was finding
myself. To remain in that community and in my familial
home seemed to others natural and, indeed, the only thing to
do. But my war experience and my grandfather's genes were
requiring that I put distance between myself and both my
familiar and familial setting. I felt the need to explore and to
experience other worlds.

It was a very difficult decision. My family did not
understand. They were hurt, as must also have been my
rabbinical great grandfather when he learned that his son
had set sail for South Africa. But consistent with that part of
the family "tradition," I was to pursue the universe of ideas
and, indeed, to examine language and texts very closely. I
would take a doctorate in the humanities and plan for an
academic career. Thus was I to respond to the desire to
explore and expand and, at the same time, hedge my bet.

The years working toward the doctorate as a teaching
assistant were as exciting and stimulating as had been my
undergraduate and high school years. And the completion
of the doctorate (albeit during the dry years between the
post-World War II veteran bulge in enrollment and the yet-
to-come explosion of college attendance when the war
babies came of age) led to an excellent appointment in
another midwestern university. Before leaving my doctoral
institution I married a pretty coed whom I had met there the
year before when she was a senior.

The first three or four of those years of my first full-time
position were productive and satisfying, both the teaching

and the scholarship. I enjoyed especially the teaching, the stimulation of rigorous intellectual activity, of consistent and coherent thinking, and of problem-solving capacities. I received happy raises and a promotion in rank. Tenure seemed assured within another year or two. But I had become restless and needed more excitement. I found a new campus in another midwestern state seeking faculty amidst what promised to be explosive growth. I had no trouble foregoing the security of tenure for that opportunity and so moved my young family to undertake a new teaching position in a somewhat less distinguished but more dynamic setting. My grandfather's instincts had overcome the conservatism of my early social conditioning, at least in this action.

Fifteen months later I was offered the position of associate dean of instruction of my new campus, which I took with enthusiasm, providing as it did some status and some additional salary. But it also offered something else. It was an opportunity to establish a better setting for learning than I had seen administrators do in my few years as a full-time faculty member on two different campuses. Another fifteen months passed and I was invited to accept a handsome and prestigious fellowship to a year of postdoctoral study which, after its completion, led to the offer of an academic vice-presidency in another midwestern university. So I left my second position without tenure.

And, as a matter of fact, I had, I believe, at that point passed the line to the province of risk-taking. I had lost my interest in tenure.

Four years as an academic vice-president with principal attention to the stimulation of curriculum and undergraduate teaching (with all the contention they brought) led to a college presidency of a fledgling state university in a large midwestern city, an institution that had just been released from the harassment of municipal control as that city's teacher training academy. My inauguration as president brought my family from the east coast for the first time to bask in my and their "success" as a professional who had made his way into the mainstream of this society, fulfilling the hopes and aspirations of those refugees when they had cut roots and made their uncertain way to America. They and I were very proud.

Eight years were needed to shape that university, to build from the municipal teachers college an able faculty and a meaningful curriculum to serve the new population of students, especially from minority backgrounds. These were the late Sixties and the early Seventies and all the conflict and contention of the time offered stimulation aplenty for that cautious lad who had become venturesome. After the eight years, which included the task of planning, financing and building a totally new campus, I took a new position in the Southeast as provost to build another new campus of a fairly new state university. This, too, turned out to be a satisfying adventure, to bring faculty and programs together and to build facilities on a new setting with funds which I lobbied from the state legislature.

By now growth had begun to decline. In some places enrollment had begun to decrease. Budget growth was levelling off. A new challenge was presenting itself, not the management of growth and larger budgets and the opportunities for educational experimentation and the stimulation of quality, but the management of decline and smaller budgets in such a way as to strengthen learning.

The opportunity came to provide that kind of leadership. I was offered the presidency of a small rural state college in the far West, one with serious enrollment decline and serious budget deficiencies. I took it with alacrity. The issue seemed clear enough to me and to others. Because the college had emphasized remedial education and had attracted a very high percentage of weak students, able students had begun to avoid the institution. Public confidence in the college had been declining for at least half a decade. The faculty and students had become seriously demoralized. Among the most important causes of this unhappy development had been the inadequate leadership of my predecessor and his administration. He had been "promoted" into the position of "systems" chancellor, functioning as chief of staff for the governing board.

My program, developed after engagement with faculty, student and community leadership, called for a vigorous campaign to recruit able students, some innovative scholarship programs to honor able students, and a redirection of the administrative staff from plodding routinism to creative and responsive reshaping of every part of the college. Very quickly morale was elevated and more able students began enrolling again. The college was on the way to renewal and stability.

From the very beginning, however, my predecessor, now systems head (that is, chief staff officer for the board governing the college and a number of similar public colleges in the state) seemed displeased. As I began removing and replacing his former administrative colleagues (some of whom he had appointed and others of whom he had retained from his predecessors), he came under continuing counsel from those administrators that I was up to no good. He then began quietly to persuade the board members that I was making too radical a change in the institution and in due time, after several failures, convinced a majority of the Board. They quietly requested my resignation, which I refused to offer. Extraordinary support emerged from among the students, faculty members and the community as well as from the local press. But it was all to no avail. The majority held. I was fired.

I was both unhappy and pleased. No one likes to have the rug pulled out from under him when he (with substantial support) is creating order and quality. I was pleased because I had a chance to face uncertainty and could test the fear and insecurity generated in my youth, which, in part, had very likely led to an academic career. That sense of insecurity I had long since shed. I had become a risk-taker. Now I had to face the consequences of risk.

I decided that I would move even further into the unknown for a new adventure. I had had significant opportunity over the years to demonstrate leadership capacity, as an academic vice president, as a university provost and twice as a university president. Surely, I concluded, that experience had value in the big world beyond the campus. And so, approaching the age of sixty, when most men are planning their retirement, I set out to seek a new career. And I found it. I was offered a senior executive position in a large and growing corporation at a salary substantially greater than I had ever earned in higher education. The challenge and the opportunities for service I now find as stimulating as any I had experienced within the academic community.

As I look back upon more than three decades of service to higher education, I find myself stuck with a singular point of view, one that may be a bit simplistic. I think it unfortunate that those of us who were youngsters during the Great Depression and experienced poverty and deprivation as the sons and daughters of working people have been and are exercising control of higher education. We brought with us deep-seated fears that place a high premium on security and guarantees against the vicissitudes of the human experience. We have been exercising leadership in higher education for the past several decades, both for our faculties and within the administrative fraternity. We have been excessively hesitant and excessively cautious. Too many of us have forgotten the intellectual excitement and commitments of our youth. To kindle that potential in our students is the central purpose of our (my former?) profession. We do not have to tear apart the fabric of academia to do that, as was attempted in the Sixties. But we do need constant, if moderate, renewal of our settings. And we need to begin with ourselves.

Allen Green

I don't like to read James Joyce, study Noam
Chomsky and listen to Schoenberg. I don't like
movies with subtitles and I can't spend more than
two minutes with the best of Seurat or any other
French impressionist. It is difficult to like anyone
who likes your dislikes or who dislikes your likes...

At our wedding we insisted on having three limousines; all
Caddys, a white one for the bride and a grey one each for the
wedding party and the parents. It was a New York wedding.
So, nearly two-hundred joined in on the dancing, the dinner
and the campy rituals. The Watermill Inn had copied from
the other Long Island wedding factories. We were their first
wedding. The paint was glossy white on the garden lattice-
work and the staff were still humble and courteous. It was
the first day of summer solstice, a grand day to recite vows
amid upper-middle-class glitter.

The parents of the happy couple melded well together.
Both had working class roots, except the bride's side was
nouveau riche. Their wealth impressed my parents, as it had
me. We had never seen such things as a five bathroom house
with north shore waterfront and Danny Thomas as a
neighbor (his east coast summer home). Their cars cost more
than my parents' home. But the two homes were equal intellectually. Neither had a significant collection of books. Only
magazines like Redbook and Reader's Digest were available
to skim or to make clutter. Nevertheless, my parents read
success in what they saw and consequently they put on airs
trying not to be their lowly selves any more than they had to.

Their wedding was much simpler. She was 19 and he
was 21. It was done in haste after they discovered I was on
the way. Three months pregnant, my mother exchanged
vows with her ex-Marine. There was no wedding party, no
tradition or anything to make it a special occasion. It was

just the two of them in the best clothes they owned, Fr. Canon, and a few friends who formalized the marriage forever that late November afternoon. My mother was a telephone operator and my father a Sunbeam Bread delivery man. He was also in the Marine Reserve. Up till then, my mother's story was one of riches to rags, my father's rags to rags and as a couple it became rags to J.C. Penney. My story involved advancing from J.C. Penney to Macy's, with occasional trips to Bloomingdales.

Both of my parents were raised in the upper-lower class during the Depression. My mother's father died when she was seven. He was a kind and respected, Mid-West plant foreman. His kindness even extended to a few alcoholic slobs, one of whom married my grandmother less than six months after he passed on. Within seven years my mother had six new siblings, the money was gone and she had become tired of her step-father's abusive behavior. So, at the tender age of fifteen she left Chicago to live with her grandmother who rented a small apartment in a small Pennsylvania town. My great grandmother was a classic spinster. She lived on the $120 she drew each month from a trust left by her father (she didn't collect social security). In order to make ends meet she slept in the dining room and subleased two bedrooms to odd, middle-aged bachelors. Naturally, my mother had to work while in high school to establish her place in the dining room.

My mother's roots were somewhat aristocratic, at least she claimed to be related to a Kaiser. In contrast, my father had poor Welsh roots. On his mother's side was a lineage of common farmers and on his father's, he drew upon a line of laborers and vagrants. Although he came from a broken family, his father was a good man—maybe too good. He was a craftsman, a tinsmith. The gutters and downspouts he made can still be seen on many of the town churches. During the Depression, construction slowed and he got a menial job working at a blue-nosed college located in town. He was proud just to be working. But he discovered he didn't like to work around college students. He felt they were too prissy, frivolous and immature. They, for example, like to throw water and rotten food on the maintenance men as they made their rounds. One day, as the story goes, grandpa retaliated. In a pestering way, a medical student asked him if he could build something to hold up a cadaver's arms so they could get at the pits. "I got just what ya need right here with me" he said, then pa calmly pulled out a couple six penny spikes and nailed the cadaver's hands to the wall.

My father and I inherited grandpa's values. We both became craftsmen, he a draftsman and I, a scientist. My father's career development was rerouted, however, by three significant events in his life. World War II, the Korean Conflict, and the 1959 recession had lasting effects on the character of my father. Dad was one of the many working class kids who quit school and lied about his age in order to be swept away by the grand purposes of WWII. He served six years during the war, was discharged, and later was recalled during the Korean conflict for another two year hitch. After eight years of the service he finally returned to night school and received his high school degree. Nearly middle-aged, he discovered the craftsman in himself through a correspondence course he took in electrical drafting. Westinghouse hired him as a draftsman, but soon let him do his own engineering work (at a draftsman's pay). At last, it seemed, he had security doing the work he enjoyed. In return, he became a loyal Westinghouse employee. Then came the recession. Westinghouse suddenly left town, leaving scores without jobs. Undaunted, dad got another job, became loyal to another company, and the same thing happened again. All of this he blamed on not having a degree, "the right piece of paper," he would say.

From both of my parents I acquired the belief that higher education was the key to success. Education was a primal force for social change; it gave us hope. We believed in education more than the tenets of Catholicism. But it wasn't for its own sake, it was for where it might take us.

What has it been like for me as a professor? With respect to colleagues, it is difficult for me to make any evaluative generalizations in academia. To begin with, I can't say I like poor folks and dislike rich folks. However, I must admit that earlier in my career and sometimes even now I feel a mixture of envy, fear and anger about my well-heeled colleagues in the white tower. There are certainly differences between myself and those who were raised in the academic elite. Through a colloquium series I have become acquainted with some of the most influential psychologists in the East. Some of these individuals have come from academic or professional upper-middle class backgrounds. Who they know is awesome; This makes me feel left out, like I felt when I couldn't get in the K-Club in high school. Their command of language and their scholarship is often beyond my skill levels; for this I envy them.

It's good that native intelligence is not measurable, for if I were sure I had their native abilities, I would also feel bitterness and a sense of inequity. (If I had been raised in their environment I would be just as good as they are. I wasn't, because of social circumstances, so I deserve more, they deserve less, etc.) A third source of negative feelings toward academic elites is our dissimilarities. I don't like to read James Joyce, study Noam Chomsky and listen to Schoenberg. I don't like movies with subtitles and I can't spend more than two minutes with the best of Suerat or any other French Impressionist. It is difficult to like anyone who likes your dislikes or who dislikes your likes.

There is definitely a more salient pattern in my feelings toward fellow academics. These feelings are driven by professional values more than a class stereotype. My strongest negative feelings are saved for incompetent peers. I dislike those fellow professors who, because of their neurotic life style, are inadequate. I truly hate whiners. These individuals know professional standards and values quite well; and they let you know they know them. However, despite their reverence for high standards, they are curiously low producers. When pressed to explain their failure to achieve, they always blame others, or external forces. "The administration," "the student," funding sources or equipment are their scapegoats. True professionals are never content with themselves, and they push for excellence in others while coping realistically with their limits. Moreover, they themselves are producers. They work hard, but there is nothing strident or desperate about it. They enjoy it. Consequently they are fun to be with—they excite, not tax your energy. This kind of colleague may tend to come from a working class background, but my experience does not unequivocally support this kind of conclusion.

Class consciousness does not seem to play a major role in my dealings with students. Information about your students' social class can be useful if the student population is heterogeneous. However, at the four schools where I have taught, the student populations have been homogeneous. With regard to class, if you've seen an example of one, you've seen them all. I do, upon second thought, have a soft spot for the hardworking lower-middle class kid, particularly if he or she has talent. Late bloomers also have a special appeal to me. On the other hand, I have come to recognize that some well-to-do students from families with high achieving parents have to struggle with the same capitalistic ideals that the Horatio Alger-working class kid does. I have a soft spot for them too.

The students I have the greatest difficulty with are those who treat their peers and me as though we were inhuman manipulandums, i.e., we're the instruments of their dimly conceived hedonistic, selfish pursuits. The working class student shows this by demanding that everything he/she learns is career (money) relevant. The well-to-do student reveals this orientation by letting you know you are a servant helping him to maintain his college-as-country-club scheme. But you can't tell them apart when they say things such as, "Will this be on the test?"

Academic authority is an enigma to me. The further up the hierarchy you go, the more mysterious the administrator becomes. Simple concepts can't explain their behavior. Often it is difficult to discriminate the causes of their actions. Are they manifestations of a new policy, sloppy planning, strange compromises, or their prejudices about the faculty? Who knows? I don't think even they do. But "they" are not entirely at fault; some of my colleagues are their accomplices. These faculty, myself included, help to maintain an excessively vertical organizational structure by functionally being line workers while maintaining the pose that they are intellectuals far above the mundane muck of college administration. Our administrators have a complementary set of myths that insure that no useful communication occur between themselves and the faculty.

This academic hierarchy is a symptom of a dysfunctional, but common, organizational structure present in many American businesses and institutions. It's the old father-knows-best model, and when you employ it, you play one of two roles; you can either be management or labor. Management directs, labor follows. It is a tiresome old game that drives me up the wall mainly because it doesn't work. Unfortunately, in academics most administrators are not scholars or teachers, and on the other hand, most faculty only dimly understand the realities of administrative decision making. It is obvious the two should get together—but that would create mutual status incongruities—and it would be dissonant with a basic assumption of the American Dream, the "ladder assumption." Remember, success is gauged by how far one moves up the ladder. Getting together at a circular table bends the ladder.

Would I do it again? No. At least I would not sign a contract to teach at a small Catholic university. The problem is simple. I work too hard for too little pay and respect. I feel like a surplus Ph.D., teaching at a mediocre institution for peanuts. Yet despite this situation, I have had fun with students, enjoyed my colleagues, used what free time I have had to work for professional excellence and have been generally more happy than unhappy. It's just that the academia I hoped to get into ain't here. I didn't expect to teach nine hours per week (3 graduate and 6 undergraduate), be the chairman of three degree programs, be responsible for five faculty members, 120 students, work eleven months a year, ten years, to get paid less than a plumber.

Moreover, the status of a professor has dropped considerably since the 1960s. I haven't changed my class position very much at all. I'm still in the working class—only now I'm teaching working class kids in a blue collar school. I'm no stranger and this is not paradise. Perhaps I expected too much. Maybe the academic life I want exists nowhere. I doubt it. There is academia and there is academia. The academia held in high regard is the upper-middle class version of it. There are numerous higher education factories in this country that only seem like colleges and universities. Their real purpose is to maintain the illusion of upward mobility while delivering the kind of education that tends to keep working class kids in their place. That other academia is still hard for working class people to get into, be they students or professors.

Fred Biltmore

...After 17 years as an assistant professor or less I have recently been informed that I will be promoted to the rank of associate professor next year. I am no longer much harassed or annoyed by moronic administrators. The environment may not be ideal but it is substantially better than any academic situation in which I have been.

I was 22 years old when I decided to be a college professor. This decision can be traced to my failure to make a success as a collegiate basketball player at a university in the Northwest. I had hoped for a career as a professional basketball player which I believed would open the door to a good coaching job. However, in the fall of my senior year I realized that not only was such a career unlikely to materialize, it was not to my liking anyway, for I did not like the values fostered by big-time athletics. In particular, I found the coaching staffs in the major sports largely devoid of any concern for their athletes, completely authoritarian in their dealings with them, and fundamentally dishonest in their bearing. Consequently, I decided to abandon athletics as a profession and become a social scientist. Since I had a good academic record I was able to obtain financial aid in a new doctoral program at a large but undistinguished university in the Southwest. I had little idea of what academic life would be like in spite of the efforts of two kind and able young professors at my undergraduate institution to explain it all to me. But I am getting ahead of myself. Let me explain my background and then relate this to my academic career.

There is nothing unusual about my ethnic or religious background. It is thoroughly Wasp. My ancestors were mostly of English origin with an admixture of German and Scandinavian blood. So far as I know they all practiced some form of Protestantism: Anglicanism, Presbyterianism, or Methodism. There is also a Mormon or two lurking in

159

my background but for obvious reasons I would prefer to forget this. I have traced my ancestry on my father's side back to the year 1661 when an English Puritan fleeing the Stuart Restoration immigrated to Maryland. Part of my mother's family immigrated from Cornwall, England, in 1880 and earned enough money working in the mines and on ranches to buy land and raise sheep.

My paternal grandfather was an itinerant laborer who left a small farm in the Ozark Mountains shortly after the turn of the century and drifted into the intermountain area. He married a girl of 14 there, had four children by her and then deserted the family, rarely to be heard from again. My father was reared in old mining camps by his mother and a step-father who was a millwright. He quit high school in his junior year and worked as a farm hand, mill operator, miner and truck driver before he finally became an electrician. He also served a hitch in the Civilian Conservation Corp during the early years of the New Deal. By the time I was born in 1939 he was employed by the federal government as an electrician's helper—later he became a journeyman electrician, and still later a foreman.

My mother was the daughter of a sheep-rancher whose holdings were heavily encumbered with debt as a result of the Depression. However, she did finish high school and attended a junior college for one semester before returning home to help her father run the ranch. In 1934 she married my father, whom she had met in high school. They have remained married for 46 years and have long since finished raising a family of six children.

My earliest ideas about class and status undoubtedly stem from my childhood experiences in a small town owned and operated by the federal government on the Southwest desert. It was a good place to grow up. We led a stable, orderly, although boring existence in a community that was made up of relatively well-paid white- and blue-collar workers. There were almost no extremes of wealth or poverty as almost every family had within a few thousand dollars of the same income. The town was also unusual in that it was overwhelmingly Protestant or Mormon. Chicanos, Blacks, and Jews were conspicuous by their absence. All of the houses in certain sections of town were owned and maintained by Uncle Sam. Some of them were larger and better built than others. If our house was furnished differently than most others, it was partly because there were six children in the family, and my father's income had to be stretched a bit further. However, he was a thrifty man with a good eye for bargains and I can honestly say I never wanted for anything that I now consider important. In any case, my mother was a devoted housewife who always kept our clothes clean and mended, the house tidy, and served hot, nutritious meals at regular intervals.

The only real poverty I saw was when I traveled through the deep South on a bus at the age of twelve. I was struck by the wretched housing along the highways and by the fact that a black boy on the bus could not eat in the same restaurants with the whites. But this was only a fleeting glimpse of something otherwise alien to my experience.

The only group of low status people that I encountered as a boy were the Okies who lived in a small settlement nearby. Although the federal government employed most of them through the same agency my father worked for, they tended to have the worst-paying jobs as gardeners, janitors and unskilled laborers. They were not poverty-stricken but they often dressed shabbily and talked a bit different than the rest of us. In some ways they were discriminated against and misunderstood. Our teachers occasionally singled them out for abuse and ridicule. I am still ashamed of the way Okies were treated and the bad effect this must have had on their lives.

When I was a small boy I was impressed by the fact that blue-collar workers like my father chewed tobacco and used foul language. I rarely saw white-collar workers who worked in offices as accountants or executives (and wore white shirts and ties to work instead of overalls) chew tobacco or swear. I think my mother was much more impressed with their gentility than my father, although he too realized that there were advantages to such restraint. What I have experienced as the habitual use of foul language by my generation of American academic social scientists from blue-collar backgrounds can be traced to our continuing revolt against the gentility to which our parents aspired but perhaps never quite achieved.

Morally, the community in which I was reared was much under the influence of the liberal Protestant denominations and, to a lesser extent, that of the Mormons. Although my family were strong Episcopalians of the High Church variety, similar influences were pervasive. As a small boy and adolescent the main message I learned was that you have to take the consequences of your behavior. This was so instilled in me at home and at church that I still believe it. It is no doubt reflected in my preference for the well-ordered life based on hard work, self-discipline and goal-oriented behavior despite an occasional backslide into drunken self-indulgence and irreverence for the mores of the Great American middle-class.

I have taught at or attended 13 different institutions in a career that spans 24 years since I first entered college at age 18. I have moved so often that my friends, all of whom are academics, sometimes refer to me as an "academic bindlestiff." The universities I have been associated with have ranged in size from 2,500 to 35,000 in enrollment. They have all been state institutions. I have had nothing to do with private schools of any kind. With few exceptions my students have come from middle or lower middle income families. What little exposure I had to wealthy students was negative. They were mostly spoiled, lazy, self-indulgent and either apolitical or politically conservative. In fact, most of what I know of the American upper class is based on reading the works of G. William Domhoff, C. Wright Mills, Digby Baltzell, etc., not on first hand experience. My strong dislike of concentrated wealth and power does not stem from first-hand knowledge of either the upper class or for that matter, the dispossessed since only on occasion have I had students who were from underprivileged backgrounds. My leftist social and political philosophy, instead, comes from two other sources. The first was my childhood and adolescent experiences in a largely middle-class community where little difference in income and status existed between top and bottom. The second is my knowledge of the literature of social sciences which enables me to give theoretical justification to feelings and attitudes derived from my early life.

My experience in universities suggests to me that academic faculty might best be divided into these categories. (1)

"Image-mongers" who flourish by distorting or even fabricating their academic accomplishments with regard to publications, academic "connections," teaching competence, etc. Often they are skilled at diverting attention from the paucity of their accomplishments. (2) Social parasites who have no serious intention of doing any productive work beyond the absolute minimum of meeting their classes and turning in their grades at the end of the semester. The 1960s produced an unusually large number of these drones who leech off their more conscientious colleagues while feeding at the public trough. (3) Egocentric high-powered publishers who contribute little to the academic community except their monographs and articles in scholarly journals and selfishly see their present position as but a springboard to a better job. Often they neglect their students because they are really not interested in teaching. Usually they will not serve on committees of any kind except under duress or promise of personal gain. (4) Vocational-technical types who do not have a broad liberal arts education, are incapable of thinking critically outside their narrow specialization, however competent they may be within it, and do not understand what a university is for. (5) Political intellectuals, usually found in the social sciences and humanities, but occasionally in the natural sciences or elsewhere. Some of these people are the backbone of the university and the salt of the earth provided they have not become too neurotic or alienated. Others of them, however, have no ethical core or moral bearings and are as devoid of scruple as it is possible to be.

My typology of administrators contains the following categories: (1) "Opportunists"—this varies from those who will do anything to advance their careers, to those interested primarily in preserving their positions and privilege since they have long since reached their level of incompetence. (2) "Authoritarians" who believe their own decisions should be binding regardless of merit and who, if they consult with others beneath them in the hierarchy, only do so in order to manipulate them. (3) "Professionals" who claim they are above and beyond mere ideological and value considerations and simply want to get on with the job. When substantive conflict arises they either play dumb so that they will

not have to make hard decisions or else they preach toge-
therness and social harmony so as to avoid taking sides.
Essentially they are moral idiots with their eyes on what
Veblen called "the main chance." (4) "Principled leftists"
who stress egalitarianism and participation and emphasize
the need for academic excellence. This last category is a
joke—I have never met a single administrator who fits into
it—if one did exist he would not hold his job long. Of course,
some administrators are better than others, but on the
whole the ones I have known are a dismal lot. They simply
reflect the hierarchical values and corruption of the larger
social order.

No doubt some of my difficulties in academic life stem
from the fact that I have changed disciplines on several
occasions. I was originally trained as a New Deal historian
with a minor field in political theory. I decided that history
was not my calling because it lacked adequate conceptual,
normative and theoretical underpinnings. I "retooled" as
the saying goes, by doing a year of postdoctoral study in
political science and economics at another large state university in the Southwest. Alas, I discovered that historians
no longer considered me one of them, while political scientists were reluctant to accept me since I did not have a doctorate in their discipline. I have since drifted from one discipline and department to another, holding appointments in
history, political science and public administration as well
as teaching economics. I was recently described by a colleague as "a political scientist who was trained as a historian but who prefers to publish articles on economics in
sociology journals." Given my research interests and teaching experience in various disciplines it is not surprising that
I no longer consider myself to have a discipline. But this
lack of disciplinary focus and credibility has complicated
my career.

My egalitarian values and stubbornness have gotten
me into trouble with numerous administrators. At one college in the Southwest I gave low grades to about a quarter of
a large section of first-year students in American history.
The chairperson of the history department, who was undoubtedly under pressure from higher-ups, said he would fire me if
I did not change my grading policies. I left this distinguished institution of higher learning after one year.

At another Southwestern university I was fired by a department head without a vote by my colleagues while I was on a leave of absence. He was supported by the administration which was, no doubt, glad to see me leave. I had been influential in getting the local chapter of the A.A.U.P. to censure the president of the university for his role in closing down a religious center run by a liberal Presbyterian anti-war activist. Also, I was one of two faculty advisors to a chapter of S.D.S. which the university refused to recognize or permit to use its facilities. It was not a militant chapter nor had it caused violence or disorder, but given the bigoted, reactionary nature of "Sergeant-General Sorebutt," as we called the fool who was president, this was too much. Naturally, few of my colleagues had the modest amount of courage it would have taken to come to my support. In any case, I was only too glad to leave this intellectual and moral wasteland for greener pastures.

Alas, my next job was at a small community college which was run by two deceitful, swindling rascals who were incompetent. For three years I tried desperately to accommodate myself to these morally diseased gentlemen for I was beginning to feel that I was at fault for almost continual battles with administrators. I organized a faculty senate, became its first chairperson, and then, seeing the need for a faculty union, persuaded others to join the National Society of Professors. All this was to little avail, however, as the powers that be continued to hire old friends, fellow flunkeys and complacent incompetents who were interested only in drawing their paychecks. To this day no faculty member at that institution has ever been denied tenure on grounds of incompetence!

I was fortunate after three years to find another job— this was probably due to the fact that I was willing to work for a low salary and had a good record as a classroom teacher and a publishing scholar. This time I taught public administration and public policy at a small state college in California. I was in a business school which had (of all things!) a liberal dean who was a very decent man. Since this was a temporary appointment the dean helped me get another job after two years at a similar institution nearby. As usual I was glad to have work but I found this new place depressing in the extreme. It was the most bureaucratic, authoritarian atmosphere I have ever experienced. I was arbitrarily assigned to committees in whose work I had little interest or knowledge. My textbooks for graduate courses were chosen for me without my consent by the department chairperson, a retired federal bureaucrat, who was a bully as well as a fool. I later learned that he had been forced to hire me by a dean who was impressed by my letters of recommendation and publications. This chairman hounded me almost from the day I set foot on the campus. I have since decided that what motivated him was his belief that since I had never been a bureaucrat I could not train the students. There was too much political economy and political sociology in my public administration courses, indeed, far too much normative discourse—and too many people were starting to think for themselves. I was told by the chairperson to change the content of my courses and the substance of my syllabi even though I got very good ratings from my students on the standardized evaluation forms. I could have stayed at this institution and probably would have been given tenure, but the revolting nature of the school and the smog-belt which surrounded it were good reasons for leaving after two years.

Presently I am teaching political science in a medium-sized state university in the intermountain area. Although the work load is heavy, I am able to function with reasonable effectiveness as a scholar and teacher. After 17 years as an assistant professor or less I have recently been informed that I will be promoted to the rank of associate professor next year. I am no longer much harassed or annoyed by moronic administrators. The environment may not be ideal but it is substantially better than any academic situation in which I have been.

CHAPTER 6

Separate Pathways

Our four contributors here share an interesting strategic response to university life: considering much of what they found there unacceptable, they quite simply *forged* ways to be college professors remarkably different from those of their colleagues. One, indeed, has actually constructed a "college within a college," a self-contained and workable world having little contact with the other one all around.

And, the other three essayists have pushed aside barriers (two of them by campus politicking) to what they considered the right and proper way for an academic and the university to be. Perhaps what is most admirable (or outrageous, depending on one's view) in the efforts of this quartet is their refusal to allow their large disenchantment with the university to descend into a cynicism that might have destroyed their productive and interesting work lives.

Another of our contributors (whose essay was not included in the book) described his own alternate path in a way that condenses an essential feature of this kind of strategy, when he wrote that:

> It's not a perfect life, but it has the great merit of being largely a product of my dreams, not someone else's. And, I feel pretty good about the fact that I never wrote a word to please a dean, and I never forced any of my kids to practice the viola.

Charles Finder

The more difficult time happened later...Kids, after the middle '70s, have no tension between career and commitment. They're just occasionally interested and they see their intellectual and critical learning as simply a way to hack a grade. That makes it very boring. It's a job. It's putting in time and drawing a paycheck. What helps me survive is that half my time is spent in Latin America where ideas are definitely consequential.

My father began as a leather worker and he used to be a peddler—fish peddler in the streets. Eventually he was a fish monger on a small scale, and that's what he ended up doing for about twenty-five years. I worked with him in the fish market for about 5 years, from about 13 to 18, until I slashed all my fingers, almost lost them. When that happened, he said, "It's time to go to school. You're not going to be a good fish cutter, so you better get an education." So I said it's time to move on to something else. My whole educational career is kind of a paradox because the lower down in the educational system you go, the worse I was, and the higher I went in the educational system the better was my record. So junior high school was pretty bad, high school was so-so, undergraduate was *cum laude,* and in graduate school I took all the honors. I was very alienated from high school. I really didn't see any relationship between high school and what they were teaching. The history teacher was a big booster of the American Legion, not that I was very political. In high school I was running around with the really tough kids in the neighborhood and was very heavily into gambling. I used to be one of the hot-shot crap shooters. One day, I cleaned out the janitors and came to class with about seventy-five bucks rolled up in my pocket. I used to hang around pool rooms a lot. I had gone through the ceiling on the I.Q. test, and yet my grades in high school were C's, B's, B+'s, an occasional A. It was at the last moment that I decided to go to college.

169

I went to a commuter college, worked during the summers, weekends, paying my way through school. The first semester in school was terrible. I can't remember clearly what I got but it wasn't much above passing. But, in the second semester I met a young English professor who started me on cultural criticism, reading George Orwell, criticism of *The Reader's Digest,* and it made a lot of sense to me, a kind of mass-culture critique. There was no political economy taught then, but beginning in my sophomore year in college, I really began to develop more or less a critical view. Because of it I spent an enormous amount of time reading, ten hours or twelve hours a day. Tolstoy, Nietzche, a whole gamut of writers.

I had very little to do with other students except for a small group of commuters, a couple of Italians from East Boston, a young Jewish kid who was from my neighborhood, who was a member of the Socialist Working Man's Circle. There was a handful of us and we had nothing to do with the whole fraternity, sorority, college scene. We really could have been in another college. Most of us worked our way though school. I think once or twice we went into Boston and broke in on one of their parties and drank up their booze. We spent most of the time studying and trying to figure out what to do, where we fit in and how to integrate what we were reading and how we were living.

Learning and political consciousness came together for me. It was a kind of existentialist trip. We started first with the whole attack on religion. Even when we would go out with women, we would spoil the date because we would get involved in political discussions with some of the girls who were Jews, or Catholics. Suddenly we were attacking and messing up the evening. Mostly we were driven by a real sense of dissatisfaction. A fellow named Benedict, who was a political theorist, was talking up C. Wright Mills. His ideas were very influential for a lot of us. Though we were very alienated, very hostile to what was going on, we certainly were not Marxist in any felt sense.

About this time I met a guy two blocks from where I lived who was an underground Trotskyite. He opened up a whole area for new reading. I started reading Trotsky's *Revolution Betrayed* and *History of the Russian Revolu-*

tion. I started subscribing to *Dissent,* I think around '56 or
'57, and it was again extraordinary in a sense that it opened
me up to a whole new area of cultural and political criticism.
I met Irving Howe and attended a few of his seances. I came
to not like him playing the role of Pope and his lacky young
graduate students and undergraduates who hung on every
word. There really wasn't a good give-and-take critical discussion. I think the thing that finally put me off was that we
had read a book by Isaac Deutscher on the Soviet Union.
Immediately this lacky jumped up and accused me of being
an apologist of Stalinism. I had no idea what a Stalinoid
was. I had just started coming to the group and, in fact, was
very sympathetic to Howe's perspective. That kind of Stali-
nophobia, and Howe's capacity to be the "master's voice,"
was more than I could take.

The last year in undergraduate school I felt Boston was
a really closed world, a conservative town. I had a professor
in Political Science who advised me to go to Berkeley, but
then I forgot to send in my application form for a Woodrow
Wilson fellowship. So I packed up and read Ginsberg, was
impressed and took the professor's advice about going to the
West Coast. There I found new vistas, new opportunities for
being involved politically and also intellectually. I guessed
that the West Coast was a much better area in which to
break new ground. And I think I needed it on a personal
level. I had been tied to home town and the Boston area. It
was a way of personally breaking loose and also making my
way academically. Berkeley was supposed to be one of the
up-and-coming graduate centers. But I was still not certain I
wanted to be an academic.

Halfway through undergraduate school, I was going to
be a lawyer. I also took a civil service exam, and when I
arrived at Berkeley I was notified that I had a job in the
social security administration or something like that. I
wasn't sure what I wanted. I was probing. I had worked as a
shoe salesman during undergraduate school. Just before I
finished, the shoe company offered me a general manager-
ship for New England. I turned that down. I had one foot in
the system and one foot out. At the time I was really becoming radical, and making career choices was pulling me in
both ways.

Anyway, I decided to go to Berkeley and immediately I found a whole number of political groups there. It was very difficult adjusting. Everybody seemed to know everybody else and I knew hardly anyone. I knew a Marxist ex-seaman, a person who was running a bookstore, and he took me in and gave me some advice. I got in touch with some political people. I went to graduate school for one semester and quit.

Basically I quit because I was really appalled by the opportunism and the careerism that I found among the graduate students. One example: I was in a class with a fellow from the Rand Corporation who later became a real hot-shot expert on South East Asia. About half way through the course he asked for an evaluation of the class. Well, nobody got up and said anything. So finally I got up and said: "Look, I'll tell you what I think. I think you're giving us the kings and queens interpretation of history; there's no role for the masses, the rulers decide everything and the masses are passive instruments of change. I don't think that's the way that it's been; not necessarily that the masses make history but certainly there have been rebellions, and protests, that these events shape the conditions under which—." He stood right in front of the class and accused me of being a rash, insolent young man. Then, some other graduate student got up and told the professor what a great course it was.

That sort of thing turned me off, even though there was nothing terribly offensive about it. But I wasn't learning anything and I really didn't feel at all a part of being in the academic world. I dropped out. For a year I was writing. I thought of myself as a writer, a poet, a short story writer. Yet I never felt confident enough about what I was doing to go public with it. A lot of it was writing for myself and about kinds of things I was feeling, and that kind of writing really was very alienated from the academic world. I became involved in a Marxist group and I decided to go into the factories.

This was not an easy decision. I knew what I was getting into. It wasn't exactly an attractive place to plug in since I didn't have the skills, and unskilled factory work is pretty brutal. I spent '59-'62 working in different factories.

After work, most of the political activity happened to be around the university. So I was doing a kind of double stint. In the factory, where I was supposed to be doing political work, in fact I was mostly earning a living. In the evening I was falling asleep at student-organized political activities. While that was going on, there was a big demonstration against the House Unamerican Activities Committee in San Francisco. I got involved and as a result the FBI got after me in the factory.

One of the things that I greatly appreciate, the main learning experience that I had out of that whole period in the factory, was the tremendous degree of solidarity that I got from the workmates, from the guys in the machine shop, especially a handful of southerners that I worked with, boys from Arkansas, one of whom was a shop steward. His brother was also on the floor. For two years, despite FBI pressures and attempts by management in response to these pressures, they were not able to fire me. I remember this fellow from Arkansas coming up and telling me about all the heat that was being put on him and his telling the foreman in effect that while he didn't agree with my point of view, he'd fight for my rights. He was a kind of Arkansas version of Voltaire. That experience was very important because in many ways it wasn't replicated in the academic world. When the heat came on, at least as a faculty member, the main response of the faculties was to shiver and cower, and pull back from any attempts at expressing overt and militant solidarity. The first thing they think about is their own job and how their own job can be saved, divorced from any sense of loyalty. I still wonder why academics are like that.

I guess most of those attitudes are shaped around individual career definitions. Personal ties and loyalties aren't important . There is not much of a sense of brotherhood in the academy. Whenever someone is on the firing line, academics might agree he is right, but they will also agree that he's self-destructive. Any time someone is outspoken, the most liberal faculty will come up to you and say, "Gee, I'd like to defend so and so, in fact I'm doing what I can, but I wish he wouldn't be so self-destructive." The whole attempt is to change the issue from one of the content of the struggle to the style of the victim. And in a sense that is a way of disassociating one's self from the issue. When I got hired in my first job at State U., there was a handful of faculty members that were politically involved, probably 25 out of 2,000. Every one of them was fired except myself, maybe because I probably had more publications than most of the rest of my department combined. Another fellow remained an associate professor for 15 years despite the fact that he published three major books. So that was the price that a lot of people paid.

Anyway, after finally getting fired at the factory, I went back to graduate school and essentially with no illusions this second time around. It was a place to engage in political activity, it was a place that I could begin to do some of my work. At the time there was some Latin American professor working in the university with whom I felt comfortable, and I began with the idea that I'm gonna do what they're doing better than they are and also go on to do my own work. It was a terribly difficult task because at the time there was no radical, intellectual tradition established. I had the enormously complicated task of learning the conventional literature and then developing both a critique of it and alternative to it.

I felt the challenge; I met the challenge. As I came through graduate school, there were huge demonstrations in '64 and '67. In that period of great student mobilization I found real community. The graduate students, and even a few faculty members, began to develop ties. But most of the time was kind of like checking in, finding out what was on someone's reading list in a course, making sure you knew the positions, the methodology, the whole bit and then outside of the classroom on the famous terrace of Cal U. is where we would have the really serious discussions, which were intellectual and political. These were some of the brightest and best people that I've known. The most illuminating discussions took place outside of the classroom. Cal U. always had the erroneous reputation that the learning experience was with the prestigious professors, but they usually were very boring and unchallenging. A good deal of the best learning times tool place outside.

My first teaching job was in the back woods of Pennsylvania. It was a big jump and a very dramatic experience.

This was 1967. A lot of people I knew were quitting college and joining full time in the Movement. It was the height of the Vietnam War, the height of the mass mobilization. I confess I felt very guilt-ridden as I accepted the job. Even though I sustained the high level of political visibility and activity the fact of not being full time in movement politics was still a point of great pressure, personal pressure, and I was constantly thinking over whether I was doing the right thing and always feeling the need to compensate by increasing political activities within the context of a professional career.

During that time, the whole American Dream and America as the democratic world leader was called into question. Even when you had fraternity boys and others in the classroom, they were very defensive, especially when they were threatened by the draft. Justification for the affluent careerism was really called into question. So most of the experiences that I had at the time involved the students coming over to a point where they were at least open to critical ideas, for whatever opportunistic reasons. For example, some Republican kids came to me for draft counseling. I spoke at Princeton. I gave a talk at Harvard. A lot of the students that would come for counseling were sort of caught in a bind. On the one hand they were going to these schools, and I would openly say, "Look, you made a choice to come to an elitist institution." The problem was how they could try to change their educational experience to be more in line with their political thinking, rather than to resolve that problem. They had to come to terms with the fact that they had made a choice to pursue a prestigious degree in pursuit of an elite career. Yet they were embracing radical and political ideas. I just threw it back at them.

The really more difficult time happened later. That was dealing with petty bourgeois kids from ethnic backgrounds, kids who after the mid '70s had no tension between career and commitment. They're just occasionally interested and they see their intellectual and critical learning as simply a way to hack a grade. That makes it very boring. It's a job. It's putting in time and drawing a paycheck.

What helps me survive this period is that half of my time is spent in Latin America where ideas are definitely

consequential. And you have to be there. The context is
different. If you lay out a particular line of analysis and the
political implications of it are that someone takes up those
political implications and develops them, they could be putting their life on the line. And it seems to me that one has to
assume the responsibilty for those ideas. That has been a
very satisfying aspect for my intellectual work. In the U.S., I
retain an enormous degree of frustration in attempting to
make classroom work consequential for the students. It
ends up that you are pitching for one or two students in the
classroom, hoping they will take your course and then go to
the South, spend six months hitch-hiking through the
Southwest on an independent study, write up a paper on
how the oil companies and power companies are destroying
the Navahos. There is probably one student a year like that.
That sort of saves the game to some degree.

I think there are variations among administrators, to
tell you very truthfully. At State U. you had the kind of
president that welcomed General Westmoreland during the
Vietnam War, tight-ass people who weren't interested in
ideas, who thought the faculty members should be home
doing their work and administrators should decide what the
university is all about. At another state university, I've had
the opposite experience; a low profile president whose job
has been to pass off important decisions to the faculty committees. He responds to any pressures and tries to avoid
conflict that will draw adverse publicity. I frankly have not
had much conflict with administrators as much as with
conservative faculty members.

I think in some ways, the last nine or ten years most of
the hacks that I have met have been certain faculty
members. And I'm not saying they're all conservatives. I
recall my last year at State U. There was an incident in
which the homosexual group on campus began to activate
itself and one of my graduate assistants was involved in the
support of the homosexual rights. The president of the university was very hostile to them. In the course of this struggle, my department chairman informed me that they would
now pass a rule in the department that assistantships would
not be granted to any students with two or more grades of
incomplete. Well, the consequence was that this activist,

and three others who had two incompletes, would be cut out of their assistantships, which meant in fact, kicking them out of the program. So I went to bat for them, and during one very intense discussion of the matter chairs almost started flying across the room. It got very physical. The vote came down, and it was 9 to 1 with 10 abstentions in favor of this new ruling. I was the *one*, of course. Most of the abstainers called me up later in the day and told me how wonderful I was, very courageous. Very supportive, but they called on the sly. I told them that I would have appreciated much less praise and a quiet vote in the meeting.

After a while these kinds of things happen and you feel that before going to bat for a faculty member or someone else you are going to wait and see whether other people are also going to go to bat. That's been my attitude ever since. After a while I decided that the bigger issues and the bigger society were much more important to me than becoming involved with faculty and administrative struggles. In one recent incident, while we were building up our doctoral program, a senior professor wrote a letter to the president attacking our program, as a marxist political program. I answered him very simply. If he wanted to discuss the intellectual merits of the program I would bring the curriculum vitae from our department and he could evaluate them in light of publications, professional meetings, etc. If he wanted to launch a political polemic against marxism I would buy him a soap box and he could carry on the discussion. That was the end of that exchange. The point I'm making is that you recognize what the academic rules of the game are and then I think the political battles fall into place.

Socially, my best friends are people who aren't in academic life. They are people who have been victimized in academic life and have been blacklisted, or are freelancing either by force of circumstances or by choice. I don't really have any close friends, or very few that are really heavily involved in the academic life. There are probably only a handful of people that I can think of and most of them are spread across the country. One of the basic problems is that I really don't trust academic people. They are so gossipy and so competitive and you really can't sit down and let your hair down and discuss with them. You don't know what they're going to do. There's such a lack of character. People that I have helped bring into the department, helped publish, helped a couple of them get tenure, suddenly turn around and act in the most vindictive fashion. I totally lose confidence. One of the things I've concluded is that not only intellectual excellence and political commitment or ideological commitment is important but character is even more fundamental. Profoundly lacking are people in whom you can confide, who will go to bat for you out of loyalty. These traits are profoundly absent in the academic world, or if it is there it is not because they're in the academic milieu, but because of some other reason.

Would I do it all over again? It's hard to say. I spent a number of years working at factory jobs, and I don't think I'm up to doing that anymore. I think the last factory job that I spent a couple of years doing was spray painting. I developed spots on my lungs, so I'm not up to going back that route. I think the fear of falling down into a difficult and grinding kind of existence is always at the back of my mind. On the other hand, I do have a couple of friends who have been able to make it as freelancers, able to write and live off of what they make as writers. I've always enjoyed doing in-depth kinds of journalism, and I do it in addition to my teaching because I think it's some of the most important aspects of my intellectual work. Some of the most perceptive, analytical, theoretically interesting pieces are written in so-called nonacademic journals that provide me with a lot more insights than what is passed off in the Political Science and Sociological Journals.

I've created another world, other than academia in which I relate to tens of thousands of people who are serious both intellectually, and politically. But I still feel a great deal of tension. I feel a need at some point to be in a society in transition, where I can apply what I've been learning, and be involved in building a new society.

George Puck

...I run my own small college within a University
two days a week. The rest of the University can go
to hell with itself. I think of myself as doing exactly
what I should be doing. And, I think that the institution needs me a great deal more than I need it.

My mother was born in the United States. She was one of
eleven children who all grew up in New York's lower east
side at a time when the teeming masses were welcomed by
the statue in the harbor. The niche has now changed; I
suppose we now see the lower east side in a romantic haze,
something that it certainly was not for those who lived
there.

She had a good voice. On occasion she sang in the
chorus of the Met. Mostly I remember her singing the Star
Spangled Banner at Fourth of July parties in Far Rocka-
way, the place where I grew up. She was very short—under
five feet; in fact, at an early age (say about 16) I was so much
taller that I could look right down onto the top of her head.

My mother had a difficult time with me. It began at
birth. The doctors said one of the two of us might live, but
not both. As it turned out, we both survived. But the real
trouble started when it was time for me to go to school. I
refused. I was thrown out of kindergarten for scratching the
teacher's face: the issue was that she wanted me to make
paper chains; I found that silly (I think now—I don't really
recall what I thought at the time). Anyway, it took a time for
me to start again. But it never went well with me through
public school. I never listened to any teacher. In fact, I
remember listening to a teacher for the first time in college.
I'm not sure why I never listened; I may have been thinking
about other things but I can't remember now, and I don't
want to try. All in all, I was said to be a bad boy—a very bad
boy.

What does all of my early school experience have to do with my mother? Well, it hurt her. She put great stock in my education—no, not in my education, but in Education. Here I was, one said to be a poor student, and there she was, with all of her great faith in what beauty and wonder there was in learning. There was and is, but in retrospect, I think that learning may have little or nothing to do with school. My bad boy image is not invented. My mother died while I was in my teens. I recall an aunt saying that I had killed her. That's not true at all; but it was said.

My father was born in Turkey. His father had gone there from France to engage in trade, in particular, goods transported via ships. The family remained French, so when World War I started up, and the French were about to call upon him to serve France, he escaped Turkey with one of his brothers and eventually reached the United States. At first, he was employed in a button factory. After a year or so, he went to work on the docks of New York where he remained all the rest of his working life. He became a clerk and was in a position to help get work for his brothers as longshoremen or checkers who checked the goods loaded or unloaded. He worked there during the difficult years of unionization. Crime, violence, etc., was as everyday as the morning cup of coffee. My father is now 90, still independent, and still strong.

My father, to this day, remains a foreigner. He is a U.S. citizen, but he touched base with the U.S. through my mother. He is a life-long Democrat (Democrats, he says are for the working man), but in the past decade he has come to doubt that. He is much better informed than most Americans. When he came to the U.S., he learned to read by studying newspapers, in particular, the *New York Times*. He has a high regard for education, but it is not unqualified. He cannot understand, for example, how a person can study French in school for three years and still not be able to converse in the language. He has known too many college educated fools to believe that education makes a man wise. He, himself, in my view, is a wise man, although he does not think of himself in that way. At 90, he has seen a lot, and he has learned a lot. I suppose one would call him self-educated, but without the benefit of books. It is not trite in his case to say that life, nature, the sea, watching, observing, trying to comprehend, seeing the view of another, and so on, have taught him a good deal.

Somehow or other, the "bad boy," who never listened to a teacher, ended up in academia. What has been my sense of belonging? I have little, if any, relationship with my so-called colleagues. This may sound strange, so a little explanation is in order. My colleagues do not talk about what I want to talk about. They talk about *other* colleagues, or about the weather, or about whom to hire, or something like that; mostly about *other* colleagues. Ideas—perhaps what I thought it was all about—come up as banter. When I first entered the academy, I thought it would be otherwise. For about ten years—the first ten—I talked about ideas. This was often offensive to others. It was offensive, touched with respect. I think they thought that I was doing right; nevertheless it was offensive. So in the last ten years, I stopped talking to colleagues. I talk to students when I do talk. Students think that they are supposed to talk about ideas to a professor, or at least they pretend that they think so. Well, even if they pretend, we do talk about ideas. I do not enjoy a sense of membership in the academy. Rather, I like to think of myself attached to a world of intellectuals—those who deal with ideas, just as a carpenter deals with wood. If I have a sense of membership at all, it is with anyone who wants to talk about ideas.

I am fortunate in working at an institution where the students come relatively well-prepared. I also spend a good deal of time working with graduate students. Most come from higher income families. Over a period of twenty years, of course, students have changed, and so have I. It is difficult to cast meaningful generalizations in a situation of flux. But I will venture a few, with some misgivings.

The first is that income differences between me and my students do not make much difference if we center on ideas. I try to cast aside those differences that appear in clothing and such. But, I notice them; I think about them; I suppose I am sensitive to them. I am always aware of that, and I think about it when I am not in their presence. But in a situation where ideas are at the center, I feel that it is rather easy to get on with the discussion at hand. Still, I must admit, I feel a personal kinship with those who aren't in the "rich" category. This is particularly true of graduate students. I *like* males who come from working class backgrounds. I tend *not to like* rich girls. But I think that I can handle those likes and dislikes such that a rich girl who is really interested in what a university is really all about is marked "O.K., sure," in my mind. Immediate, first glance, repulsion on my part, is replaced with a positive attitude as soon as the subject gets interesting, as soon as I have a hunch that there is something worthwhile to talk about.

Because the institution where I teach is high in prestige ranking, the students think they are supposed to respect the professors. I believe this makes one hell of a lot of difference. They do not seem to believe that I am there to serve them. They seem to think that I would not be a professor at X institution if I were not good at what I do. All of this helps. It is a fiction, for sure, but it makes my job easier. They come in thinking that I must have something to say. I try not to disappoint them, and most of them respond in a positive way.

How has life in the academy worked out for me? I think of myself as a happy man. But it must be clear that I have had the opportunity to make my work in my way. I limit my four courses per year to 15 students each. I do all my teaching in my own office. Three of the four courses, by my choice, are graded satisfactory/unsatisfactory only. All four courses are of my own design; they exist at no other University. I spend two days a week on campus. One of these days, I teach: two seminars, one in the morning, one in the afternoon. On the other day, I have office hours all day long. At these office hours, I talk with students and others who visit with me. I *never* visit the office of another professor except when I must do so on business. I serve—by choice—on no committees, or perhaps, one every four or five years, that I determine to be unimportant. The other three week days, and often on weekends, I read at home. My "research" at the moment consists in sculpture which I do in a studio at home. I am making a series of Americans for Americans to see themselves.

The above routine has been going on now for ten years; I have not been hurt in salary as far as I know. I do what I do because—in effect—this is the way I can enjoy my work. I do not know what would happen if I were forced to change my pattern. In my view, I run my own small college within a University two days a week. The rest of the University can go to hell with itself. I think of myself as doing exactly what I should be doing. And I think that the institution needs me a great deal more than I need it.

I believe that in my work I have obligations to knowledge and to students. The college and university as an entity is a sham. I am not. I do what the institution says it is engaged in doing. I don't think we can change the institution by tinkering with it. You have two choices: (1) Change the entire cultural fabric of late western culture, or (2) become an exception within the system, and at least keep your self-respect. I can't do the first; I'm lucky to be able to do the second. I have great concern for ideas and for the people who deal with them. I think it is unfortunate that the university, by and large, does not provide for their needs. I will, in the midst of them, in spite of them. They put up with it because they know little about what I do to begin with, and I provide what they claim to provide, but don't.

If all of the above sounds arrogant, so be it.

Would I do it again? I suppose so.

Would I seek some kind of other work? Maybe. My ideal would be to be a very highly-skilled worker with lots of education to enjoy books and music. If I could, I would do art (in particular, sculpture) full time. But that would be only if I were truly independently wealthy.

There are all kind of academic authority. A chairman, I suppose, is an academic authority figure. With these types, I have had few problems. For the most part, I ignore them, and they, in turn, ignore me. By and large, this is my experience. I find that in my particular situation I can go ahead with my affairs while paying no attention to such authority. They do not touch upon what I do, at least not yet. I draw a tight line around my affairs, and as long as they do not cross it, nothing whatever happens. Non-serious encounters have received enough anger and noise from me to turn them back quickly. I think they think they can't move me. When they cross that line seriously, (if they do) I will fight them very hard, or leave. I don't know which I would do because I have yet to be tested on that one.

There is no way to conclude all the above. Lots more could have been said. I am not a stranger in paradise. It—the contemporary academy—is the stranger. Whatever it once was, or professed to be, it is no longer that.

John Adamson

The worst of professional administrators are social climbing, bourgeois hustlers. The Dean at my college has a rowing oar on his wall. I like and respect academic life so much that I can no more understand someone who would cease to be a professor in order to be Dean than I could if the principal cellist with an orchestra suddenly decided he'd rather be the bookkeeper.

I was born in Cincinnati, Ohio, on the tenth of May, 1947—Mother's day, as it happened. I was the second child born to Evelyn and Joseph, my birth having been preceded three years by my sister. My parents had met in Chicago, where my mother, having left her home town of DeKalb, Illinois, worked as a waitress, while my father was a draftee in the Air Force, completing his training before being shipped overseas. At the time of my birth, my father was employed in a cooperage, making barrels for the flourishing whiskey business across the bridge in Kentucky. There is an interesting story concerning how my father happened to be employed at the cooperage. The barrel factory was owned by a fairly prominent local family named Oaker. One of my father's aunts had been employed as a maid in the Oaker household (one of a number, I was brought to believe) and she often brought my infant father along to work with her. So the Oakers, having lost a son in the Great War, became very attached to my father, and spent considerable time with him in his youth. They also occasionally provided him with small luxuries, including a bicycle, and this apparently caused a certain friction (in those Depression days) between my father and his seven brothers and sisters.

My paternal grandparents were farmers in what was then land outside the Cincinnati urban area; my grandfather and his brothers had bought the farm with the proceeds from the sale of a small dairy which had been run, without noticeable success, by my great-grandfather. My grandfather's approach to farming seems to have also been a bit lackadaisical: as late as the 1950's he was still plowing with mules. And in his later years, he lived mostly by selling off pieces of land, and by such auxiliary enterprises as selling to passersby pint mason jars of the meats from black walnuts, which he had spent the winter extracting from their shells. He also made fine elderberry and wild blackberry wines.

My maternal grandfather, Hollis "Roy" Miller, was raised in Grand Rapids, Michigan, but moved in his youth to DeKalb, Illinois, where he became a worker in a U.S. steel mill, which at that time had a thriving wire nail and wire products business there. The last remnants of U.S. Steel, in the form of the Englander Mattress Company and the Cyclone Fence division, left DeKalb when I was in high school. The vast, crumbling brick buildings that once housed its plants are still in evidence in the oldest part of the town.

In 1917 my grandfather left the steel mill to volunteer for the army, and spent considerable time in the trenches in France, where he acquired, among other things, an extremely low opinion of the British, who in his days had no positive attributes whatsoever. Through a twist not uncommon at the time, my grandfather was fighting the Boche in France while my grandmother, a woman from a farming hamlet south of DeKalb, was unable to find a job in the area because of her German name.

Upon his return form the army, my grandfather resumed employment at USS, where he worked until the onset of the Great Depression, when that industry collapsed in DeKalb as elsewhere. From what I gather, he was then without steady employment for nearly seven years, during which time a number of students from Northern Illinois State Teachers College (now Northern Illinois University) continued to live in his house as non-paying boarders. The Crash had left them with the same absolute dearth of money as my grandfather, but he didn't have the heart to throw them out, so they lived there until they graduated, contributing what they could when they could. Many of these students still contact my grandfather; one, at least, is a reasonably successful architect. Sometimes in the late 1930s, my grandfather finally found a job with the DeKalb Fire Department, a job which he retained until his retirement.

In late 1950, my own family moved from Cincinnati to DeKalb. My father had just failed as entrepreneur; he had started a business selling and delivering Seven-Up soft drink to stores and taverns, but his business sense seems to have been on the par with his father's. In DeKalb he got a job with the Fire Department, owing no doubt to my grandfather's influence, and worked there until his retirement. On his off-days, he worked first as a deliveryman, then as an assistant to a truck mechanic at a local GM dealership. He and my mother also Simonized cars on weekends, $15 for a regular car and $20 for Cadillacs. My mother worked from the time my younger brother entered school until after I graduated from college, first as a school secretary, later as a secretary at a finance company.

I had attended kindergarten in Cincinnati, but entered first grade at Haish school in DeKalb. (This school was named, incidently, after Jacob Haish, who invented but did not patent barbed wire.) I remember clearly that my first years in school were extremely disorienting. I had learned to read precociously—spontaneously, so my mother holds—and I could read quite well when I entered first grade. But the assumption was that I couldn't read as well as the sons and daughters of college professors and of the local gentry (a word that *really applied* in DeKalb). So, I was placed in the lowest reading group, and remained there long after it became evident that I could read at above grade level. By the end of third grade I could read off the scale on the standardized Iowa tests that marked the end of every school year in DeKalb, and thus gained the luxury of not being required to take them. On the other hand, I was extremely slow to learn such things as the multiplication tables, and was also unable or unwilling to tell time until I was in second grade.

My education in Dekalb was for the most part uninspired. I did reasonably good work, but was usually far from outstanding. The main memory that I have is one of boredom. At one point in second grade I somehow discovered that the process of counting was recursive, so that in theory one can count as high as he wishes, and I spent a great deal of time counting to some astronomical number. At the end of each stint of counting I wrote the final number on a small piece of paper which I kept in my desk, so that I could start from there when more time was available. Along with the boredom, I was aware of the displeasure directed towards me by the school officials, who frequently chastised me about the disparity between my high scores on standardized tests and my less than spectacular performance.

My academic career in high school was also pretty lackluster; I spent the lion's share of my time being a jock, acting in plays, working to provide myself with spending money playing bass in some very bad bands, and thinking about women. The academic curriculum at DeKalb High School was very bad; my algebra teacher was the football coach, and one fascist American history teacher actually threw me out of class for reading ahead in the book. My weak performance convinced me that I wasn't really very hot stuff, and apparently my teachers by and large shared that view. When I scored very high on the qualifying exam for the National Merit Scholarship Program, one of my teachers told me, that "if I'd known you were smart I'd have made you work harder."

I had always shown aptitude for Science, and in the 60s that seemed to be the place to go, so when I applied to colleges I applied to be an engineer. I wanted to go to Dartmouth—why I honestly just can't recall—but my academic record was too anemic for Ivy League. I ended up enrolling in a small private college in Wisconsin, which at the time had a cooperative program in engineering with MIT. As time went by, I gave up the idea of engineering, majored in physics, and later, to the amusement of my physics professors, added a major in philosophy.

My undergraduate education was financed by some money from the College, some money from my jobs, money from my parents, and vast NDEA loans. My first two years in college were hardly sparkling; I had no notion of how to study, and I think my high school career had left me a little skeptical that someone standing in the front of a classroom might have something worthwhile and interesting to say. I also lacked the discipline to deal with the array of activities vying for one's time, and by the end of the fourth semester, I was on both academic and social probation. In my last two years, however, I was extremely successful, and had decided, on the advice of a professor of mine, to try to get into a graduate program in philosophy, with the intention of becoming a college teacher.

I had by then grown very fond of the academic atmosphere; I genuinely liked the world of ideas and thought I could happily spend my life in it. The Ivy League university to which I had most wanted to go admitted me, but with no financial aid. This presented me with a difficult decision, since I now had a wife and a baby daughter. We decided to go to Ivy U., and I spent the summer of 1968 packing peas and corn in a small family cannery in Pickett, Wisconsin (where one day I killed over 300 flies), as the more fortunate of my classmates celebrated our graduation in Europe and the less fortunate in Southeast Asia. My wife and I lived on brown rice and eggs and saved what little money I made for graduate school.

My decision to go to graduate school was met with a good deal of amazement by my family. I have 54 first cousins, and I was the first of us to go to college (one other ultimately did), and much less graduate school. The whole notion of being interested in academia seemed absurd to my aunts and uncles, especially when combined with the fact that I had a degree in physics which would have landed me a reasonably lucrative job.

I was able to get an NDEA loan to finance tuition, but my wife had to work full-time for a local temporary agency, while I spent my time as a scholar/baby-sitter. Fortunately I did well enough to be offered a tuition grant for the second semester, and an assistantship for the next year, so we lived for the next two years on the princely sum of $220 a month. My class background was brought to me quite clearly during this period: my fellow graduate students seemed to have inexhaustable sources of funds. One friend, who accepted a job for $11,000 (keep in mind that this was 1970), told me that she'd have to cut back her lifestyle, since her mother sent her more than that while she was a student! In the spring of 1971 I finished my dissertation and was offered and accepted my first full-time job, which was at a medium-sized, fairly prestigious university in Pennsylvania. I left in 1982, after a long fight that involved being recommended for tenure by my department and rejected, in what was an unusual move, by the president and his cronies. So at this point I can look back with some distance on my academic career.

Did I feel as though I belonged, now that I was formally a part of academia? I think that I have enjoyed a sense of membership in an academic community, even though I think those communities are deeply and gravely flawed. In fact, it may well have been this sense of participation in a joint endeavor that made academic life so attractive to me, and encouraged me to remain in academia. But I also think that this community is in many ways more ideal (based on the way in which we choose to speak of ourselves in public) and more artificial (the physical arrangement of the university buildings, the illusion offered during faculty meetings that we are making joint decisions) than real.

Part of this increasing artificiality is due to the increasing prevalence of university administrators who have either never been teachers or scholars, or saw being a scholar-teacher as merely paying one's dues towards being an administrator. These folks obviously see the university either on the corporate model—we produce a commodity and we have to shape the commodity that we offer to meet the demand—or as an arena for upward mobility. The current president of Liberal Arts University (L.A.U.), for instance, has several times said publicly that he wants junior faculty members to "compete with one another," the laurels presumably being academic tenure. It's very difficult to see these increasingly common conceptions of the nature of the university, held in high places, as being very conducive to community. It may well be, of course, that these administrators envision some academic version of the "invisible hand," mapping small-scale self-interest onto large-scale harmony. But such opinions tend to bring to mind Schopenhauer's reaction to Hegel's glorification of the existing Prussian monarchy; "and from this truth is supposed to come?"

It is of course possible that the acquisition of truth, or perhaps even education in any real sense, is not the goal of many university administrators. In response to the charge that many students at expensive private universities have very narrow, uncritical and bourgeois perspectives, I have heard the answer, "we like it that way , such people are our constituency, and this is what they pay for..." The catalog of the University for which I worked was pretty outfront about how safe the campus was, not only physically, but also in the sense that you can be damned certain your kid won't come home with any crackpot ideas.

My views towards my immediate colleagues are divided, too, into the real and the ideal. During a long period in which I underwent three separate tenure reviews, I became deeply and painfully aware of the extent to which many of my colleagues view their scholarship as a *commodity*. As one friend put it, "some guy writes, 'you're a good teacher' on a piece of paper and that doesn't mean shit." One colleague of mine, who was instrumental in denying me tenure, has regularly cranked out an article or so a year in an obscure field of philosophy that time has bypassed. He once said to me, with respect to a particular (important) book, that he had "gotten a good quote from it."

I sometimes say facetiously that many of my colleagues want to get *old* awfully fast (and some no doubt do), but a more sober appraisal is that there are certain rigidly delineated patterns of behavior which are acceptable, and these patterns and roles are by and large imitations of how middle-class academics envision an elitist society. For example, a colleague of mine insists that it is necessary to keep some "distance" from the students to be respected; apparently the respect is supposed to accrue not to the person but to the *role*, and the role is marked by characteristic dress, speech, modes of behavior. Indeed, one of the more unproductive members of the faculty of L.A.U., who is very popular with the administrators, *looks* and *acts* like what Buick dealers from Bergen County, New Jersey, *think* a college professor should look and act like. These roles are, of course, usually (and deliberately) antithetical to normal working-class modes of behavior and it is extremely common for working class academics deliberately to disguise their characteristic patterns of speech and behavior. One friend of mine, an academic from a working class southern background, would never dream of betraying his origins through something other than the cultivated neutrality of his accent.

What I have said here reflects, I think, a current academic trend. On one hand, we set forth the ideal of a community of scholars, and the pressure to conform is real enough, yet on the other hand the system of rewards is so aggressively individualistic that any community remains, for the most part, a wistful ideal. I can certainly attest that the values which my University projects in its catalog are radically different from those which determine the amounts in the pay envelopes on the 15th of each month.

But beyond the universal difficulties facing all academics today, I think that there is a special problem posed for those teachers from working class backgrounds who teach in the upper echelon of private colleges and universities. The typical student at the university at which I taught comes from a family which, while not wealthy by its own standard, is certainly comfortable. But this comfortableness is by and large a relatively recent phenomenon for these families; grandpa started out with nothing and now dad is the biggest Buick dealer in Bergen County. This peculiar "new wealth" background makes it very difficult to talk with them about *real* politics, that is, issues of class relations. These are the people for whom the American dream, at least in its economic and social guise, has worked; if Dad has lots of money and Uncle doesn't, then it *is* usually due to the fact that Dad has worked harder than Uncle, or was smarter. Thus the ongoing nature of class distinction in America is masked; unlike being black, which after all can't be *helped*, I think most of my students regard being of modest means as a reflection of a lack of talent or effort, and in this atmosphere it is not surprising that the working class student might feel a little intimidated. (I'm not certain that this lack of class consciousness is merely a sign of the times; I had a friend in graduate school who talked great radical politics, but was so rude to waitresses and salespeople that I couldn't handle going out in public with him.)

But on the other hand, many of the most reflective of my students sense a certain tension: whatever economic rewards the American Dream may have brought, these kids don't see their parents as being particularly *happy*. Many, in the course of their studies, have come to realize that there are *desiderata* in the world beyond selling loaded Buicks, and they come to see this in spite of pretty determined efforts by many in the academy to conceal it. Perhaps this is to be expected; I suppose Deans hate getting phone calls from irate parents whose children have returned home disillusioned, not with the university but with selling Buicks. And yet there is a paradox: the very background which they now increasingly question was a necessary condition for their being in a situation where such questioning is possible. That the University is by and large a bourgeois institution is pretty clear, and I'm sure that many people would point to corporate support of education as evidence of the "openness" of American big business. Whether this openness is anything more than illusion is of course debatable. The rise of career-oriented studies is not, I think, so much a corporate response to economic conditions or real needs as a reaction to the late sixties, when the academic community *did* seem to represent a real force for change, and thus to represent a real and present danger.

Have I found my career as an academic fruitful, enough so that I would do it again had I the chance? I guess the answer is yes; I get a great deal of satisfaction from what I do, and feel I'm *good* at it (although as I have pointed here in the mind of some this is debatable.) I almost never see what I do as *work*; I look forward to the start of the school year and fret through January and the summer. But further, the university, as I have said above, offers at least the *illusion* of a communal meritocracy based on reason, a rational community governed by curiosity. How long even that illusion can stand in the face of increasing pressure from within and without to treat ourselves as a commodity, to "respond to the market," is again questionable.

I've thought of other careers, and there are some things that I think I could enjoy. I've often thought about being a professional musician, although I probably couldn't handle the bullshit connected with that sort of career. I went to college to become an engineer, and I have little doubt that I could be happy doing that; I like making things work. But it would be hard, I think, to alienate myself from the arena of ideas, and I hope that choice does not materialize.

Louis Potter

The year I went to NEU they hired nine people in economics, all from the Big Ten and Ivy League-type schools, except for one Southern hick. I spent a lot of effort my first year trying to lose my accent. I felt people in the northeast associated a Southern accent with ignorance. But, I later came to believe it isn't geography that matters, it is class. People were looked down upon for their "Chicaga," "Joursey," "New Yawk," or even "Baston" accents; like Lisa Doolittle, they represented the wrong class.

Understanding one's feelings, or even knowing what they are, is at best a tenuous thing. It is so easy to be confused or even dishonest with one's self after years of building ego defense mechanisms and working out complicated rationalizations to square understanding with feeling. But even recognizing this difficulty suggests a personal insecurity that I think or feel has something to do with this working class kid passing himself off as Doctor Professor Intellectual, having a higher income than ninety-five percent of the people who work for a living. I spent most of my career trying consciously to "live down" my past while subconsciously failing. When will they find out that I am a fraud? Probably the central condition of my personal development was, as it is for most people, family. I was a middle child of twelve children who were born to my parents over a twenty-year period from prior to the Great Depression until the end of World War Two. No, we were not Catholic and no, we did not live on a farm.

Both of my grandfathers were ministers, of sorts. One attended a two-year fundamentalist college after finishing whatever education he received in a one-room school. He was killed with an axe while inviting the wrong man to a religious service; my mother was twelve.

My father's Dad was a seeker of fortune in Texas and in New Mexico. He had little formal education, farted away several potential chances for a fortune, and ended up as an itinerant preacher. He died broke in a Nursing Home at age 99.

My father quit school at age 16 to go to work, and my mother dropped out of high school in her senior year, to get married. But though my parents were not highly educated in a formal sense, they were intelligent and talented. They read books when time permitted and always kept up with political events. We were generally poor, but then we thought everyone was, except for the Rockefellers in New York and that Jew guy down the street who gave us treats to do things like light his stove on Saturday morning.

Growing up in a family of fourteen must have established some basic values that have been with me since. Sharing physical things and mutual psychological and emotional support, were necessities for survival in a tough outside world. The idea of equity became equality. Survival of the fittest just wouldn't wash. You didn't win and you were not better just because you were bigger, stronger or smarter—that just wasn't fair! So we were taught to root for the underdog and do battle with the powerful. "I may not be better than anybody, but I'm just as good," was my mother's admonition.

We also learned a healthy suspicion of slick arguments and were taught to trust our gut in values of right and wrong and also to appreciate simple common sense. It made us more argumentative and hard-headed, but much less likely to be bamboozled by selfishness masquerading as intelligent analysis.

After an undistinguished career in a public high school I went off to a state college. I didn't know what universities did other than play football. Of the six brothers and sisters older than me, only one had gone to college for one semester before dropping out to help support the family. I'm not sure I was ever on a university campus until my senior year when I decided college sounded a lot better than working full time. Several high school friends were going so I guess the peer pressure, along with the encouragement of our guidance counselor and my parents telling me I could get a good job if I went to college, sort of allowed the decision to get made. I'm not sure it was a decision that I made.

I entered a good state college as a freshman in the Fall of 1954, as an engineering major, like everyone else. From the time I stepped on that campus I questioned if I belonged, but was determined to stay until they found me out and kicked me out.

The first two and a half years were a struggle. I voluntarily dropped out to go to a dinkier school for the second semester, then I returned to flunk out after my fourth semester. Then I plea bargained with a compassionate Dean for re-admission on condition of changing majors and making a B average. My junior year I learned how to make A's, largely due to the challenge and guidance of a couple of wonderful teachers. In my senior year academic success was easy, and I was adopted by the faculty as their promising undergraduate.

In my mind they didn't know how much I was fooling them. That year I was offered a graduate assistantship to go on for a masters degree Do you mean they will pay me to go to school? Such a deal! I guess I will go on until they "find me out." When they gave me a bachelors degree it lowered my opinion of the institution more than it raised my opinion of myself. The two year master's program was easy and I was a star, but that was easy in a school I had decided was marginal; or maybe I had just fooled them again.

In 1961 we moved to the real State University (S.U.) to try my luck at the Ph.D. program. They were not only going to pay me to go to school but were going to let me teach my own classes! I was going to be a college teacher! It felt so good I went out and bought (charged) a new wardrobe so I could look like a college teacher.

My first year at S.U. was a shock. By chance, probably, the entering class of graduate students was a collection of brilliant, crazy (in the clinical sense), argumentative, mostly political lefties, socialists, communists, activists, etc., whose common denominator was that they read everything they could get their hands on. They were interesting and interested and so intellectually aggressive. For the first time I encountered what was, in my perception, a real academic environment, where ideas were pursued, no holds barred, nothing sacred, nothing out of bounds and where the only penalty for being on the wrong side of an issue was to be forced to reevaluate your position.

We all gathered in "the coffee room" almost continuously, when we were not in class, to argue, debate and intellectually beat on each other. When I arrived in this "pit," I found that I was well trained in neoclassical economic theory but I was ignorant; I had not read any books except textbooks. I had spent six years being trained, but not being educated.

In self-defense, I read everything mentioned in those coffee room brawls; history, psychology, sociology, you name it. I read more books that first year than I had read in my previous twenty-four years. And for the first time I felt that I belonged in academics. I was no longer there because it beat working for a living, though I did like the idea of having a lot of holidays and summers off to have more time for politics and reading.

In those first two years at S.U. I also found out that I was an exceptionally good teacher. The students really responded to me. It was probably because most of them were kids from working class backgrounds, like myself, and I could empathize with their feelings of not knowing why they were there and not giving a shit about anything of a social or political nature. My job was to convince them that it isn't queer to care about ideas and it isn't that hard to learn how to learn.

When I left S.U. in 1963 (with all my courses finished, but without having written my dissertation) with my confidence far exceeding my experience, I took a job as Assistant Professor of Economics at Wisconsin State College. My perception of the academy at that point was the open debate of ideas I had experienced in "the coffee room." Was I shocked! The first week I was on campus in my new job, my chairman took me to the faculty coffee room. By chance we joined the chairman of the Biology Department at a small table. Very quickly the issue was joined when he began his argument that "Negras," as he called them, were biologically inferior. We, or I, got louder and louder as the debate progressed, until the whole faculty present gathered around us like we were two dogs in a pit. By then the other faculty members at the table, including my chairman, had moved to give us room. They had never seen anything like this. It ended when my opponent abruptly left the room refusing to discuss the issue any further; his mind was made up. He was driven from the room, probably more from my volume than by my logic, and I always thought he was a coward for leaving. But in any case, I had quickly established a reputation as one who would challenge, so the "Negras are inferior" fella, and others avoided me when possible. It was not easy after that to have, as they say, intellectual discourse with my colleagues. They were into minimizing their contact with students, colleagues and ideas, while maximizing their salaries and fringes. I gained a reputation as a teacher and my economics colleagues as well as the administration, (and I would like to think, the students) were truly sorry to see me split after the first year.

At Western College (W.C.), the next stop on my sojourn for academic excellence, I was still young, inexperienced and naive, thinking W.C. was an aberration, and not like most universities, where the faculty were scholars, if not philosophers. It took me two months to get into the first of several major battles in the two years I was there.

My Department Chairman, being an economist, was an income maximizer. He always scheduled himself to teach a large lecture section of five hundred students. He then ordered a dozen, or so, desk copies of the textbook for his (non-existent) teaching assistants and then sold the books to his students, one dollar below bookstore price. What bothered me more than the textbook graft, was that he was a horrible teacher who was monopolizing several hundred students. As a young idealistic Assistant Professor, this didn't seem right to me, so I organized my first academic battle.

The lesson I learned from this first battle was the general indifference faculty and administrations have toward right and wrong. They don't want to get involved. But in the end, my dogged and loud threats at exposure and calling in the FBI, IRS, AAUP and a whole can of alphabet soup, along with my getting the book companies to cut him off, finally ended with his resignation.

My second year at W.C., I had my first confrontation with the public at large and learned, for the first time, how university administrations view academic freedom. My colleague (the first real one I had up until that time) and I wrote a letter to the editor of the local newspaper in response to an editorial. It was an innocuous letter, we thought, explaining that the mere existence of a national debt does not necessarily spell doom.

The response to our letter was incredible. We quit clipping the editorial and letters to the editor responses after twenty-one, all hostile, were printed in a period of two weeks, We, and the president of the university, received anonymous letters and phone calls demanding we be fired, if not shot. We were called socialists, faggots, pinkos and one person accused us of being part of the "Hoover, Catholic-Communist-conspiracy."

That same year, 1965, the anti-Viet Nam war movement at W.C. began, and since nothing intellectual was going on except for my classes, I became involved. We had all of ten faculty and students in the movement. When we planned a demonstration for the town square, the city council passed a new law requiring a parade permit, and denied us the permit. We sued for a permit on grounds of free speech. Where the "national debt issue" had created controversy, this issue actually started a town *vs* gown war. We were denounced in every forum in town as unpatriotic communistic perverts. There were not only demands that we be fired, there were threats on our lives. Once again the president of the college gave us his old "don't stick out your neck" routine and shut up, hoping we would go away. Once again, naively thinking the faculty would at least support free speech, we circulated a carefully worded petition supporting same. Out of three hundred faculty members, we got eighteen signatures. It was indeed a fine day for the academy.

I resigned that year to return to S.U. to complete my dissertation. I was fired the day after I had resigned. It didn't make sense to me either, but the Department Head explained that I was "too much of a trouble maker." Perhaps the administration was afraid I might withdraw my resignation so they fired me to make sure.

Probably because of the very tight labor market in economics in 1967, I was offered a position at New England State (N.E.S.). At last I would be finding that intellectual community where ideas mattered and they would be freely pursued under the protection of true academic freedom. I had doubts, but I hoped I could measure up in the big time. After all, I was lucky to get a chance to make it in a growing university bent on becoming first class.

I hit N.E.U. with little timidity, organizing the non-tenured junior faculty to demand a democratic department where people served on personnel committees, budget committees, curriculum committees, etc., without regard to rank or tenure. We won the battle and set the stage for a continuous struggle, bordering on war, within the department for the nine years I was there. The struggle always came down to personnel matters, hiring and firing decisions and the criteria for making those decisions. One group or another tried to "build" a "first rate" faculty by hiring those they wanted and firing those they didn't want. And whether the issue was developing one breed of economics or another, the outcome was a fight over hiring or firing someone.

While at N.E.U., I taught part time at Green College, a small neighboring private school, almost every semester. It was there that I first encountered the children of the upper-class as students. They were the daughters of wealthy industrialists, high-ranking government officials, university presidents. Even the daughter of the President of the United States was there, though fortunately not in my class. These students were different. They came from another world. They were not like the kids from the cities and small towns I had taught elsewhere. The students at Green were all well-dressed and healthy. Their uniformly straight, white, beautiful teeth represented fifty thousand dollars in orthodontists fees for every class of thirty students (four million dollars for the whole student body).

They were bright, well schooled and highly motivated students, but what set them apart, in my mind, was that they knew they belonged at Green. They knew they would go on the the best graduate schools or law schools and would move on to run the large corporations, law firms, banks, universities, governments, etc., or at least they would marry men who would.

In one sense, teaching these students was easy because they needed a teacher less than most, they didn't need to be shown that it was okay to be intellectual. They didn't need to be convinced that it was easy to learn and that ideas were important. They just needed someone to organize their reading and guide them toward important issues.

In another way Green College students were difficult to teach. They had trouble feeling or empathizing with hunger, poverty, unemployment, powerlessness and other things they had not experienced or even witnessed. The system had worked so well for them it was difficult for them really to understand that it doesn't work for a lot of people. I guess I was much more cognizant of class differences than they were. More than once I wondered what I was doing in trying to mind-fuck the kids of the power elite; without much success I might add. On more than one occasion, when I would meet my students later on down the road, I would discover that my student "radical" had become a banker at Chase Manhattan.

I left N.E.U. after nine years, to move on to the Southwest and the University of Ulcer (U.U.). I had to escape the elitist Northeast. Though I had security, friendly colleagues and political allies, they were able to mind-fuck me subconsciously so that I felt I didn't belong. I just was not one of them. I did not have their background and education, and I was not into publishing abstract esoteric, irrelevant economic theory. And I was not willing to teach their students while they hid away at typewriters; that was rational, not subconscious.

The colleagues I left at N.E.U. were the brightest, best educated people I have ever encountered, and I cared a lot about several of them, but others had, from my perspective, some of the most fucked-up values in the world. Whatever strain of economics they represent, left or right, orthodox or whatever, they think they have found truth from their analysis and have a right to profess it to the world. Some are simple hustlers who know rewards and status come from getting things in print. Others actually believe they have successfully constructed a general theory of the universe.

As I reflect back on my twenty or so years as an academic my feelings are very ambivalent. On the one hand I feel very lucky to be where I am, in a relatively easy high paying job that gives me a lot of freedom. On the other hand my egalitarian values leave me with guilt feelings because faculty, like most businessmen and professionals, are paid too much for too little work while most people in the world, through no fault of their own, work hard in shit jobs for low pay.

Some of the faculty I have known were good people and a delight to be around, but a majority were either ignorant or abrasive, egotistical assholes. I feel fortunate to have known those few very special academic people with such intelligence and talent who go on doing battle with a basically unfair system and shit culture. I don't know that I would have found as many of those people had I been shuffled off, at one point or another, into selling insurance, drafting for an oil company, or whatever, outside a university. It is just a shame that most of my colleagues have been dull, boring, hustlers or weird, crazy people who really think they are important.

The literally thousands of students I have known have also been a mixed bag, some bright, some dumb as a bag of cement. Some have had good basic values and others were selfish and obnoxious. I guess most of the students I have either liked or at least understood how society had them fucked up. I have mixed emotions about my classroom experience as a teacher. No amount of positive feedback has been able to lift the apprehension I feel about what I am really accomplishing in the classroom. I have continuously received compliments from students, outstanding student evaluations, several standing ovations for lectures, a distinguished teaching award, and I have seen a number of "my" students go on to the "best" graduate schools. And though it feels good to be appreciated, I still wonder if I am appreciated for the right reasons. Do I really influence their values, their perceptions of themselves and of the world, or am I just another consumption good where they, or their parents, pay for a performance? After twenty years I am still nervous before every class, wondering deep down if I really have anything to say, or am I just bullshitting them.

It is, of course, more comfortable teaching working class people, probably because they can better relate to my values. It is hard to get rich kids from the privileged class to think very long, or very hard, about changing the system to remove their privileges. And I probably feel more sense of belonging with people of my own class background. We understand each other better.

Throughout my career I have done battle with academic authority from Department Heads and Deans to University

Presidents and Trustees. But the problem I have faced is when hierarchical decision making has been broken in favor of faculty or student democratic (more or less) decision making, I have mostly had to face majorities of assholes. It has been my experience, more often than not, that faculty and students tend to be as conservative, authoritarian and arbitrary as any administration.

Universities are unique in that they have faculty who hire and fire each other with only some guidance from above. This has always presented me with a problem because in one sense I think of myself as a worker and where I come from, workers didn't fire workers. But when I see some of the faculty creeps, who pass themselves off as humans, inflicting themselves on students, it is hard for me to deal with keeping them in the classroom. On the other hand, most of the battles I have fought were trying to protect the job of decent, intelligent people who were thought not have the "proper" credentials, like publications in this or that stupid journal.

When I look back over my career and ask myself if I would do it over again, I really don't know. I don't think I made a conscious choice to get into academics; it just sort of happened. And I obviously haven't made the choice to get out, though I have thought about it from time to time. I have fantasized about becoming a craftsman of some sort or running a small business like a motel in some obscure place, but the reality of making a living and maintaining some freedom ends the dream rather quickly. As one of my colleagues says, "in the real world people have to really work!"

I also like that part of the academic environment which allows me to read, discuss, teach, learn, and otherwise be involved with what is going on in the world. As much pretentiousness and sham as there is in academics, I know that I would miss the intellectual stimulation if I were not a part of it. I would miss the students and those few faculty who provide contacts and allies for political activity. If I had to choose between academics and something else in "doing it again," even with perfect hindsight, I have no idea what I would do. Perhaps I would have gone to law school to better equip myself to fight evil; but then I may have ended up as just another ambulance chaser.

CHAPTER 7

Balancing Class Locations

Nowhere in our book is there more persistent demonstration of estrangement and inner conflict than in the following six autobiographies. And, nowhere is the struggle to balance the new and the old more eloquently described. Loyalty to one's "friends and folks" is a noble and admirable trait in our society; but, of course, sometimes the friends can range—when one's lifestyle has ranged widely—from (say) an old buddy at a honk tonk back home to (say) a sophisticated and nationally known psychology professor. Further, one can have learned to love and respect common gritty labor in a part of one's life; then learned to have respect, even love, for the mere words on a clean piece of paper. These are quite common experiences to most of our contributors, and especially they appear to have influenced the strategies of those who wrote the essays here.

In these essays, we don't find "acceptance and attainment" most prominent; nor do we find especially discernible alternative pathways taken. What we do find is one after another of straightforward accounts of the time and effort (and talent and imagination) necessary to remain faithful to remnants of the old life while developing a growing attraction (even loyalty) to the new one.

Earlier, in our own shared voice, we said that at its root the myth of upward mobility was fraudulent because it denied the fact that social class structure generates qualitatively different ways of being human. To be two types of persons in a single life is not the stuff of happily ending tales, and that truth is exceedingly well demonstrated here.

Jane Ellen Wilson

I was born in a hospital, and I grew up on my family's farm three miles east of the Susquehanna River in a fertile valley of central Pennsylvania. My great-grandfather was a druggist in a small town for most of his life, but when his health demanded it he bought this farm and moved his family upriver twenty miles. My grandfather and father were actually born here, as well as my great aunt, great uncle, and uncle. My sister grew up here with me.

My father's family, of their generation in this country, boasts a few ministers, some schoolteachers, and a lawyer ("Uncle George"). They also farmed and worked in factories. When I got my Ph.D., I became the most educated person in the family—a subject much and proudly discussed at the recent family reunions. My mother's family holds farmers, loggers, laborers, and many nameless women.

I grew up close to all four of my grandparents. My father's father farmed all his life, raising bumper crops and building up a Holstein dairy herd. Towards the end of his life he wrote poetry: about the land, the animals, the weather. He showed me plants and trees and taught me some of their names and uses. His wife farmed, cooked, milked cows, and taught me to read at the age of four. I learned to play piano using her old upright and the pump organ in the parlor.

My mother's father was a cheerful man with a strong sense of justice. He smoked Camels, tickled me with his whiskers, and let me play with his wooden leg (I liked to put things in the holes in it.) He left his real leg in the Argonne during the first World War. Even with his wooden one he farmed, worked in the limestone quarry, and, as he got older, began sharpening saws for a living. My grandmother grew up on farms and in logging camps, helping her mother cook for the loggers. In spite of her regular education she was valedictorian of her high school class. She married and quickly had three children, going on to work as a cook, a nurse's aide, and finally an LPN. In her fifties she began to paint, and now paints wonderful pictures of the activities of her early life in the woods and farmland of Pennsylvania.

My father graduated from high school and wanted to go to college, but was prevailed upon by his family to stay and help with the farm. In addition to farming, he was interested in music, and learned to play guitar and call square dances. After he and my mother married they put together a country and western band (she played bass and sang) and played for local festivals, at square dances, and on the local radio station. They still do this, taking off very little time from their work. When his father died, my father went on to become a carpenter and local contractor, farming in the evenings and on weekends, trying to make ends meet. Besides helping with all the farm work, my mother has worked as a cook, housekeeper, and companion to elderly ladies.

The people I come from get up at dawn, work hard all day, go to the Lutheran church on Sunday, abstain from liquor, get married, stay married and have children (there are a few old maids), and live close to their family and close to the earth. We had little cash but lots of food and a beautiful piece of land to live on.

Among these people farms pass to sons, not daughters. Although my parents had no sons—only two daughters—it was expected that we would marry and leave. It was never expected that we would become farmers and stay there. This bothered me; I felt dispossessed by default. My family decided that I had a gift for music, so they brought me up to play into their band. They had me sing as soon as I could talk, and taught me to play guitar as soon as my hands were big enough. They decided I had a gift for schooling, too. I read everything I could find and was "smart." Like every-one else on the farm, I did all I could to help in the fields, at the barn, and in the house: making hay, butchering, doing daily chores, sewing, cooking, gardening. They imagined futures for me: I could be a nurse or a teacher; I could marry a farmer or a factory worker and stay near home; I could marry a rich man (that future came highly recommended and in fact my mother still mentions it); I could go to Nashville and become a country music star. They had no better idea than I did how to reconcile my abilities (which they wanted me to develop) with traditional women's roles (which they wanted me to follow).

By the time I was twelve I had opinions about everything, most of them different from my parents'. Country music: didn't like it; Christianity: thought it was hypocritical; country living: I wanted to go to the city, hear "folk music" (ie. Bob Dylan), and visit Europe; government: I was generally against it; war: didn't like it in general and in particular was concerned about Vietnam (this was 1965). My folks were appalled; a revolutionary ancestor was ok., but a revolutionary teenager was another story. My voracious reading and musical taste had given me ideas. I was stuck with these ideas, however, three miles out of town in a household with strict parents. I was sure the exciting, real world was going on elsewhere and I was missing it. By the time I graduated from high school I had built up a tremendous head of steam and was out to find what I had been missing.

I went to college. Getting married or going to school were the two acceptable ways to leave my family and I bet on education. However, I was still only sixteen, and my parents wanted me to stay close to home; of the nearby colleges I chose the most intellectual and radical and moved to the dorm to enter another world. What I found was more middle and upper class people than I knew existed; and for the first time I met people who didn't know that trees had names.

I expected to find intellectual stimulation and community; fun and companionship; new ideas and political concern; and all the things I had been missing just ten miles away in Rural Delivery Route 2. I also strongly expected academia not to discriminate against women. I knew that if I married someone who worked at Chef Boyardee or AC & F that I'd be expected to conform to traditional women's roles.

I also knew that physically I couldn't work the way that men did; I didn't like baling hay when I had my period, for example. And though I had a lot of endurance for physical work, that didn't seem like strength to me; strength meant picking up a hundred pound sack of grain. (Little did I realize how hard that was for men, too.) But clearly (I thought), being an academic didn't involve physical labor or childbearing, so I trustingly assumed that the academic world did not discriminate against women.

What I found at college was disillusioning; but I had invested heavily in my bet on education, and I lasted two years the first time. I found some intellectual stimulation; and I found lots of people making themselves miserable with their intellect: agonizing over Hegel and Nietzsche and talking in (I thought) circles. I found a great deal of personal freedom: to come and go, talk and dress as I pleased. I found some companionship; my first boyfriend was from upper class suburbia. While I had no expectations about women's roles there, I did believe (for years) that the long-haired pacifist men of the late sixties extended their gentleness and egalitarianism to women as well as to the Vietnamese.

I had a scholarship and I borrowed money; I worked in the library. I found people who shared my taste in music and I played with them and by myself in college coffeehouses. I tried to be a music major, since I was more interested in music than anything, but found that I didn't have enough of the right kind of training—classical—to do much, instrumentally. My music instructors were very authoritarian, I thought, demanding class attendance and sign-in sheets at concerts; although I breezed through music theory, I couldn't bring myself to abide by the letter of their law. Finally the chairman politely told me I wasn't suited to being a music major, and suggested if I couldn't get up in the mornings for his class, I should see a psychiatrist. This was my first major disappointment with academia.

I dropped out and spent the summer on the farm. Eventually I got a job as a waitress at a local Pancake House. In a few months, I had saved money and wanted to go to England, although I couldn't quite figure out how to go about it; in the meantime, two of my former professors convinced me to return to college as an English major, saying that the campus needed "creative people" like me, and that they had designed a new program with more freedom. I believed (I was nineteen) and signed up again only to be told by the dean that I was, as a junior, too old to be part of this new program. I slogged through English courses, writing poems and songs instead of term papers.

Because academic reality seemed reductive, flat, lifeless to me, I kept seeking other realities. I worked occasionally as a musician (coffeehouses) and as a music instructor for children, in summer arts programs and in a hospital. I also worked at a small, local hotel as an all night desk clerk. Although just downtown—seven blocks—this was a world away from the college. I had begun to realize—through my high-class, crazy boyfriend—that most people at the college came from a middle class suburban world, with its own trappings, values, customs—most of which I did not find congenial, even though I was supposed to be aspiring to them (by virtue of betting on education). At the Hotel I dealt with truck drivers and their girlfriends, with women from New York and Philadelphia come to visit their husbands and lovers in the nearby federal penitentiary, with small town dramas and informal prostitution. In a way I felt at home with this—country music on the juke box, drinking, adultery, high drama in a small pond. I did not feel at home with truck driver machismo, but started to learn to deal with it. When I became friends with a driver from Cincinatti, I was shocked to learn that his wife wrote poetry and he thought it was great. Mostly I was shocked by my own arrogance in assuming that this class of people wouldn't know or care about art. After I realized that my own assumptions had been cutting me off from people, I started to feel a little more at home in the world.

I graduated from college and moved to my boyfriend's hometown. He lived in the high class Philidelphia suburbs, and I lived in a house in town, as did some students, and all the black people. For many reasons, I was't very happy there. Thus, having discovered that there wasn't much room for my voice in the working world, and seeing little room for my voice in a suburban lifestyles (sic), I bet again on education. Well, maybe I couldn't get an interesting job because I wasn't educated enough. (The extent to which this was also influenced by my being a woman and by my class background was just beginning to dawn on me.) And maybe, I thought, I just hadn't found the right subject to study in academia.

I had always felt there was something missing in academia's view of the world. In literature, for example, they studied Englishmen writing literature; I knew that people exercised verbal creativity in many more ways than that. My grandfather told stories, my father told stories, every truck driver that walked into the hotel had a story to tell. In music, academics studied classical (mostly European) music; I knew that people exercised musical creativity in more ways than that. My political concerns had led me from the first to an interest in folk music (and vice versa). From somewhere, it occurred to me that people in the academy might actually study these things. Maybe one of my professors told me how I could look that up—maybe it was a librarian that showed me the index where universities were listed according to the majors they offered; I don't remember. But in any case, I started applying to graduate school in folklore; I also applied to my alma mater to study for an M.A. in English. My experience in the working world had upped the ante on my bet on education.

Another reason to keep betting on education was that I had rejected my family's way of life and values. More accurately, I couldn't see any place for myself in it. Laboring from dawn to dark was not my idea of a good time, even if I had been a man. Still, I loved living in the country and growing food. But what farmer wanted a "smart" wife? That was not part of my family's imagined future for me.

My family didn't always see much sense in my ongoing education. When my friends from suburbia wanted to drop out of school and become carpenters, farmers, musicians, their families were horrified. The family of one woman I knew threatened to have her committed to an asylum when she persisted in her desire to do physical labor and live in the country. My family, on the other hand, often said they thought I should go to Nashville and become a country music star. While they saw some sense in going to college for four years, they hoped I would become a teacher at the end of that (one of their few models of educated people, I guess).

When I found only menial jobs and then went back to school, they were mystified. To their credit, they were fairly supportive. But, even when I was an undergraduate, they had little money to spare for education, and when I persisted in this system, they told me I was on my own.

Two schools accepted me as a graduate student in folklore; neither could offer any financial assistance. My alma mater offered me a scholarship to get an M.A. in English. It seemed easy to do. I had also figured out a way to deal with their system, I thought, and I was already living in that town. So I deferred folklore for a year and went back to my first school.

Taking four courses a semester didn't daunt me; in fact, I was quite nonchalant about the experience at the time. Nights, I worked at the hotel again, taught some music, and lived cheap (the garden vegetables helped). In twelve months I had an M.A., and it was on to grad schooling folklore in the big city...and, at a famous Ivy League school.

Again with some nonchalance, I borrowed money to finance the first year. I was very excited about having found a field that, I thought, expressed my innermost concerns and would provide me with the socially, intellectually acceptable means to bring forth those concerns into the world. The second year, I got a scholarship which paid my tuition; I still had to meet my living expenses. By this time I felt comfortable enough in the city to begin playing music for money. I did this with the new man I had taken up with, a good talker and interesting character, a high school dropout from the Jewish suburban middle class. The rigors of being straight academically were compensated for by the field-work I was doing as part of that—I had begun to interview people in my home County about folk medicine.

Active as I was as a graduate student, the methods of academia still seemed alien to me. Although I conceived of my discipline as subversive within the larger intellectual reality of our culture (as did a number of my colleagues, explicitly), on a day-to-day basis, we felt as oppressed by our own discipline as by those disciplines we had come from. The hierarchies and game playing which seemed essential for survival in the system were offensive to me. It also made me sad to see my fellow students so cowed by authority.

I was disillusioned when my discipline (committed at least intellectually to the views of the "folk," the peasants, the poor, the disenfranchised) had to debate whether or not to become involved in political issues. Many folklorists said that an academic group should not have political views. It seemed so obvious to me that we were living in the same world as Phyllis Schafly, Gloria Steinham and millions of women and should recognize the fact (that mysterious, physical, universal world which we were all part of— although my faith in this had become hazy). *The Journal of American Folklore* published a scholarly article on the involvement of folklorists in the Third Reich. A number of women and myself planned a conference on Women and Folklore and boycotted the larger meetings in Utah, which had not ratified the ERA.

During these years I was also playing music three or four nights a week in city and suburban bars. Being in the city was stimulating musically as well as intellectually. I felt that I had finally learned to use my mind, to stretch my abilities. I felt I had finally met large numbers of people who were just as smart and smarter than me, just as talented and more talented musically than me, as crazy, radical, poetic, visionary, anything! In the city I was no longer the eccentric I was at my rural High School. I had finally been to the place where everything was happening and had measured myself against it, had jumped in with both feet and found the water fine. I got comfortable with my abilities and felt less disenfranchised than I ever had. However, at the same time, living in the city and being a graduate student was strenuous and downright dangerous.

The whole process of becoming highly educated was for me a process of losing faith. I was taught not to trust my perceptions, but to refer to the bibliography and the traditions of my field; my original reasons for taking up folklore had been translated into the particulars of twenty courses and many conferences, parties, guest speakers, administrative wranglings, by the interdepartmental feuds and machinations, by papers and newsletters and meetings, by the anger I felt at my discipline's shortcomings and its treatment of women, by the cultivating of professors, by the hairsplitting which is essential in European intellectual culture.

As I did my studies, I also began working by myself in the city. It was an educational and terrifying experience. Fortunately for my financial situation, I was hired to play three nights a week in a little bar/restaurant near the waterfront, near a newly hip section of the city. What I liked most about the place was its mixed clientele: longshoremen, businessmen, beautiful people on dates from center city, gay men and women, artists and craftspeople of every ilk, Catholic Italians from south Philly, and occasionally some of my fellow graduate students. Because I played mostly for tips, I had to learn to communicate musically and verbally with all these people. I enjoyed that challenge and its contrast to the academic world across the river. Crazy as the Left Bank was, I felt at home with the folks there and gained a lot more poise. I also learned how to deal with obnoxious drunks of all ages and classes; and noticed that the whole scene got crazier when the moon was full.

The main drawback to working at the Left Bank and elsewhere as a musician was that I was no longer under a man's protection. Aside from the expected barroom hassles, I often went home alone, and had to park far from my house and walk there—four, five blocks, in the middle of the night. In order to survive, I had to think defensively. That sounds sensible enough, but what that meant was walking home from work every night considering how I might or might not be jumped, robbed or raped. That made me very angry.

Finally, after a few minor street incidents, I tangled with serious crime. I found that my house had been broken into, robbed, and set on fire. I lost cash, instruments, all my cloths, personal belongings, stereo, everything valuable. Most of my papers and all my notes for my dissertation were o.k. The police thought it was the work of a psychopath, but had no clues. My friends and neighbors were freaked out, and so was I. I pulled myself together enough to finish writing a paper and delivered it at the folklore society meetings that month, and then I left the city and my close association with the academic world.

What living in the city and living in the academy have in common, for me, are two things: both took me closer to the realities of mainstream American culture than I had ever been (you know what I mean: official culture, high culture, the majority consensus of reality; the trappings of the American dream, or depending on your point of view, the "heart of the dragon."); and both were the opposite of what I grew up with, the farthest poles, that I had to explore in seeking what was missing from what I knew. Well, what I discovered (as many people before me) was that what I was searching for didn't exist "out there." Only by coming to terms with my own past, my own background, and seeing that in context of the world at large, have I begun to find my true voice and to understand that, since it is my own voice, that no pre-cut niche exists for it; that part of the work to be done is making a place, with others, where my and our voices can stand clear of the background noise and voice our concerns as part of a larger song.

As I have come to realize this, to come full circle to where I started, I have found more and more people who share some part of my vision. This makes me very hopeful and also makes confronting the realities of America somewhat less grim. I have also come to believe that most people feel like strangers in the world.

Specifically, my sense of community comes from both inside and outside the academy. Recently I have found a number of people my age who now have Ph.D.s and are functioning inside universities—often we share some past in the 1960s, some transformation of those concerns and times; and recently I have come to realize that many folklorists come from working class backgrounds. Last year at our annual meetings (which have the character of a festival, family reunion, academic racetrack, business luncheon, and singles bar) I had several conversations with people about coming from "the folk" and how strange academia was, how strange the assumptions of the middle class, and how strange our families found our bet on education (though not necessarily in principle: a number of our families espoused onward and upward). What they found strange was either that we were women doing it, or that the realities of it—years of study, poverty, academic power trips—did not match their image of the dream. One of my fellow graduate students, from a working class English background, had difficulty explaining the ins and outs of academic life to his family until he compared interdepartmental politics to the cutthroat business practices with which his family was familiar. And then they were appalled to realize how similar academics were to the rest of the people.

A more positive connection for me, comes from the subject of my field, and my own interests into that field. It's no accident that I've studied the people that I came from. It's their reality I'm trying to describe, to affirm, to give voice to. Doing this gives me great satisfaction, because I can put my intellect (whose restlessness forced me to leave what I knew) and my academic experience (for better or for worse, it's part of me now) to use for the people and the place where my heart lies.

When writing my dissertation I lived on my family's farm. Instead of paying rent, I worked in the fields and garden. What I resented as a child, I then enjoyed as a choice that I made; I came to see the positive values in my family's way of life as well as all the negative ones which I had rebelled against. I came to see that those values have been part of me even while I thought I was doing something very different. My folks, too, while they couldn't understand the purpose of my education while I was going through it, enjoyed reading my dissertation (which is about a kind of folk medicine they both know and it's written in a style meant to be useful to both academics and the people whom it's about).

I feel the same way about academia; it's like an eccentric member of my family whose company I enjoy at annual reunions and family dinners. My intellect, as well as my background, is a part of me that I can't deny. I would rather give a lecture on mythology for an honorarium than work as a waitress for the same amount of money. (I would also rather play music in smokey bars than work as a factory supervisor for the same amount of money.) I'd rather spend the day writing than driving a tractor, five days a week. I would rather do any of the above than be wife to someone whose support bought my subservience.

What I value and begin to find, even in the academy, is: cooperation, a sense of community, a concern for the disenfranchised, an attempt to lead a balanced life. My first job teaching was at a community college where most of the

students majored in forestry, nursery management, horti-
culture, welding, wood products technology, graphic arts,
nursing, etc. I taught freshman composition; a required
course, though there were no English majors there. I liked
this job because these people were "down to earth." That's
how I find myself putting it. What I mean is they came from
the same class background as I did. This made me comfortable. I tell myself that I enjoyed these people more than
students with pretensions about themselves and their backgrounds, and with illusions about the class value of education. I felt silly, sometimes, teaching them English grammar (I call myself the grammar police) and, I felt ambivalent about the fact that it might have enabled them to get on
in the system that values education; but I liked to talk to
them about writing, about communication, about ideas,
about how to write resumes and letters to the editor.

I found it significant that some of my former professors
considered this a low class job. But it's all the same to me
whether I correct grammar or whether I try to impose some
standard of writing style. While I might rather have been
talking about some fine points of folklore, still, it was a job;
and one way or another, my working class background
makes me want to keep working in my second job. It makes
me want to survive in this cash economy, and to work to
bring forth in the world a voice that speaks for my vision
and for the vision of the people and place that I come from.
Those people and that place gave me life, beauty, dreams,
and purpose, and to speak for them is the least I can do.

Thomas Hall

...I was getting excited about the academic world for it was there, in the pristine ivory towers of thought and the muddy streets of debate that these issues in their full ramifications could be dealt with, or at least engaged. It turned out to be something cheaper, shoddier, and more corrupt than I could have ever imagined.

All along it seems as if I have been pulling, hauling, shoving, fighting — screaming, at times — to enter an alien world that ultimately cannot exist for me; that has been my experience in brief, an experience frought with the feelings of privilege, of guilt, of values in conflict, of alienation, of soaring freedom and shattered dreams. I quite frankly have no clear conception concerning the birth of those feelings, and I will simply try to tell you what I think now.

I am about one-quarter "dad" and three-quarters "mom," with a large stochastic element, none of which I can explain. That ratio begins to take shape in the early years when my father wasn't around: he was steering a cargo ship for the U.S. Navy, carting beer across the ocean to satisfy the cravings of thirsty servicemen at Southern Pacific outposts of war. When he returned I went through much the same experience that Flannery O'Conner, I think it was, writes about in "My Oedipus Complex." That fucker came home and took my mommy. As a result, I guess, he and I didn't have much to do with each other. Nonetheless, I am left with traces of him which now and then surface, sometimes to my chagrin and other times to my salvation.

For most of his life my father was an awning salesman and an ailing man caught in an age of economic transformation which rendered his work an anachronism. He worked long and hard hours to please others — a wife, a boss, a customer, a fellow worker and friends — and didn't have much left over in the way of love for his family. While he attempted to please others he exerted his own influence and authority within the confines of our household; he was a sycophant and expected the same from me. In many ways I still feel the way to "get ahead" is to follow his lead, and I often think about how my "superiors" evaluate my professional performance.

But that is the substance of small dreams and his were certainly limited. He lusted for nothing more than what could realistically be attained by someone else telling him his job was well done. He wanted nothing more than a desk, a damn desk from which to conduct his work and worldly affairs. He made it too, and he died.

All the while he practiced values that would be important in the world of business affairs. He was practical wherein his practicality took the form of noting that the shortest distance between two points was a straight line. He believed and taught a strict division of labor within the household. His recreation was fishing and hunting, not for pleasure but for the bag; it was edible. He was a straight shooter, though. He could put a .22 shell up the ass of a fleeing rabbit at a hundred yards, and he never told a lie. His morality was honesty, an honesty which became a powerful obstacle in his path of accomplishment. His conflicts left him emasculated and silently cold to the ones that somewhere, somehow he just didn't know how to love.

I spent a number of years trying to build a father image of which I could be proud; the university is where I found it. I entered the university to study civil engineering because it was practical, and my father in his authoritarian way had made it clear that such pursuits were what he preferred. I listened even though he didn't finance a penny of the pursuit, believing I would appreciate my education more if I paid for it. Truth is he was a cheap bastard. I enjoyed the freedom and soon met a professor, a man with a powerful voice and commanding presence who was instrumental in altering my allegiance to practicality. When that man told ME, in a class of hundreds, that supply and demand worked just like two edges of a pair of scissors to determine price, I discovered magic and became enamored with the man who had introduced me to it. He worried, professionally, about one thing: that workers got screwed. And he was damn well big enough and bright enough to enforce his view, or so I dreamed. There it was, and I was caught. I followed him around like a puppy taking each of his words, each of his thoughts, each of his actions as the correct and important way of thinking and acting about the world. It wasn't long until I wanted nothing more than to be just like him and began preparing myself for entering the academic world. It was an exciting time.

I think I know why it was an exciting time. It was more than just finding or constructing a father image. I felt something magical about studying the worker-employer relationship; it was mystical, somehow holy and transcendental. There was much more I wanted to know about; there was something in the mysteries of that relationship which kept me inspired. My father, the impeccably honest one, had been fired once upon a time when an employer found some inventory missing and the books awry. That firing was arbitrary and ruthless, probably, in the end, designed to cover his own ass. While that experience was not really part of me, not part of my psyche, it did affect me. I remember distinctly going out of my way on the journey home from school to destroy that former employer's flowers, throw rocks at his windows and tantalize his dog. Maybe that's the genesis, maybe not. Maybe it's that experience coupled with a set of fundamental Christian values which were impressed upon me by my mother. Most likely it was a combination of the two with strong random influences.

My mother was a deeply religious woman who did not seem, somehow, to understand the implications of Christian thought and values. The depth of her understanding extended only to the requisites of martyrdom and the utility of guilt. Though it was not her intention, she put me in touch with abstract thought, with the possibility of being concerned with something outside self. I was taught, indoctrinated perhaps, that there is a distinction, useful and necessary, between God and devil, love and hate, peace and war, and justice and equity. But the area of organized religion was at one and the same time restrictive and incomplete in its ability to face the implications of those issues. I was getting excited about the academic world for it was there, in the pristine ivory towers of thought and the muddy streets of debate, that these issues in their full ramifications could be dealt with, or at least engaged. It turned out to be nothing like that at all; it turned out to be something cheaper, shoddier, and more corrupt than I could have ever imagined.

My naivete sometimes overwhelms me. But I was quite slow getting started, having read my first book of any substance during that first year in the university. I was just beginning, still had the fervor of a potential preacher, and firmly held the view that rational discourse could lead to tipping the scales of justice in favor of those "less fortunate" than myself. I felt somehow ordained to take the message to the people, to tell them that there was a world that can be better, that harmony and fairness in all human relations is possible and desirable. There was nothing practical about that; I was struggling with a world of thought that was alien to me as real poverty, and as real work.

The civil rights movement convinced me that the level of injustice and inequality was broader and deeper than I, untutored and parochial, could have ever conceived. But it sprawled out before me in ugly confrontations between white masters, their dogs and enforcement officials, and unfortunate blacks who never had a chance. My interest and enthusiasm shifted direction, but the rudiments remained. I went to study under another man who specialized in the study of discrimination and had earned a reputation as one of the leading advocates of equal employment opportunity. I quickly replaced my first father figure while my fervor remained real and vibrant. I came to believe more deeply that justice would triumph, that good would overcome. I believed that it would come about through study, research, effort, influence and the application of a set of public policies.

I dreamed grand dreams. While most of my colleagues were interested in learning the few technical principles necessary to keep the great economic machine roaring I worried about poverty and discrimination, education and jobs, with a goal, however dim, of creating the Great Society. A nasty little war drained our common sense. Along came Nixon and dismantled the Great Society just as it began. The decade of the seventies ended like it began, a time of disillusionment, of faded hopes and tarnished dreams. Those events affected me profoundly and somewhere in the decade I escaped.

I chose my escape carefully, finding a semi-academic post which allowed me to travel the world at the expense of Uncle Sam. In the post I came face to face with the horrible reality of working for someone, someone whose judgement and whim could mean my success or failure, my livelihood. I found within this quasi-academy the necessity for a practical outlook, an outlook I had avoided or at least not come in touch with for a number of years. Survival and opportunity rested upon the successful performance of tasks defined, dictated, and designed by others. I found the need for specialization and well-honed technical skills. I found the benefits of respecting and believing in the righteousness of authority. It was a shock, a shock from which I have not fully recovered.

There were, simply, things and tasks which I had to accomplish to be readmitted to the academy. Teaching would not suffice, neither would preaching. The work had to be acceptable through review to a broad spectrum of the profession; it had to be published. The work had to consider common themes and use common techniques; the privileges of teaching rested on successful performance in other arenas. I did the job laid out for me reasonably well. I jumped through all the right hoops and learned who to suck, when to suck, and how to suck. I reentered the practical world I had long left. I did what was expected of me. In one way that exercise served me well. I moved back to a university, quickly received tenure, and served as an administrator at the department level.

I staked out an administrative position in academia for the express purpose of training for the post of university president. Two things came together to define that quest: the first is that lingering respect for authority and the attendant respect I could expect to receive. Second, as I saw it, was an opportunity to set the academic tone for first a small group and then an entire institution.

Can you begin to imagine my naivete? The respect and admiration I sought derives from a deep-seated insecurity that somehow I'm not good enough. The desire to lead has always had that connotation for me, and I have never, simply, felt adequate. Almost immediately upon accepting the administrative duties my views began to take another distinct turn, swinging back to an interest in abstract thought, to a consideration of those issues which are bigger than myself and in no way immediately applicable to the problems of the world. But the process was a torturous one.

I entered the world of administration with the objectives laid out for me by colleagues who defined necessary duties prior to my arrival. As a result I was instrumental in securing the dismissal of one colleague and levying salary penalties on others who were not in favor. One of the most profound experiences of my life was watching two colleagues come to my office and cry about the manner with which I treated them. I was sick, sick physically from the power of the revelation that I could be instrumental in doing that dirty work, in changing the course of an individual's life, in separating an individual from his employment. God, I was sick. But I did what I was asked to do. I had had no previous idea or notion of what would be required, and my initial reaction was one of acceptance rather than abhorrence.

It is at this point, a trusted and dear colleague had a big influence on the way I now think about things. He made me come in touch with a set of values I had conveniently set aside in my quest to satisfy that other side of myself, that side which needs acceptance and strokes. As I engaged in that transformation another arbitrary and ruthless act penetrated my world—the denial of the department's request for that colleague's tenure. I was completely shocked and angry, angrier than I have ever been. It brought back visions of my boyhood, visions of going out of my way to hurt someone. The bastards hurt me. They hurt my sensibilities, they shattered my dream and made me know once again and for evermore that we are but workers in a factory where the strings are pulled by the bosses. And my reaction, though stoked by bile and guided by political cunning, was no more effective than tantalizing the master's dog. With that bitterness I ran away—once again.

I am writing this now at the end of a year of reflection, a year devoted to the search for what I think is important, and how I might relate to whatever it is. But reflection, the

realms of abstract thought, of reading, thinking and writing
are still alien to me. The joys of traveling in that realm are
very personal, very intimately private, and free. The only
freedom I do not now and never will have is to fuck off, to
play. Even with that, academic life is a luxury, a luxury for
which I get paid damn well. The price I pay for it is guilt, a
profound and lingering guilt.

To assuage that guilt, while not doing permanent dam-
age to my practical training and nature, I must attempt to
contribute to making this world a better place, a little less
evil, a little less authoritarian, a little less unjust. But my
ability, power and influence to accomplish those objectives
are miniscule. In my case, insecurity and guilt drove me to
accept a second-class education and spend my life working
in a second rate institution on social problems over which I
have absolutely no influence. But it is only in such institutions as this that the working class perspective is alive at
all. We are, to be sure, the elite of the working class but
working class nonetheless.

The nagging dilemma is that to pursue one side of my
nature, very practical, upward mobility toward a position of
power, prestige and influence with higher income is to deny
the other, the side where opportunity is the pursuit of an
abstract personal freedom of thought and action. On either
hand, whichever impulse is extant, I do build grand dreams
while other powerful personal influences are truncated. It is
that kind of conflict that I carry to the classroom; I tend to
fight my personal battles in front of the collective, captured
audience of students in hope of igniting within them a conflict of similar proportions and encouraging them to wrestle
with the result. But teaching and preaching is an alienating
exercise. Those students come and go, and I cannot know
what they learn, what they will do, or where they will go.

At one and the same time this experience has been
mundane and metaphysical, banal and rich, frustrating
and exhilarating, crude and holy. I hate it, and I love it.

Alice Trent

> There's always another rung on the (academic) ladder. In some ways I know that's wonderful—the job always changes. You keep the mind alive. But other ways it looks like a never-ending treadmill. I sit and have tea with art historian friends who discuss seeing Nureyev that night. They look at me funny when I talk of my find of the day, a T-shirt that says "Fuck Art, Let's Dance."

Immediately before writing this biographical essay, I was informed that my writing would be most welcome because women working-class academics were as scarce as the proverbial "hen's teeth." Although I certainly was never aware of statistics, I have long carried this fact around with me as part of my psychological baggage. Not only am I an academic, but I am an art historian. While most intellectual disciplines are strange territory to the working class, for many reasons art history is predominantly an area nurtured by the leisure classes. In a word, I have lived daily with the knowledge that I am "different." For some time, I felt that this different-ness was created by my career and situation. In part, I believe this notion was developed because of my adjustment to an Ivy League School. After being away from that school for a year now and after teaching for the first time, I have been able to see that this differentness had been there from an early age and is reinforced by my being a female working-class art historian. In effect, I believe that the importance of my status upon my life is neither economical nor sociological, but psychological.

My father's parents came from Italy. His father died of Black Lung contracted in a Southwestern Pennsylvanian coal mine. This happened when my grandmother was pregnant with my father. During the Depression, my grandmother would walk five miles a day to do a load of laundry for 25 cents. My father quit school in the 8th grade and worked on a farm. He was drafted into the Army; he was

called to Pittsburgh for a physical and was taken immediately—didn't even get a chance to say goodbye to his
mother. When he came back, he worked in a steel mill, then
in a bar called the Pig-Whistle, then on a garbage truck, then
in a food market.

I'm not sure what he did when he married my mother.
My mother's parents came from Poland. Her mother left
Pennsylvania to work as a domestic in Brooklyn when her
father couldn't work during the Depression. After graduating from High School, my mother and her sister also went to
Brooklyn to work as domestics. With the money my mother
saved, she went to nurse's training in Altoona. She quit
working as a nurse when she married my father, but went
back part-time when I went to grade-school. I've never identified strongly with the Women's Movement, but I think this
is largely because I perceive it as dominated by an upper-
class female mind-set. In my life, there has never been a
question as to whether I had a *choice* in working. In my
background, women work—it's as simple as that. When my
female colleagues at the university discuss "women's issues," I do not feel comfortable. In many ways, I cannot
relate to their personal experience.

Of course, while working-class women are more likely to
have jobs, the type of job they will have is usually restricted.
Certainly a move to academia is out of the ordinary. My
course of development owes much to my parents, and particularly to my mother. While my mother has a career, she
identifies strongly with her maternal role. Before I was
born, she carried a boy full-term and he was born dead.
When she became pregnant with me, the doctor recommended a therapeutic abortion because of her health. Need-
less to say, when I was born, I became the object of intense
love and mothering. I was to receive everything she was
denied. Never was anything held as impossible because I
was a girl.

When I was five, I was registered for kindergarten. I
looked forward to this "room with all the toys" quite eagerly.
For some reason, my mother decided to take me to have an
IQ test at a nearby teacher's college. We didn't have a car,
and I remember what seemed like a long bus ride and carrying out all these "games." The result was that my mother

was told that I was smart enough to begin first-grade. I still remember sitting at the kitchen table and crying at the thought of not going to kindergarten. Right then, I knew I was "different."

In first grade, although younger, I was taller. I always had discipline problems with teachers, I could never understand the need to raise my hand. Most of the time, I was being punished for something that wasn't really "bad," but for some creative project I wanted to carry out. In the 4th and 5th grades, I suffered seriously from constant abuse from teachers. My parents considered sending me to a private school. But because there were none in the area in which I lived and because I would have to live away from home, I wasn't sent.

The way in which my mind operated also seemed to separate me from my peers. I remember vividly being teased in the first-grade for coloring the dittoed uniform pumpkins with tinges of brown, for "who'd ever seen a perfect pumpkin." My height meant that I was nicknamed "Gorilla." In second grade, I was the first one to get glasses. At the same time, while other girls were going to be teachers and nurses, I was going to MIT to be an astronomer. My family moved to an apartment downtown—not near other children, but near the library. So, it was books that became my friends.

In junior high, I became even weirder. I fell in love with the Beatles—grew my hair long, wore madras smock dresses, and textured tights. I was singularly ugly and attracted much active taunting from those my age — male *and* female. The teachers, who came from the same stock, resented me as well. The only way I "survived" was through a friend, who happened to be weird too; and through my creative efforts, such as writing for the school paper.

The most important thing to me was to get out of that small town. So even though I come from a working-class background, in reality I have never really identified with the working class. In fact, I have felt detached from it and oppressed by it. When some of my colleagues rhapsodize about the glories of the working class, I feel just as uncomfortable as I do when my female colleagues talk about the Women's movement. The most important thing about my being working-class is that I identified with no group—I don't subscribe to any "organized religion."

My interest in the Beatles opened me to many new worlds. Here were "four working-class lads" who had "conquered the world." When one of them said he read *Lady Chatterly's Lover*, I read it. When one of them said he was interested in art, I looked at art. My goal in life became to go to London. Yet, there were other forces that had long before been exerted upon me. From the first grade, I was "college material," and so upon graduation I enrolled in a college in Pittsburgh. It was small Catholic college where all the girls wore circle pins and their hair in flips. It was 1967 and I wore granny dresses and paisley dresses.

At that point, I made one effort at rebelling against the inevitable. Although I was one of the selected honors freshmen, my grades were inconsistent. I had a "C" average. To the consternation of my parents, I quit school, went to London but couldn't cope, and left after a week. I lived in a slum for a year and worked at various jobs for a Pittsburgh department store. Some of them I failed at miserably and I never identified with my workmates. So the next fall, I registered at the University of Pittsburgh.

At Pitt, I discovered Art History. While other courses were work, art history was pure joy. It allowed free reign of a study of various disciplines. As an excellent student, I became a favorite among the professors. I had never planned to go to graduate school. When finished at Pitt, I planned to go to London and work at a gallery. But I began to think it might be easier to get a foot in the door by going to graduate school there. My professors were horrified at my only applying to one graduate school and strongly encouraged me to apply to other schools. There were a few things about Ivy U. that looked interesting, so I applied there. To make a long story short, I was rejected by the school in England and was accepted at Ivy U. with a fellowship. When you're a working-class kid from a small town in Pennsylvania, you don't say no to a fellowship at a "big time" university.

Going there has probably made the biggest change in my life. I certainly don't regret it for an instant. Yet because of the way the whole thing happened, it has made me feel that there has been very little choice in my life. People look at me and say how much I've "accomplished," but I feel that

I've been shackled by my working-class origins—that I *couldn't* say no to fellowships. Quite frankly, I don't feel very comfortable around academics—I find most of them boring. At the moment, I work in an Art department and feel I get along best with the artists. I constantly think I should have gone into fashion design.

Upon entering Ivy U., I think I first became conscious of being working-class. Most of the other undergraduates had gone to prestige schools such as Harvard or Smith. Similarly, most of them had been able to travel abroad to see the works of art we were studying. So, I felt out of place at lunch time discussions about mutual friends on the crew team, the little restaurant across from the Uffizi, and the like. So, it became easy to attribute my graduate school difficulties to my working class origins.

And there were difficulties. The sort of education I had received at Pitt wasn't inferior, but it was of a different sort. I found myself floundering about for the first two years, and I found it particularly difficult to take since for most of my education I never had any sense of competition. The effect was pretty devastating to my self-confidence. I think I've finally been able to deal with this — both intellectually and personally.

I think that this sense of inferiority made me go through a period of watching my "P's" and "Q's." I didn't want to do anything amiss. Now, I'm finally feeling a sense of liberation, and perhaps am even going to other extremes — deliberately provoking the sensibilities of others.

In the final year of my graduate course work, I found my stride. I took my oral exams and then went off to England to do research for my dissertation. I stretched it out for as long as possible, three years. Because England is so class-conscious, the sense of myself as being working class deepened. At the same time, I saw how much education permitted me to move in prestigious circles: visiting Lord and Lady So and So. In fact, at this time, I began to see how I actually had an advantage over many others in being able to move among different peoples with ease: I was just as comfortable talking to an old "ba-ba" from Polish Hills as to a former English ambassador to the United States. In essence, I felt a tremendous sense of liberation and power from my "differences" by that time.

Upon returning to the States, I finished my dissertation and received my Ph.D. During that period, I felt a tremendous sense of pride in what I had accomplished for both myself and my family. I was selected by my department to give a talk at the Frick Museum in New York at an annual symposium. This particular honor was made even more succulent in my mind, because of the irony of a coal miner's grand-daughter speaking in a museum established by the Grand Prick Frick, the most bad-ass robber baron of them all.

I think that lecture was the height of my working-class pride, consciousness, whatever. I think, in fact, it was the last gasp. For now I have been an assistant professor for two years, and I can no longer even make a claim to be working-class—neither socially nor intellectually. One of my biggest problems of these last years has been searching for a way to relate to my parents, the very people who have helped to make the whole thing possible. Once again, it is this differentness that I feel.

I teach at a so-called liberal arts college in Pennsylvania. I tell people I worked like hell to get out of a small town in Pennsylvania. The students came from very different socio-economic backgrounds. The student body is very homogenous: upper-middle class suburban kids from about a four-state region. But in a very short time, I saw that it was precisely because I came from a different background that it was *important* that I be there. Possibly I could open them to a wider range of thinking.

At the same time, I've learned about myself from my students. In becoming good friends with them, I've found that we have things in common that I once would have attributed to my being working class. In fact, this essay was far more difficult to write than it would have been just a year ago. In many ways, I feel I'm leaving the past behind.

Now that I am a professor, I find that my "different-ness" works well. At a university, professors can be individuals — do not necessarily have to worry about getting on with colleagues. In fact eccentricity is woven into the mystique of the profession. My "different-ness" works well as a role model for people who are beginning to move out of the comfortable and familiar. My being a women in an area not dominated by women also works well. Yet, I still have doubts about whether I will remain in the profession, even though I know I am good at it. This has to do with my feeling like I didn't have much choice in the matter. And it also has to do with the fact that I do have to depend so strongly on students for a sense of reinforcement. I worry about the personal consequences. Ironically, after years of "differences," such strong acceptance is difficult to put in the right perspectives. It leaves me open and vulnerable. My emotional life suffers the most as a professor.

Perhaps this is the crucial element in being a female working-class academic. The male working-class academics I have met are usually extremely driven. They have to "prove something" by succeeding in their careers. Often this makes them rather single-minded. As a woman, I don't feel a career — whatever it is — is enough. I seek emotional fulfillment as well. My "differentness" has meant that I've gone through my teen years alone, and graduate training, as for many women, made me undesirable to many men. After years of self, I now seek an other and wonder whether such will ever be possible in my life as an academic.

Would I do it again or will I continue to do it? Now that I have a Ph.D., now that I have shown that I can teach, I feel that I can do anything I want. But I realize at the age of thirty-one there are limits as to what I can do. At the moment, I'm in London to do the research to write the article from my dissertation, so that I can take the next step on the academic ladder. There's always another rung on the ladder. In some ways I know that's wonderful — the job always changes. You keep the mind alive. But other ways it looks like a never-ending treadmill. I sit and have tea with art historian friends who discuss seeing Nureyev that night. They look at me funny when I talk of my find of the day, a T-shirt that says "Fuck Art. Let's Dance." I go to the pub where other academics talk of the dialectical and cynical qualities of Blake. I want to yell "Bull Shit!" at the top of my lungs. I want to go to the Roundhouse and see the latest new wave groups, but dread standing around with no one to talk to. Academia has been a way out of my small town in the river valley of Pennsylvania, but what will be my way out of Academia?

Tom Jones

> I'm very happy doing what I do. It sure beats sel-
> ling cattle at the stockyards. If I ever stop enjoying
> it, loving it even, I'll get out.

In the eyes of my father, I'm pretty sure I'm a failure. That's a little hard to take, but it helps that my mother respects what I do Respects it, though she doesn't really have much understanding of what is involved in being a history professor.

Mom was valedictorian of her high school graduating class in 1932, and wanted to go to college, but it was just not an option for a poor girl in rural Arkansas during the Depression. Instead she married my father the night after she graduated, had three children within the next seven years, and worked at odd jobs. Interestingly, her intellectual abilities were so easily recognized by that whole little town that one of those odd jobs was substitute school teacher. Pretty amazing, with no college. But it also helps to show why she, unlike my father, is proud of my academic accomplishments. Vicariously, I think she's really gotten off on the fact her son became the first in the family, on either side, ever to even get a college degree, much less get a Ph.D. and become a professor. (Why else would letters from her to us be addressed to "Dr. and Mrs."?)

But why Dad's attitude? I'm not sure I know. Maybe I'm even wrong. All I know is that he seems almost proud of the fact that he only went through eighth grade. When I began to respond positively to school, when I began to want to practice on my cornet or read (or write) science fiction after school—in short, when I did anything that departed from the pattern he had set, and my older brother had followed, of working out-of-doors, mostly with cattle—my father clearly disapproved. And, finally, when I persisted in following my own path, always with considerable support from Mom, I pretty much lost touch with Dad, and I have not really communicated very well with him about anything of importance since. (Not that I really ever had, of course, but I think clearly the potential was there, if I had just gone in the "right" direction. Certainly my brother—who has been at various times a farmer/rancher, truck driver, feed salesman, etc.—seems to have kept considerably better communication with Dad than I have.)

Dad had a job for $1.25 a day as clerk at a country store during the Depression. Like John Prine sings about his grandfather who "voted for Eisenhower 'cause Lincoln won the war," Dad always voted Democrat "because FDR saved the country." (Well, with one exception, and that perhaps significantly, was in 1964 when I foolishly tried to convince him how dangerous Goldwater was, and he voted for Goldwater.) His next job was as a cattle salesman for a commission company at the stockyard. And that's the one he kept until his stroke a few years ago made him unable to work anymore.

I was a 19-year-old virgin the first time I got married. She was seventeen, and, of course, I thought she was one too. Several years later, even though my values had changed considerably, when I found out she had not been, it almost broke my heart. As you will see, I recall this event with a purpose.

What does that have to do with being an academic of working class background? Well, you see, "working class" for me—and it's important to note, I think, that none of us would ever have thought of calling ourselves that—had to do with a lot more than just what kind of job your father had. It means a whole complex of values, including virginity at marriage and, of course, implicitly, marriage itself. It also meant: sex was purely for the purpose of having babies, and you had to feel guilty about it even then; divorce was out of the question; country-music; a form of religious fundamentalism (combined Methodist/Baptist—the men of the family became the former, the women the latter) that saw "sin" in smoking, drinking, dancing, sex, and boating on Sunday;

not playing a neighboring school in football because they had a "nigger" on their team; neighborhoods where cars were always propped up being worked on; and, of course, that the only jobs for real men involved purely physical labor.

I'm sure even that list doesn't say it all. But maybe you begin to get the idea. I guess at one time or another in my life I've rebelled against all of that. But some of it has had a great deal of staying power for me. And some of it has been a source of much pain, especially the part about sex. I was in and out of marriage like a revolving door for a few years before I realized that the major problem was the value system that had been inculcated in me in such matters. Interestingly, I've been happily married now for six years, and plan to stay that way. Part of the values stuck. And I'm glad they did.

In religion, I'm a Unitarian—properly speaking, a member of the Unitarian Universalist Association. You don't have to know much about that to know it's considerably different from Methodist/Baptist. But notice that religion in general, and involvement in a church in particular, stuck.

After years of rejecting country music—first for jazz, then for rock and roll—I now listen to it about as much as any kind. I find it deals with the things that are important to most people.

After years of thinking of my home town as just a place to be from, and never a place I would want to be, I made the down payment on a little piece of land there a couple of years ago. My wife and I are going to build a place on it when we can afford to, to get away to on weekends or whatever, and maybe to retire to one of these days.

I guess the part of the working class value system I'm describing that I've rejected most completely is in the area of race. I've already mentioned our high school's refusal of athletic competition with another team that had one black guy. In those days I didn't know there was anything else to call them but "niggers." There were no blacks in our little town except for one elderly couple, Jim and Fanny, who I thought were liked by everybody. It seemed perfectly natural that black kids were bussed from a nearby small town where they lived, through our town, to an all-black school in a larger town.

Later I learned Jim and Fanny were tolerated only because they knew their place and that they had had children who had to go to school elsewhere. I also came to feel that it was pretty strange that forced busing of black kids to keep people apart was okay, while forced busing of black and white kids to bring people together was bad, even somehow un-American.

The turning point, of course, came when I began to get to know some black guys in history courses as an undergraduate and began to realize they were pretty much like me. I'll never forget the first time my first real black friend, Robert, rode home with me, then caught a bus to his home in Alabama. I had a '56 Ford with flarefender skirts with "Arkansas Traveller" painted on them. Robert was driving. When we went through Shamrock, Texas, I pointed out a place for him to stop that I had eaten at before and thought was good. He seemed hesitant. I had no idea why, and insisted. He stopped, but insisted I go in and get the food to go. Finally, it got through to me. First I was embarrassed, then madder than hell that this guy, my friend, couldn't eat where I could. No big deal, I suppose, but an eye-opener for me. My mother, by the way, after the obvious initial shock, was more than decent to Robert in the couple of hours he had to wait at my house before going on to catch the bus. Dad, as I recall, never said anything.

Mom, as a matter of fact, God bless her, stayed with me through my changes in all things pretty well. Martin Luther King helped her do this—he was, after all, a Baptist preacher. She even seemed not to disapprove when I took part in civil rights demonstrations when I was in graduate school with the black guy who became one of only two good friends from those days that I've kept.

Which leads me to the area of the value system inculcated in me in which I seem to have changed *least*. *How* it leads me there, will, I suspect, take some explaining.

You see, I feel like I get along basically pretty well with most of my professional colleagues for purposes of the necessary day-to-day academic activities. But they're *not* the people I want to be with otherwise. They're certainly not the kind of people my wife and I want to live around. So about four years ago we bought a house in a...well..."working class" neighborhood. Nobody else I know of from the university lives anywhere close. Our house payment is only $126.15 per month. (Fortunately, that means that, in addition to liking it, we can almost afford to live in it!) It's not, obviously, a very "desirable" area to live in. There are lots of vacant lots, lots of empty houses, lots of rundown properties, lots of old people, lots of unemployed people. I played on a community softball team the last couple of years with a guy who does lawn work, two janitors, a wrecker driver, a service station attendant, a school bus driver, a guy who works for a scrap metal company, and several guys who are most of the time unemployed. And there are *always* plenty of cars propped up being worked on. And I love it!

But, at least to make clear the relation between this and my previous topic, the one last thing I *hate* about it is the pervasive racism. The other day I was visiting with some neighbors whom I consider really good friends. We were discussing how friendly their dog was. So friendly it would probably be useless as a watch dog. "But you ought to see her come alive if a nigger tries to come into this yard!" I just bit my tongue. But should I have? Isn't there anyplace you can get away from that? (Certainly the university is not the place; Arab students there are sometimes referred to as "sand niggers.")

How did I get to be a historian? How did I get to be as "radical" as I am? I am a historian. I do think of myself as a radical, though I insist on defining that term for myself.

My high school band director helped me a lot, in both of these. He read history on the side and frequently shared his enthusiasm about it with us. When I started college, I was a music major. But I changed to history. And that made me a radical.

For my radicalism has little, if anything, to do with socialism, communism, or any of that other "foreign" stuff. It's as American as baseball. It grows primarily out of my study of American history. It's the kind of radicalism that means "of or pertaining to root or origins; fundamental." If you inquire—the root word of history, "historia," means "to inquire"—into *this* country's origins, you'll find a revolutionary tradition indeed: life, liberty, the pursuit of happiness, freedom, liberty, equality, democracy, the right of rebellion itself. A long and honorable radical tradition, that I'm proud of, with heroes like Sam Adams, Tom Paine, Abigail Adams, Henry David Thoreau, Fredrick Douglass, Charles Beard, and Martin Luther King. I think it's sad that so many people, including but not limited to the working class, have managed to forget all that. One can even make a case that to be a good American historian is automatically to be a radical *and* a patriot, for patriotic means "of our fathers." A word game? Admittedly, but more, too, I think.

Of course, more was involved in my radicalization than becoming a historian. Civil Rights struggles and Vietnam both moved me also, as they did so many others. I remember the first time, as a faculty member, I spoke at an anti-war rally. Interestingly, among the other results, it lost me some "working class" friends.

Since I've said that I consider being a historian and being a radical very closely related, the relationship between the two is evident in what I teach about and the way I teach it. Among the subjects I've worked in the last 15 years are black history, radicalism in American history, women in American history, and American environmental history. And in my "regular" courses, largely in the pre-Civil war era, my approach is one which emphasizes differing interpretations as a device for showing students that history can be something interesting, important, even, God forbid, relevant—and as a device for challenging their value systems. I think college should challenge everybody's value system—it certainly did mine!—and so many of my students have a value system that so deserves challenge.

Many, if not most, of my students are, to put it bluntly, rich/conservative/Republican/spoiled brats. Without, I feel, compromising my role as a historian, I manage to get through to a few of them each semester. By getting through to them, I should be quick to add I don't necessarily mean getting them to agree with me on anything, but rather just getting them to open up and think and be willing to question their beliefs. Many of them, certainly, have a hard time relating to me. Perhaps I'm naive, but I don't think that has anything to do with class origins. Perhaps significantly, I find myself not very conscious of students' class origins, to the point that I'm not sure I can tell.

My experience with academic authority, as I think back on it now, hasn't been all that bad. Oh, at times I thought it was. I've suffered professionally—raises, promotions, sabbaticals—for personal things like appearance, lifestyle, politics. I thought that was wrong, and I fought it. I still think it's wrong, and I'll always fight it. But I'm not inclined to think any of this has anything to do with class; not when faculty members of similar persuasion but different class background have had the same problems.

Maybe acceptance of authority is an aspect of my working class background that has never been particularly difficult for me. In any case, it seems natural to me that there are those who have authority over me—and that there are those, students, over whom I have authority. (Though I do not feel compelled to respect a dean, vice-president, or whoever, who acts in a childish, biased, authoritarian, arbitrary manner. Nor do I expect my students to respect me unless my behavior is worth it.)

I've already said that I get along well enough with my colleagues, but am not, do not choose to be—perhaps could not be—really close to them. The only thing—well, the *main* thing, anyway—that *really* bugs me about them is the game of one-upmanship with intellectual bullshit and how many books everybody's working on that never get published, etc., that takes place, especially at professional meetings. I just have to get away from that, and mix with some "real"—working class?—people.

I'm very happy doing what I do. It sure beats selling cattle at the stockyards. If I ever stop enjoying it, loving it even, I'll get out. You're being fundamentally dishonest, even immoral, it seems to me, to do something like teaching when you're not really giving yourself to it. You're not just hurting yourself, after all—we can think of lots of people, in all social and economic classes, who don't enjoy their work—but your students as well if you don't really care for what you do. And most of your students are sharp enough, of course, to know.

Sometimes I even feel lucky, making a decent living—

not outstanding, not as good as it "ought" to be, but decent—doing something I not only enjoy, but consider rather important, something that makes a bit of a contribution. Oh, we're not going to save the world, we historians. No academic discipline is going to do that, least of all those that most often claim they're going to. But...well, like the graduate student in literature who replied to the sociology graduate student's cocky claim about saving the world by saying "Okay, you save it then, and we'll make it worth living in!"—maybe what I hope is that history can make a small contribution to both.

George Pappas

Now at the age of 36 I am an associate professor at Prestige U...I have tenure...a beautiful family...a fantastic home on the top of a mountain...I teach the children of the rich in order to have this comfortable existence...Is this what I ought to be doing?

On a cool Saturday in early October, I sit at this typewriter struggling to find the time to pound out a few lines about myself in an effort to communicate to others how the "American Dream" worked for this working class kid, and, more importantly, how I manage to continue to do what I do without having my identity shattered day-in-and-day-out.* That is, how I daily walk the tightrope of reality/insanity at ole Prestige U. here in the secure glorious rural beauty of Pennsylvania. Ah, 'tis almost kickoff time, as the band begins to play. It's parents weekend and the crowd is moving in force toward the stadium. It's somewhat incredible to me why it is that I have no interest in this game given that I spent the better part of my life from the age of 8 to 22 literally entertaining people by inflicting harm and injury on others in stadiums.

Dad has always amazed me. He was the son of a candy store owner and grew up in a poor section of Norwich, Connecticut, of Greek origin. Dad was a hard working kid—always worked, as he tells it. Paper routes to earn money to give to his Mom—especially after his Dad died during the Depression when the family lost the candy store. The money Dad and the other kids earned served only to complement

---

*I would like to dedicate this simplified caricature of the evolution of my being to my lovely children, in the hope that someday they will understand their need to participate actively in the making of a just and humane society.

243

the meager income his Mom earned at the local textile mill. Life became unbearable for Dad and even his pool hustling didn't help alleviate the urge to get out of Norwich.

Unfortunately, it took Hitler and the Japanese to provide him an avenue of escape. He lied about his age and enlisted in the Navy. Dad spent the war years on a ship in the Pacific. I never realized the impact of this experience on him until those dinner conversations in the Vietnam War period when he would argue violently about the war; the fact that I would not go, the fact that my friends would not go, the fact that his son, going to college, was not only a pacifist but a socialist as well. It would not be until I was 34 that I would learn from Mom that Dad for years after the war in the Pacific, would wake at night in a cold sweat crying—he lost many friends in combat, saw his best buddies severed in half before his eyes...yet, 26 years later he demanded that war continue.

After 26 years in the Navy, Dad entered the private sector—the banking industry—as an appraiser. In time he worked himself up to being a branch manager. By the time he was 55 he began to understand some of the things that I had been saying to him for years about capitalism as an economic system. Now at 58, Dad is bitter...but that is his story.

Mom was the daughter of Pete and old Ma Schaeffer, also from Connecticut. Pete was a construction worker and a heavy drinker. In my youth, he would sit at my bedside during visits and drink his beer (Ballantine) and tell me stories about his youth and his soccer days.He was a proud Dutchman but unfortunately no match for his English wife—it is certainly complex to be sure, but the word was that she put him in his grave much too early. Mom, like Dad, was looking forward to escaping the hard life on the farm, cleaning rich folks' homes after school, and listening to the endless fights between Pete and Ma Schaffer. So, at the tender age of 19, she married Dad and shortly thereafter became the mother of me.

At the age of six-months, we went off to Alaska to join Dad. From there we went to San Diego...then to Guam...then back to San Diego...then to Norfolk, Virginia...then to San Diego. Those were no doubt critical years in my life. Arriving in San Diego at the age of 16 wasn't easy. The military life—the traveling, the housing projects, changing schools, meeting and leaving friends, having little money, and not having Dad around very much at all—somehow shaped a kid, who, by 16, had a pretty strong self-concept. More than anything else, I suppose sports were my savior. Being athletic always gave me a place to go, ready-made friends to meet, and something to feel proud about. The notion of teamwork and cooperation and collective goals always seemed to motivate me.

The last years of high school were very important for me. Being an Athlete-scholar (as we were called then), I was placed in the college prep program taking the "heavy" courses with kids who wore glasses and whose skin was always pale. (Yet, they always made great lab partners!) Having to study so hard and spend enormous amounts of time on the practice field made life difficult aside from the social/personal traumas of being that age.

Selecting a college was something that kids I went to school with thought little about and knew little about. I did not even know at the age of 18 that there was really any difference between schools other than their geographical locations, the extent of partying that went on and the reputation of their football team. The old T.V. show "College Bowl" did lead me to believe that there were places where people took school very seriously. But, then, who would ever seriously consider such a place? Then, all of a sudden, I was standing outside the Dean of Students office at Pomona College waiting for my interview. I said to myself "What am I doing here?" This is what you get for playing football and being smart. "Christ," I said, "This is not the place for me! Looks too hard, too serious;" so, I enrolled in Factory U., in San Diego and, *in spite of the odds,* I managed to get myself an education. part of my getting through stemmed from being in a fraternity for two years, part of it came from having to work through college (grocery bagger, janitor, lemon picker and landscaper), but most of it came from self-discipline and hard work.

I discovered early in college that while I was fairly intelligent, I was no genius. If I were going to get anywhere, I was going to have to work and work hard; but without

motivation the hard work could not come; fortunately for me
as the nation was collapsing around the Vietnam War and
race riots, I managed to take some classes from some rather
special faculty and that was the turning point for me. Studying Latin America, in particular, opened up my eyes to the
nature of U.S. capitalism and the nature of imperialism. It
was my interest in political science, history, and economics
that effectively turned me loose intellectually. During my
last year in school, I even borrowed money so that I did not
have to work and could have more time to study. By 1969,
having finished college, I started graduate school in Political Science...after a semester I realized that I was "burned
out" and bored with abstraction and theory. I wanted to do
something!

Sitting in the cafeteria at Hoover High School on Saturday morning with a terrible hangover, I was about to go
to a qualifying exam for a position with the San Diego
County Dept. of Honor Camps. Looking at the other 300
people competing for five positions (ostensibly requiring a
degree in Psychology or from the behavioral sciences) this
frustrated social scientist felt the odds were against him;
yet, somehow, in the mail several weeks later came the
invitation for an interview..."Have you ever used drugs?"
said the person in the center of the interviewing panel. "Well
ah...yes," I replied. There went that job, I thought. Six
months later, I was a different person. Six months working
with addicts, alcoholics, and others who had for one reason
or another transgressed against private property, put the
world into perspective for me. In addition, working with
mainly Chicanos and Blacks sensitized me to the realities of
racism in our society. I loved my work in the camps. Most of
the time, I felt like an inmate rather than a staff person. The
camp system had potential and several of us "young turks"
did our best to twist the system around. We tried to make it
responsive to people's needs. We tried to make it an environment capable of treating people as human beings; but, the
system was rigid and oppressive as were the majority of
staff. And, week after week, I was becoming more and more
emotionally drained, depressed, and inclined to think that
while this kind of work was important, it was not for me,
certainly not for the rest of my life. I left the camps with a
new-found sense of direction and purpose.

Knowing that I wanted to go back to school but not knowing where or what to study, I decided to let some time pass—just "flow" as we use to say. One night while attending a performance of the San Francisco Mime Troupe in San Diego, I ran into an old friend and teacher. This man was supposed to be in Peru, but for some reason was visiting San Diego. After exchanging stories during the intermission, he mentioned to me that a good friend of his from Ohio was going to be on campus interviewing students for a new rather unique graduate program in "Social and Applied Economics" at a new State University outside of Dayton, Ohio. The next day I met his friend, who turned out to be a guy dressed in a suit, sporting hair down to his shoulders, carrying a black briefcase. He invited me to sit and talk for a few minutes. It was another one of those "magic" moments—another "turning point" in my life. Within minutes I was offered a full-scholarship. And, without any hesitation I accepted. Days after, I put my suitcase, typewriter, and books in my VW and made the trek to Ohio.

A year and a half later, I was finished with the M.S. degree. My experience there would be a book in itself. Suffice it to say that under the direction and support of friends and faculty, I emerged as a student of political economy with a long-time commitment to social change. Much to my surprise, I emerged as a student with very strong ambitions with respect to teaching; yet, I could not imagine going on to graduate school for a Ph.D in order to become credentialed to be able to teach. I returned to San Diego to reflect upon my Ohio experiences (Antioch College, living in Yellow Springs, May Day '70 and '71, Kent State, more Vietnam, a trip to Mexico, the coup ousting the head of the economics department at Wright State, URPE, Baldemar Velesquez, FLOC, and many others.)

One day while teaching in the educational program that I had set up for the San Diego County Dept. of Honor Camps, I was summoned to the office for a long-distance phone call. It was a Dean from my alma mater in Ohio telling me that a predominantly Black university outside of Dayton had called him inquiring about any possible recent graduate from the M.S. program who might be suitable/interested in a teaching job. This Dean said essentially that if

I wanted the job there was a good chance that I could have it. I would have to come for an interview and take that risk. I took about an hour to think it over—called him back and said to arrange the interview. I resigned my job in San Diego and once again loaded up the old VW and returned to Ohio.

I owe much of the success that I have enjoyed thus far in my career to the "seasoning" experience I had teaching in Ohio. During the three years I taught there, I kept notes about all the bizarre experiences I had and intended some-day to write a book about the place. Luckily a woman named Ann Jones wrote such a book about being white and teaching in a predominantly black institution, called *Uncle Tom's Campus*. Being white, being successful at relating to Black students, and being political, all eventually contributed to my being fired. The official reason for my termination was that the chairman felt that my relationship with the students was *less* than professional, i.e. I was not an authoritarian oppressor. Yet, in my grievance process via the AAUP, at a meeting with the university Dean and Vice President, my African chairman publicly denounced me for being a communist. As the tape rolled on, I smiled and said that while he may believe that to be true, his naivete about academic freedom allowed him to make a sizable political blunder by saying this out loud.

Well, the tape somehow disappeared after that session and I decided that it was time to move on anyway. Fortunately for me, during the three years of teaching I was enrolled in a Ph.D. program. I finished my degree in 1974 and began searching for a place to work that would allow and encourage academic freedom. In fact, *academic freedom* was my major concern as I looked for my next job.

At a meeting of the AEA in New York City that December, I had surprising success in marketing my wares, especially since I had a rather unconventional degree from an experimental graduate program. Yet, this was what most schools found to be attractive. Wanting to teach political economy also made a difference. Finally, I signed on with ole Prestige U. Weeks later I was on campus, thinking that while the place itself and the students did not really turn me on (in fact intimidated me more than anything else) the Economics Department was exceptional—especially the emphasis it placed on academic freedom. It took some coaxing for me to convince my spouse that coming to prestige U. was a good idea. In fact, I returned with her to tour the campus on Sig Derby Day—a horrible fraternity event. She cried—urging me not to take the job. We worked that through as we have almost everything else in the 18 years that we have known each other.

Now at the age 36 I am an Associate Professor of Economics at the prestigious liberal arts college. I have tenure—a job for life, in essence. I have a beautiful family and a fantastic passive solar home on the top of a mountain just three miles outside of town. I have an income that is more than sufficient to guarantee my family a comfortable standard of living for many years to come. I teach the children of the rich in order to have this comfortable existence. For the time being, I have committed myself to living and working in this environment. I have continually struggled with the agonizing questions that confront and often times haunt professors like myself from similar class backgrounds: Is this what I ought to be doing? Is this the place where I ought to be doing it? If not here, then where? Why would *there* be better or more important than *here*? If not teaching, what? This questioning and the resulting internal dialogue never cease; yet, for the time being, I have managed to come to grips with the dilemma and the predicament. The struggle against capitalism continues as does the desire to develop as a human being. One's work, that is to say one's job, is only a part of one's life...there are other things...being a person for me means being a husband, a father, a citizen in the community...but no matter the activity context...being alive means being a human being and that means being *political*; and to be political one needs to know who one is, and where one is going.

Norman Frost

> ...I too have learned the rules of the game and feel that I can survive as an academic while being actively engaged in struggles to change a world which is dominated by the wrong class. Simultaneously, I feel privileged to be able to utilize my time and energy to learn, teach and do research, and I feel outraged that the type of behavior which is largely rewarded is that which supports this insane (social) system.

Some years ago, when my father was hospitalized and feeling like "the end was near" I took a tape recorder into his hospital room and interviewed him. I wanted to know his work history, I told him, what kind of experiences he had in his life, how he felt about them. Some months later I did the same exercise with my mother who not only had a similar background (working class) as my father, but also spent most of her life as some type of clerical worker. To me, preparing and now listening to those tapes has been extremely helpful to understanding my parents' attitudes, values and behavior which have always appeared to me as very middle class. Some of the generalizations which have formed about my parents background are:

> Both sides of my parents' families were tied to employment on the railroads. Such employment was relatively steady but somewhat dangerous, and industrial accidents were important in determining key moves in my family's history. They all came West as the railroad re-assigned them, and it was the job that determined who they were, how well they ate, etc.

> Apparently labor unions were not part of my family's life until the second decade of the present century. My own father participated in strikes in Reno, Nevada, at that time, but always the union was "busted" and repeatedly he had to start over again, at another job.

Because of the hazardous and precarious nature of railroad employment my father, whose formal education ended with the eighth grade, attended a commercial/business school in order to move out of blue-collar employment. The majority of his working life he was employed as an insurance salesman, partly salaried and partly commissioned. My father's boss lived in a big, expensive house about two miles from us and was, in numerous ways, a typical "Scrooge type." One of my favorite memories of my father came late in his life. Shortly after retiring we got into an argument about politics. He violently disagreed with my position until I explained to him the concept of "surplus value" and together we calculated the approximate dollar value of the output his boss had extracted from him in his 35 years of employment. Somehow that exercise gave him some satisfaction: knowing that he was not the only person so exploited and also putting a label on what he already knew.

My mother, whose education ended with a high school diploma stressing secretarial skills, worked for a variety of large and small businesses and government agencies. She too did her best to transcend her poor origins. Most of her relatives exhibited most of the behavior characteristics that she associated with working-class folks: divorce, large (unstable) families, drunkeness, unemployment and an absence of thrift. She, more than my father, actively pursued the middle class, Protestant version of the "good life" which stressed stability, thrift, community service, honesty, a nice home, hard work, education for the children, distrust of labor unions and an allegiance to the Republican Party.

My reaction(s) to my parents' values and lifestyle have varied over time and with my state of mind. When I was young I was dissatisfied that we lived on the "poor side of the street" in Sacramento, California. The rich kids just a few blocks away seemed to have so much more fun and more "things," were prettier, more fashionable, etc. My parents, however, appeared to me to be overly strict, overly protective, overly demanding, and we had less of everything than they did—time, money, things and prestige.

But, as I grew older, I began to envy those folks less and developed a deep distrust for the rich and privileged in general. As a teenager I began to work as a musician in private clubs, bars and regularly at the only country club in Sacramento. My conversations with the bartenders, the waiters and waitresses and my own observations of Sacramento's leading citizens led me to the "discovery" that there were two sides to most of these folks. The side they showed to the public displayed nice houses, cars and clothes coupled with polished manners, community service, and a religious and family orientation. However, the side I saw at the Country Club was quite different. There the liquor flowed freely, the "servants" (e.g., waiters, caddies) were treated paternalistically and frequently exploited sexually. There also shady business deals were cut—exclusively among the Country Club "set."

By the time I was 16 or 17 I had become disenchanted with the rich as role models and took my first concrete step toward my own liberation; I refused to go to church and informed my parents that many of their parishioners were hypocrites, drunks, gamblers, and unfaithful to their spouses...something they undoubtedly knew but didn't quite know how to discuss with me. From then on I was convinced that I had to find my own answers as to how to live and what to live for.

As a youth I had a variety of jobs from gardener, to newsboy, to a messenger and later on as a cannery worker. My main job, however, was as a musician playing for dances, shows and bars. There, as noted above, I got most of my "education," my income and my introduction to labor unions, Local 12 of the A.F. of M. While not a model of democratic processes, I did feel that the union did help us and the community and did not get in our way too much.

My favorite music was jazz. Playing jazz I learned about both skill and art and I was introduced to a new part of life—what are now called "peak experiences" by humanistic psychologists. I also learned from my experiences as a musician that if I worked hard, in a disciplined way, I could accomplish a lot. But, being a musician also set up a conflict; should I try to go to college or go right out and start traveling as a musician? My parents wanted me to go to college (a junior college in Sacramento), but I wanted to go "on the road" with a band.

The selection of what college/university to attend or whether to go at all was, in retrospect, one of life's most important decisions. At that point "class" became an important determinant of each individual's life. Those with grades *and* money went to U.C. Berkeley or Stanford. Those with grades only went to junior college and those with neither went to work. There were few sizable scholarships or work-study opportunities.

I went to junior college for a semester. Then, because my parents would not let me go on the road, I volunteered for the U.S. Army, which I learned to distrust as well. But the army helped me to see the "real world" better by sending me to be part of the army of occupation in Korea (in 1955). While I was anti-communist and racist as most of the other white boys, what I saw there opened my eyes to the international differences in living standards and instilled in me a basic distrust of U.S. foreign policy.

Returning to the U.S. after 18 months abroad was really shocking. After the horror I had seen in Korea, the apathetic '50s of the U.S. were too much. But, during my two years doing military "service," I became aware of the potential advantages of a college education and the G.I. Bill. So, I went to Sacramento State College, first to major in music and later in economics. Despite the largely orthodox/neoclassical orientation of professors there, I began to understand something about why jazz musicians were largely a poor bunch, and why Korea was an "underdeveloped country." But again, orthodox economics seemed to tell only half of the story, and it wasn't until I met with an "institutional economist" that I began to gain significant insights into "developmental processes"—the relationship between the past, the present, and the future, the social and the economic dimensions of society, technology and social relations, etc. That's when I started to "cook" with economics.

College was, for me, four years of exploring. I explored my own philosophy, my own politics, beliefs and those of others. I soon discovered that Republicans were usually rich (or wanted to be) and conservative and that those kinds of folks weren't my cup of tea. Soon I identified myself as a Democrat, then later on as a democratic socialist. By the time I was ready to graduate, I was convinced that the Swedes must have the ideal social life, democracy and socialism. So, I packed up and emigrated there, and for 1 and 1/2 years I lived, worked (as a musician) and briefly went to school there. But after a time, I saw that, as the critics say, there was "trouble in paradise." So I left and continued my search for paradise in other parts of Eastern and Western Europe.

Eventually I came back to the U.S. (in the early 1960s) and worked once again as a musician trying to figure out what I was going to do when I grew up. The availability of a graduate fellowship at the University of Colorado attracted me to graduate study in economics, more as a "learning experience" than as a career enhancing one. Graduate school was a disappointment, however. While in Europe I had become accustomed to talking frequently and openly about politics. Europe at the time was teeming with young Third World intellectuals who simultaneously wished to learn about the technology of advanced countries while wishing to impress upon those countries the fact that they were fed up with colonialism *and* capitalism. U.S. graduate schools were (are?) by comparison cloistered islands for the preparation of the mandarins who hear, see, or feel no evil with respect to their sacred capitalistic, "free market" system, which, in turn, rewards them for their uncritical allegiance.

It was in graduate school that I again was confronted by the subtleties of the U.S. class structure. By contrast, Europeans are very conscious and open about their relatively rigid class divisions. Fortunately, such divisions also breed a certain sense of solidarity within classes which makes life a little easier to endure. In the U.S. it's "every man for himself" (there was only one woman in my graduate classes and she eventually dropped out despite, or because of, a very keen mind). Those who were articulate, were facile in mathematics, could write well and read fast, were the best performers in the graduate school game. The students who understood the nature of the game were the real winners in the long run, however, for they knew what to expect/what not to expect, the explicit and the implicit rules of the game, what is "Saleable" in research, the politics of the public and private sectors, etc. In short, those who came from upper-class families were usually better prepared cognitively and affectively to do battle on the intellectual field than we who naively thought that what we were going to get was an objective view of economic realities. For those of us who looked at the economy "from the bottom up" it was a difficult and frustrating experience, but for those who were accustomed to looking at the world "from the top down" graduate school merely conformed to their view of the world and better prepared them to administer it.

Perhaps my perspective can better be understood by my saying that it was not until I was handed my Ph.D. diploma that I believed I could possibly be a "Doctor." For a nobody like me who was not even sure he could get into college, this was an unbelievable experience.

I have now been functioning as a college professor for some 16 years. I now teach at what most Harvard graduates would call a second—or even third-rate (state) university. Most of the students here are from middle-class families. A typical profile would be: the (white) father is an engineer or accountant who came to California after doing military service here. Mother is usually a housekeeper in a ranch style house. Family income is somewhere between $30,000 and $50,000. Life has been amazingly comfortable with major strains emanating from popularity contests in high school and a feeling of aimlessness that usually seems to stimulate conformity rather than rebellion. There is a smattering of minority and poor youth, however, but they do not represent their views well in the class room discussions which are largely dominated by the middle class defenders of the *status quo*, as they damn labor unions and praise the Establishment. One main difference between students at the State University and other more affluent schools where I have taught is that these students here are much more convinced that they can succeed only by "fitting in" or "adjusting to" the system while the more affluent are more convinced that they can "make their mark" usually by pursuing entrepreneurial ends in a variety of business activities.

So, what's it like being an academic with "working class" roots? Well, I too have learned the rules of the game and feel that I can survive as an academic while being actively engaged in struggles to change a world which is dominated by the "wrong" class. Simultaneously, I feel privileged to be able to utilize my time and energy to learn, teach, and do research, and I feel outraged that the type of behavior which is largely rewarded is that which supports this insane system. I feel hurt when I hear corporation executives talk disparagingly about workers and unions or when I am confronted with a glib defender of the *status quo* who is able to articulate his empty views better than I— knowing full well that he/she was prepared to do just that at Stanford or Harvard. And I despair when I see working-class families walk out of the supermarket with $100 worth of "crap food," destroy the desert with their off road vehicles and defend reactionary governmental politics at home and abroad.

Being a working class academic is sometimes very lonely. It's difficult to relate to most colleagues, but it is also difficult to relate to working-class folks, who tend not to trust you since you got to be a "Doctor."

CHAPTER 8

Outsiders

I f you don't *buy* in to the values of the academy, you get *left out* (assuming you don't get *bought out* along the way). But, then, you can be outside the tent and—if you can handle the anger and avoid cynicism or self-pity—have a lot to tell those others of us who stayed inside, accepting, attaining, balancing, or whatever. You might be able to tell what we would find in our own buried fantasies if we quit being nice and proper and accommodating, if we stopped trying to be middle-class (even though the tell-tale signs on our boots have been apparent to all, all along).

Our last essays, we believe, hold important truths for all those academics who did not start their lives in the upper-classes. For many such people, lurking somewhere in their minds we suspect there is hot anger at all the bluebloods who started and stayed at the top, feelings that might find connection to this final grouping. Two of the following essays explicitly (and two other more obliquely) have anger as their motif, experienced because the balancing act did not work, if indeed it was ever tried at all. And, our last contributor speaks, not angrily, but sadly it turns out, about how, in his adventures on campus, no strategy at all would allow him to forget his alienation from those around him.

Karl Anderson

I have never been to Chile, or Turkey, or South
Africa, or the U.S.S.R., but I doubt that anywhere
on earth self deception had been institutionalized
more thoroughly than in the U.S., and above all, in
higher education in this country.

My father worked with his hands all his adult life; my
mother was a receptionist for a large corporation before my
parents were married. I'm their firstborn, and my birth
almost exactly coincided with the coming of the Great
Depression to that part of the country. In one year, my
father's wages were halved, but he was lucky, and managed
to hang on to his job until the company he worked for was
liquidated about 1940, shortly after he had finally finished
paying for the household furnishings the newlyweds had
bought almost ten years earlier.

I grew up in a Southern city with a population of around
300,000 in the thirties; it has since mushroomed to more
than a million, and I have no more feeling toward that place
than I have toward New Delhi or Moscow. The neighborhood in which I grew up has long since vanished, but the
houses were never expensive ones, anyway. Nearly all were
one story, two bedroom, frame "bungalows," with an occasional duplex. Most of our neighbors rented, but some were
paying on mortgages. We rented, until the landlord, who
lived 2,000 miles away, decided to sell the house in the late
1940s, whereupon my parents undertook the mortgage,
which they managed to pay off in less than ten years.
Almost none of the women in the neighborhood worked,
about half the men were skilled laborers, the other half
clerks or office workers. Very few belonged to unions, or had
the opportunity to do so, but the working men, those who
wore work clothes instead of white shirts and neckties,

always seemed to me to be more respected than the men who didn't get their hands dirty each day. The only adult I knew who had been to college was an ambulance-chasing lawyer who was liked by no one, including his own wife and kids. About half the families were Roman Catholic, of Irish, French, and Italian descent, and there were a few Jewish families, but I was unaware of religious prejudice until I was in high school. Blacks lived in ghettoes (though they weren't called that), and Chicanos, though considered "white," lived, for the most part, only in certain neighborhoods.

Within my own neighborhood everyone was considered (by her/himself and others) to be among the "poor people," and everyone voted for FDR. The one family that was thought to be "rich" lived in a two story brick house, owned a big black car, and the children rarely played with the rest of us. We always thought of those kids as "sissies" and certainly didn't envy them. Only after I had graduated from high school did I discover that every member of the family worked nearly every day in their small business across town. The elementary and junior high schools I attended were extensions of my neighborhood. Parents (mostly mothers) and teachers would sometimes speak of the possibility of a few of us "going to college," but even that far back, I was aware of their lack of confidence that any of us would. As it happened, maybe half of us went, perhaps half that number graduated, and I ended up with a Ph.D. and a professorship at an expensive, exclusive Eastern private college. But I'm getting ahead of my story.

World War Two came and there was more money; even teen-aged kids had jobs. My family began to "eat out" about once a week, usually at the local hamburger joint. I was given an allowance, with which I usually bought a comic book or magazine, and my brother and I got for Xmas a small radio of our own. When I was twelve I got a bicycle for Xmas. I thought, or just took for granted, that most people's lives were pretty much like mine.

Then I went to high school. It was the "best" public high school in that city because it drew students from the richest neighborhood in town, and received twice the money that any other high school did. Less than a quarter of the kids were from families that were really affluent, but they, and the teachers, set the tone for the school. If I hadn't been a fairly good athlete, I would have completely hated high school, and would probably have dropped out, as some of my friends did, to work as a helper on construction projects, which were booming at that time.

As it was, I became a kind of "pet" of a group of rich girls, who had their own cars, and at the same time I began to learn about sex with girls of my own class whose parents worked or were separated, allowing us to meet and experiment in their house during the afternoons, when I wasn't at one kind of athletic event for another. All the teachers, and most of the students, in that high school, talked as if *all* of us were "going to college," but I never thought much about it until, during my senior year, everyone took some sort of exam, comparable to the S.A.T.'s today. Nor did anyone I knew attach much importance to the scores of that exam, and I didn't even know that I had scored high on it until much later. Most of my high school grades were B's and C's, though I was especially good at mathematics, or perhaps I had good teachers in that subject. I remember two of them.

One thing I knew: I did not want to "go to college" if it was merely an extension of that high school. For example, there were three boy's social clubs, something like fraternities. I was invited to join one, and I declined, because its purpose was clearly nothing more than snobbery. Also, I didn't want to ask my father for money for the dues, and, most important, no one from my neighborhood belonged to it. To my surprise, my refusal resulted in near ostracism, not only by club members, but by many others, who concluded that my refusal to join was evidence that I thought myself "too good" for even a self-defined elite. That hurt. At baseball batting practice one day, the pitcher kept throwing at or near my head. When I challenged him, he said something about my having a "big head." He was a better ball player, as well as more popular with girls, than I was. I found out later that he hadn't been invited to join any social club (through some mix up) and his resentment toward me for having been invited was only increased by my refusal to join. (Maybe that kind of response is merely "human," but I've found it repeatedly in American academia. My public achievements have never had the adverse repercussions that my refusal of "honors" has had.)

I chose to attend the state land-grant college because its students were "poor," and that was a good choice for me, socially. But I caught hell not only from teachers and my parents, but also from friends, when I declined membership in various "honorary" groups, or when I refused to compete for academic prizes. The truth was, and is, that I enjoyed meeting new people, seeing new places, and learning new things, but I never wanted to be any sort of celebrity, nor have I ever wanted to own a house, or a sailboat, or stay in expensive hotels. I like good food, but not expensive, ornate restaurants. I don't enjoy being served or waited upon. Nor do I like to dress for any occasion. I've worn academic robes only once, in order to protest a political commencement speaker during the Viet Nam War. Nor do I like classrooms, chalkboards, or curricula. Or even most libraries, though I'd waste away without books to read.

And that's how I became an academic. As everyone did at that time, I went into the army directly from college, and when I got out in the late '50s, no job that was available to me was anything more than a way of making money, though I tried a couple of them. A friend who was going to graduate school on the GI Bill explained to me that, as a veteran, I could get free tuition, and be paid $90 a month. Because I had a "B" average as an undergraduate, I couldn't be refused admission as a special graduate student in that state, but I was told by various advisors and bureaucrats that I would be wasting my time to begin studying a completely different discipline at the age of twenty-seven. I had a B.S. in agriculture, from the land grant college, and I wanted to study literature in graduate school.

I registered in literature against all the advice, thinking that I would read interesting books and talk to interesting people for four years before "going to work" like everyone else. My first shock came when I discovered how dull so many of the graduate faculty and students were. These privileged, comfortable, people seemed to be suffering from some form of anemia or a tropical disease that resulted in a kind of mental and emotional lethargy. I found out quickly that my own excitement and enthusiasm at being able to read and write whatever I wished was, at best, embarrassing to most of the people with whom I came in contact. Not all, however. I quickly discovered, and made friends with, a couple of dozen graduate students and a few faculty who shared my enthusiasm if not always its object. People, that is, who were interesting to talk and to listen to because they were genuinely interested in what they were learning and teaching. People who repeatedly shoved books and ideas at me and insisted that I respond to them, listening intently even when (or especially when) my viewpoint or judgment differed from theirs. That was a huge state university and, in the five years I spent there, I discovered many such people, in various academic disciplines, but they were never in a majority. And many of them, as I discovered sooner or later, came from backgrounds similar to mine. I think we all felt enormously fortunate to be able to spend most of our waking hours learning and teaching, thinking and talking, about what we cared for and considered important. Moreover, we knew that many other people weren't as fortunate.

The second shock I experienced in Graduate School was the discovery of the greed that dominated the consciousness of the majority of my peers and professors. Open self-aggrandizement was an accepted way of life, with professors spending whole class periods bragging about having a paper published, often ahead of some rival, and graduate students alternately clawing for grades and other honors, and whining about those they failed to get. I never knew most of these people well enough to know a great deal about their origins, but the few I did know well were, without exception, from families who had paid their way through private schools and colleges, and were supporting them in graduate school. Many had done no military service, and those that had were in something like Naval Intelligence, stationed in Honolulu. None had ever worked at more than a summer job as a lifeguard or camp counselor. None of these men had ever worked in a factory or been inside a whorehouse or supported himself. And most of these women were openly looking for husbands, as I found out when their interest in me waned, upon the discovery that I was living on $90 a month and a weekend job in a country store and service station.

Social class was, of course, almost never mentioned, not even in classroom discussions of the 19th Century English novels. Dickens wasn't on any reading list that I ever discovered in the Department of English, and a young, highly-regarded Professor of English dismissed *The Grapes of Wrath* (in a course on American Literature.) Even so, through careful selection of my Doctoral Committee, I was able to find four graduate professors who allowed me (grudgingly) to write a dissertation on what some people have called "proletarian" literature.

But I'm getting ahead of myself. I never expected to get any sort of a degree when I entered graduate school (and I don't have an M.A.). I simply intended to learn as much as possible, and to pursue my own interests until my GI Bill benefits ran out. So I took courses in English, American, and European Literature, and in Philosophy. It was in those philosophy classes that I really learned to read. I had always loved to read, and had developed various ruses throughout my adolescence and young manhood to avoid being thought a "bookworm." Now I was among people who were paid to be bookworms, and I discovered slowly how many of them *didn't like to read.*

The third semester I was in graduate school, there was an unexpected need for a few additional graduate assistants. One professor I had studied under, who shared my enthusiasm, recommended me for one of these teaching assistantships, even though I had completed only eight or ten courses in the Humanities. I had an interview with the Assistant Dean of the Graduate School, a Professor of English with a famous reputation for scholarship. I didn't expect to get the job, and I decided not to be anything less than candid with the Great Man. His first question was to ask why I was studying literature. I began an answer with the words, "I've always liked to read..." when he interrupted me, came around the desk to sit beside me and reminisce over his life as a midwestern farm boy who also "liked to read." That was the "interview," and I got the job. It puzzled me at the time, and I only found out much later how few people who study and teach literature do genuinely "like to read."

What I discovered, of course, is that things haven't changed significantly since Mark Twain wrote about his school days. Power and hierarchy, and not teaching and learning, dominated the graduate school I found myself in. "Knowledge" was one-upmanship, and no one disguised that fact. Pettiness and rancor were applauded *when successful.* The one thing I learned absolutely was the inseparability of free speech and free thought. I, as well as some of my peers, were refused the opportunity to speak, and sometimes even to ask questions deemed "irrelevant" when the instructors didn't wish to discuss or respond to them. We weren't, at that time, intent upon rebellion or disruption. We genuinely wanted to understand why, for example, Shakespeare often seemed to revere hereditary aristocracy, and how citizens of a democracy could understand that reverence. We loved Shakespeare, but we *couldn't* pretend that we shared the attitudes of Elizabethan English, Anglo-Catholic entrepreneurs, as most of our superiors and peers did pretend.

Fortunately, I realized after a while that I wasn't as disadvantaged in this new world as I had assumed. So I selected a Doctoral Committee, passed the necessary written and oral exams on my first try, and wrote a dissertation. The Committee disapproved of my conclusions in the final chapter, so I simply threw it away, and the dissertation was approved with no conclusion at all. (The ghost of Joseph McCarthy still lingered on in the minds of these men, who visibly winced at the word "socialism" although "fuck" had entered some of the books they assigned, if not their own vocabularies.) During these years, I married a beautiful woman, and after four years of marriage, we had three sons. She was middle class, and eight years younger than me. And, though I love her now more than I did then, she still is. She is an editor, dresses and behaves every day like a businesswoman, and manages not to tell the corporation she works for what a crime against humanity it is. I admire her courage and persistence, and do not consider her work in any way inferior to mine, but I don't think I could retain my sanity sitting in the editorial conferences she attends every day.

I mention my wife because nearly everyone I've known well in academia has married "up" in class and "down" in age; this is true of women as well as men. My sons are, I think, working class in their outlook; I don't expect any of them to earn a college or university degree, although I wouldn't prevent them from doing so. My daughter will almost certainly be middle class and earn a degree, no matter what I do. Few of my colleagues understand my attitude toward my children, all of whom are bright, talented, and have won various artistic, athletic, and academic prizes. Maybe I'm a bad father, but I've tried to be candid with my children about what I understand to be the true nature of this country and its institutions, which I believe are the greatest threats to humanity now in existence. I don't hate the United States, but I do fear its power, concentrated as it is in so few hands. And, I resent the role that schools play in that power game.

But I digress. I got my first teaching job at another large state university, mainly as a result of a recommendation from one of my graduate professors, who had been a graduate student there on the World War II GI Bill, an Irish Catholic from New England whose father, a day laborer, had died of alcoholism when my teacher was in adolescence. Two other new Ph. D.'s were hired in that department of two dozen members the same year I was. One had a degree from the Ivy League, and was heir to a chain of appliance stores in a large city. The other was the son of a chemistry professor at a small eastern private college. I liked them both, as I liked most of my new colleagues. They were all nice people, and generous to me and my family. They were also, I discovered quickly, intent on "helping" us. For example, we were told early on that the "important" people in that town attended the Presbyterian Church and that people with "taste" were buying new houses in a certain part of town. Very, very few of my colleagues, then or now, have had the faintest glimmer of understanding why I never had any desire to own a house.

I taught at that university for two years. Football and fraternities dominated student life, although only 20% of the students actually belonged to Greek letter organizations. And the Viet Nam War was getting more publicity, as were marijuana and long hair. So one night, Federal, State, and Local cops raided a house in which a dozen or so students lived, one of those big, old houses that could be rented cheaply if enough people shared the expenses. I didn't know the students at that time, but I could see a frame-up when I saw the first newspaper stories. Two of the students (all of whom were male) had hair long enough to cover their ears (this was in '65) and they were involuntarily committed to a state hospital for psychiatric examination. The "evidence" the cops discovered was an anti-war poster and a few buttons, together with a large number of cigarette butts, an ordinary tobacco pipe, and a few small medicine bottles. Some people later said that the cops hit the wrong house, while others claimed they had planted a small amount of marijuana. In either event, six months later, a judge threw the whole case out of court.

Immediately, I had written a letter to the newspapers, objecting to their sensational treatment of the raid. (Reporters had accompanied the cops.) Before mailing it, I showed it to a friend in the law school to ask him if it was libelous. It was an angry letter. My friend asked if he could also sign the letter and suggested circulating it among the faculty. We did, and perhaps 10% of our colleagues signed it, while many more declined out of overtly expressed fear for their careers and/or that it would bring discredit (and the legislature) down on the whole university.

What did happen was that the publication of this letter resulted in my discovery that one powerful publisher controlled all of the big daily papers in that state, and that the same publisher had donated and maintained the buildings and equipment of the School of Journalism at that university, and that he had a good deal of influence in the choice of its faculty. That turned out to be something that "everyone knew." Everyone, that is, who attended the Presbyterian Church and lived in the right part of town.

Because of this event, which became a state-wide controversy in the media for a couple of weeks, I suddenly achieved a notoriety I had never expected, and I received some anonymous letters and phone calls. The students involved had all been suspended, and missed a whole semester before they were readmitted after their acquittal in court.

Not one of them had money to hire a lawyer on his own, and all of them together couldn't get enough together for one of the big names in that state. I never got to know any of them closely, but I did learn that all were attending that university on very little money.

Despite all the public controversy, not one of my departmental colleagues ever discussed this matter with me, although some of them had signed the notorious letter. That was, for them, gentility and dispassionate liberalism, two characteristics I have found to dominate middle class academic behavior. Candor is in "bad taste," anger and indignation are *always* "irrational," and concern about anything more than one's own narrowly defined self-interest is highly suspect. "What," I was asked recently, "do you *really* want?" after I had spent an hour patiently explaining how capitalism cannot survive without advertising, which in turn, can only corrupt thought and language. "Socialism," I replied, to which the only response was deep embarrassment.

As Kurt Vonnegut has written, the taboos on words referring to human excretion and reproduction that became so strong in the nineteenth century only touched the surface of much deeper language taboos. Nice people may talk about sex more openly today than they did one hundred years ago, but they still don't talk about wealth, except in the broadest, most general terms. That is genuinely embarrassing to most of the academics I have known. When I have become impatient with endless complaints over coffee about low salaries, high prices or taxes (or both) I've often said "I make $25,000 a year; how much do you make?" And, the only answer I've *ever* received has been an embarrassed grimace, as if I had misunderstood the point of the conversation. Which I had, of course; the subject is not really money but malaise.

Academics often use the word "work" to refer to what they do, but, *as a class*, they do less productive work than any group I know. Teaching is tiring, and many people put much energy and effort into it. Half the people in my present department teach the same courses with the same reading, semester after semester, and year after year. The other half of us rarely teach the same course more than once every two years, and we constantly change the readings in our courses. Therefore, we spend much time preparing classes. But the actual exhaustion results from the time spent in the classroom, the intense concentration upon 25 to 50 other minds for an hour, or an hour and a half, or three hours at a time. Teaching in colleges and universities as they are constituted today takes much time and energy, as do other jobs. Its *results*, however, are highly questionable, except for a very small percentage of students. I have often felt like a man working on an assembly line who doesn't know which 80% of the products he is working on will be worthless.

I resigned from my first teaching job in disgust with the lack of intellectual energy I perceived within that institution. I now believe that it wasn't such a bad place in comparison to others, but that its faculty was exhausted and/or cowed because it had never achieved the collective solidarity that could have resulted in the dignity that organized manual workers and individual small craftsmen often have. Nor do most academics seem to realize how recent our proletarianization is. Individually, we may have much freedom of action and belief; collectively we only strengthen and support institutions which are defined by stronger forces, so our individual efforts are often quixotic, at best.

I now teach in a private university with very high tuition and an enrollment of 3,000. Five times as many prospective students apply for admission each year as enter as freshmen. Most pay full tuition, many with the aid of loans. There have been surpluses at the end of each of the last three academic years in the school's budget, yet the administration constantly warns of hard times ahead, and raises the specter of cutbacks and bankruptcy at every opportunity. So do many of my colleagues. There is a great deal of pretension about "research" and "scholarship," but most of my colleagues are happy living small town, middle class lives. Fraternities and athletics dominate student life, and the faculty and administration ignore, for the most part, how little genuine intellectual activity takes place. Public speakers and official honorees are more likely to be celebrities, office-holders, or merely rich than they are to be artists, intellectuals, or scholars. The local slang is borrowed from TV and corporate jargon, so that sophomores write about

Shakespeare's "bottom line" with no sense of irony, and academic Deans exhort faculty to attend public lectures by "movers and shakers" who are corporation barons.

Finally, the university is not a great place for candor. It is embarrassing, at best, and disruptive, at worst. Here's an example: last year, the average family income of our students increased by 25%. This was widely known and discussed by administrators. When a colleague mentioned it in a faculty meeting, the shock couldn't have been greater had he advocated infanticide. A shocked *silence*. And, that, I think is the most oppressive aspect of middle class life myself. It thrives upon people keeping their mouths shut, unless they are actually endorsing whatever powers exist. The "free marketplace of ideas" that is so beloved of liberals is as much a fantasy as a free marketplace in oil or automobiles; a more harmful fantasy, because it breeds even more hypocrisy and cynicism. Just as teachers can control what is said in their classrooms, most also have ultra-sensitive antennae as to what will be rewarded or punished that is said outside them. And these antennae control them.

I haven't intended to represent myself as a modern day Huckelberry Finn, but neither have I been a Sid Sawyer, and all too many of the people with whom I've come in contact with during my years as a teacher have been. I do share something with Mark Twain, however little of his talent I may possess. I'm bitter, and most of what I write and think is not taken seriously by most of the people I know. That is, I suppose, why I'm bitter.

I'm too old to go back to working for a living, and too accustomed to a regular paycheck to quit teaching before my pension begins, though I often think about it. Three of my kids are grown, and my wife has learned to live with consumerism and the daily hypocrisy inherent in her job. I spend as much time as possible away from my university, and out of the United States. I have never been to Chile, or Turkey, or the U.S.S.R., or South Africa, but I doubt that anywhere on earth self-deception has been institutionalized more thoroughly than in the U.S., and above all, in higher education in this country, which accepts the middle-class credo:

Don't think about it, and it will go away
Don't notice it, and it won't exist
Don't talk about it, and it will never have happened.

Hugh O'Malley

> I feel quite unapologetic about my prejudices about colleagues. I feel they are deeply worthy of contempt. They parade a sense of inflated self-importance, take pleasure over feeling smarter than students, pretend they contribute meaningfully to GNP, dance for favors, create parochial empires, cower before symbols of authority, wallow in bogus professionalism, and submerge themselves in their narrow expertise, which for many is their ticket to a legitimate place in the "academy."

I was born in Queens, New York, the same year the Great Depression hit. My parents had hard workers' lives and were not educated beyond the eighth grade. They had no particular ambitions for me other than security, safety and a "clean" job. School was a place where I played dumb, kept my mouth shut and was afraid most of the time. I never associated the experience with learning much of anything. My key interest was avoiding beatings and other humiliations. I managed, somehow, to graduate from high school.

The script for my life was fairly well set by my class position. I had no aspirations for a big time career, and college was for people much richer and smarter than I. I got a clerk's job, white collar and all. Thirty bucks a week. Soon I would have a clean wife, clean kids and a clean apartment, in perhaps a slightly better neighborhood than my parents. My life was on the working class track, heading nowhere.

The Korean war was heating up, and the Army was after me. I joined to avoid the draft. Leaving home opened the world for me. Among other things, I discovered ideas, books and my mind, which turned out to be a good one. The G.I. Bill offered me the opportunity to attend college. With some doubts and reservations I took a chance. Things took off from there. I did well in college, married into the solid middle class, went to graduate school and ended up a professor. I left the original life script behind, and I was happy

275

276 STRANGERS IN PARADISE

to leave it. I knew I was on my way to something better. I
guess it was better, but there were lots of surprises along the
way.

Ah, life as a professor, a professional, a scholar, a man
of means and position within the community; such a distance to travel from the early days in the old neighborhood.
It came into perspective one day as I was reclining in the
lovely backyard of my spacious and attractive thirteen
room house, reading, dozing and bitching about the humid-
ity and other minor discontents. Suddenly I had an image of
my father treading down the street on a similarly hot
August day, dirty and exhausted. It occurred to me at that
moment that I don't work very hard when I work, have the
summers off and live quite comfortably. My discontent
seemed more like petty annoyances when compared with
the physical, material and spiritual hardships endured by
my parents. I felt lucky, but more like I'd hit the number
with $5 riding, as opposed to an earned place in the shade on
a hot August day. The sense of being lucky, as opposed to
receiving just deserts for talent and effort is a theme I would
like to return to later. But, for now, it seems important to
mention that I feel like (have felt) as someone fortune has
smiled upon. Suffice it to say, as a lucky outsider, my sense
of legitimate membership in academic life was tenuous.

As I did not feel as though I had any clear entitlement to
membership in the academic community, I really never fit
very well in its various structures. I had (have) particular
difficulty with the structure of authority, both with respect
to my authority as a professor and in my relationship to the
college administration. As a teacher in the classroom, I
always had (have) a great deal of difficulty getting students
to do their work, admonishing or punishing them. Similarly, I had much anguish assigning grades to pieces of
work and for course performance. I preferred to create some
sense of intimacy and egalitarianism. In addition, and
somewhat aside, I felt the need to be very careful in what I
said and how I said it, a bit like a state department press
secretary attempting to explain the latest U.S. hanky-
panky without exposing himself to a critical assault for a
mis-stated word or phrase. Also, "talking academese" for
me is a bit like a translation process from native to foreign

tongue. It takes time and hard work. Further, I never enjoyed standing "up there," all eyes upon me. But being cautious and careful with my expression and articulation stands out for me as symptomatic of my sense of vulnerability as an interloper.

It is this same sense of interloper that has, I am sure, influenced my reluctance to exercise authority in the classroom. I suspect this strain around the exercise of authority is intensified by the fact that, for the most part, I have taught students from social classes higher than mine in origin. In a sense they "belonged," and I really didn't.

On the other hand, I have also resented the exercise of authority over me. It seems puzzling to me that given my uncertain sense of legitimate community membership, that I have not been more solicitous, or cautious before my bosses. My sense of my actions is that I have, on numerous occasions, stood for unpopular causes, stood strongly against administration excesses, risked my good fortune and my "place in the shade" to resist or insist that the administration do things differently. One stand that I recall amounted to demanding that the faculty council investigate misuse of federal work-study funds by the Vice-President for Finance. These funds were being placed in the general student aid category, and consequently, not reaching the targeted group for this much needed support. I knew that raising this issue in a public way would be the only chance I had to get some change. Appropriately thereafter, I never identified very well with the boss, not being one, as in the classroom or as department chairman, or having one. I guess my preference for egalitarian structures and mutual respect is somehow rooted in my experience with the stings of indignity and humiliation that are visited upon society's losers. Further, my experience in my schooling and lower class status has made me sensitive to the hurts that are a consequence of hierarchial power relationships. I cannot clearly untangle the web of personal circumstances that have shaped these attitudes or directed me to embrace egalitarian values. Nonetheless, I'm certain that these dispositions are an integral part of my professional and personal make-up.

I have had a great deal of emotional upset with my colleagues around questions of authority. A source of great anger for me has been to see the "annointed" few snap into line and sell the latest administration line, and the multitudes of willing sycophants, looking to be invited to the inner circle and that, yet, other group of faculty, too frightened or self-interested, to look up from their texts, to notice the mangled bodies and principles strewn around them. And, a corollary seems to be that they are quite comfortable with their authority in the classroom, which, in my opinion, many of them use excessively and punitively. The power of the hostile emotions within me towards these behaviors at times astounds me.

The assessment of authority relationships takes me on a rather direct route to my relations with colleagues. There have been few for whom I have felt positive regard. The cutting edge for these judgments relates to their dispositions toward authority and their professional styles. At my college there are only a few archetypes who exude manners and styles I ordinarily associate with the wellborn. There are a handful of highly ambitious and successful careerists who pretend to some notoriety beyond the campus, and a gaggle of self-contemptuous strugglers who are neither. My friends have been a handful of fellow outsiders who share my contempt for the rest of "them." I feel quite unapologetic about these prejudices. I feel they are all deeply worthy of contempt. They parade a sense of inflated self-importance, take pleasure over feeling smarter than students, pretend they contribute meaningfully to GNP, dance for favors, create parochial empires, cower before symbols of authority, wallow in bogus professionalism, submerge themselves in their narrow expertise, which for many is their ticket to a legitimate place in the "academy."

The tone and the anger of what I've written above gives some indication of the depth of my alienation.

In those occasional clear moments I recognize that some of my contempt is related to my own struggle to "make it," to compromise myself in the process of climbing. On especially clear moments my heart opens to those caught in the vicious web of demands associated with the quest for dignity, respect and security. Lord knows, we sure make these items scarce in this society, and if attained, tenuous. Indeed, the struggle is ongoing. On these especially clear moments I also forgive myself for either "selling out" or not "measuring up," whichever is foreground at the moment. This problem is compounded by the growing preoccupation of students with careerist concerns, and their instrumental approach to their education. The problems of feeling some affinity with students is intensified by their class backgrounds. For the most part, the students I teach are rich, in the $30,000 family income range and upward. As each year passes, I'm more offended by their complacency, ostentation and self-indulgence. I recall once teaching a class on inequality. I laid out my story, from the guts, a living chronicle of the pain associated with upward mobility. The blank expressions before me hurt very much. Simply, they could not, understandably, relate to my trip.

Whether strained by zealous, compulsive achievement motives or blocked from any serious intellectual engagement by learned indifference or other injuries, students seem alternately contemptable and courageous in their struggle with the grim program the culture offers. These feelings fluctuate within me as I engage them and as I embrace my own struggle.

So let's look at it! I make a decent income. Teach more or less what I want to, have the summers off, do not labor by the sweat of my brow, have the security that tenure can bring. On the other hand, I'm deeply alienated and when I'm not in an especially clear and high consciousness, I hate most of my colleagues, despise my bosses, resent my students and eschew their values, distrust intellectualism, hate the pretense and rationalistic nonsense of academic style. Am I doing O.K. in this life? Sometimes I wonder! Let's look at the intellectual dimensions of the professional role.

What kind of scholar am I? How proficient am I at my craft? What is my orientation toward learning and knowledge? I have evolved as a critic of the tendency of many establishment intellectuals to separate thoughts and feelings and facts and values. I believe the prevailing metaphysical assumptions about objectivity rooted in the social sciences to be fundamentally in error. This position is interesting in light of my early graduate school indoctrination. I bought positivism and emotional detachment, hook, line, and sinker. Partially a function of my need to be accepted within the community of scholars, I suspended my good sense and adopted the prevailing party line. Fortunately I recovered before it was too late. Further, I did not embrace narrow specialization. Though I realize that becoming an expert on a narrow piece of knowledge is a way to plant one's flag in the academic imperial scramble and thereby gain a niche which has an equalizing function. It seems to be a path to community membership. Yet, my interests have been more directed toward larger questions of meaning and purpose, and increasingly, to questions that have personal significance to me. No longer are scholarly interests defined for me by the discipline of political science. Instead, I attempt to take my agenda of concern to the world and attempt to facilitate my enlightenment and those others who share my concern. In the process of unlearning the harmful indoctrination of graduate school training, I do not feel I have lost any intellectual balance or ability. I do feel that I have a much better sense of personal ownership over how and what I think. Hence, in the area of scholarship, I do experience much alienation between me, my concerns, and the things that I study and think about. I am pleased about this aspect of my professional growth and development. It would seem that the further away from professional orthodoxy I get, the better I feel about what I am doing. My teaching and scholarship are now much more concerned with the problem of personal authenticity, injustice, indignity, the problem of authority, the human consequences of hierarchy, the integration of fact, value and emotion, the meaning of satisfaction, contentment and inner peace. In short, I try to bring the essential meaning of my intellectual and personal journey to them with the hope that they can make more enlightened choices about related personal and societal concerns. As the line between what concerns me and what I teach narrows, what I do seems much more purposeful.

Given a choice, would I do it all over again? If "it" is the academic profession, I think not. Often, the pretensions of academics are almost more than I can bear. The recognition that academia is not a world apart from the rest of society has been disillusioning. In some critical ways, the world I hoped to find still needs to be created, rather than discovered. Further, membership in the academic community did not heal my class injuries.

Concerning upward social mobility in general, I am aware that I live in a culture which punishes those who do not acquire skills and credentials that are highly valued in the market place. I know that I would not like to live a life victimized by those who are empowered to issue badges of indignity. I would not want to live in the jaws of chronic insecurity. Further I really didn't have nurturing roots to stay close to as an alternative to the mobility trip. Hence, staying within my original class location offered very little. The U.S. is not a land that affords much structure or sense of place, but rather a land which offers some choices, and occasionally, opportunities to seek that which might be worth having, though the appearance is often different from the reality, and the problems of a class based society cannot be remedied by an individual action. I guess, if I had to do it over again, I would look, as I have in my life, for purpose, meaning, and a way to change things so there would be more of everything that people need to feel good about themselves and their lives; where there is authentic communication, an opportunity to be oneself. Perhaps I would recognize more clearly with the knowledge of this life behind me, that these conditions must be created. They are not out there, to be discovered. Within the protective walls of the academy the same old struggles go forth, for status, advantage, personal aggrandizement, and approval. I imagine that the degree of social distance from which I saw the academy, colored my sense of life within. I looked for these life affirming essentials in academia and did not find what I was looking for. Indeed, again, I was confused about what things need to be created in this society and what can be discovered. I looked to academia to resolve my class injuries and again, came to realize these injuries do not heal. The pain diminishes only as the injuries are identified and examined, and the system of oppression comprehended. Indeed, the academy is an integral part of that system of oppression, snobbery, gentility, and invitation to interlopers to leave their true identities at the gates and assume the alien postures and personal styles of the professional archetype. And for those who do not enter, there is little respect and not much caring.

At this point in my life I trudge along, taking what is meaningful to me into the classroom, hoping to spark an interest. I attempt to deepen my understanding of how the class system works and how it affects people's lives, particularly my own. Meanwhile, I plot my escape or engage in rich fantasy that places me in that world yet to be discovered, where people affirm each other, rather than judge. I think I will soon be ready to join the road gang, building the way to a good society. I don't think it can be done inside the ivy covered walls.

Douglas Brent

> Middle class folks expect to have rewarding careers.
> That was a pact between God and their families.
> Other folks have jobs. And if they are lucky the jobs
> aren't too bad. Compared with the rest of my fam-
> ily, I'm lucky.

I was born in a small New England town—population
substantially less than a thousand—and raised in another,
only slightly larger. My father's side of the family can be
traced back to the early 17th century; they were English
fishermen, apparently, and made small settlements here,
and finally came over for good. They abandoned fishing
and soon became small farmers and that is what most of my
ancestors did for a couple of hundred years. Sometime in the
1880s my Great Grandfather founded a small factory. It
prospered, and he and his immediate family became—by
small town standards—quite well to do. Gentry almost.

My father was born into these circumstances in 1907.
His father was a foreman in the family factory. They also
did a little farming and owned a large farmhouse. My father
grew up assuming that there would be a place for him in the
factory. As a boy he worked after school in the mill: like most
boys, smoking cigarettes and riding motorcycles seemed
like more fun to him than Latin and social studies. He was
thrown out of high school for smoking two days before the
completion of his Junior year and never went back. He had
vaguely thought of college, had had an abortive year at a
local area school even, but this apparently ended his academic career. He went to work in the factory full time from
then on. In 1925 my Great Grandfather died and the business was run by various members of the family. In 1931 the
business folded, a casualty, as I later learned as an econom-

ics graduate student, of Big Government pursuing an Incorrect Monetary Policy. My father was out of a job.

In 1930 he had married my mother. They had met in 1927 while she was a college student at the University of Massachusetts, and had courted until she graduated, and a year after while she taught school. After the factory folded in 1931, they moved to another small town where he worked briefly in another mill which also went under, I believe. He then sold cars for a while. He made very little money; they lived in a house his parents had bought them, and in the winter they heated with coal also donated by his parents. In 1938, again with family money, he bought a small grocery store which he ran, all by himself, for ten years.

My mother was born in Fall River, Massachusetts, in 1908. Her father was a bank treasurer. He was the son of an English immigrant who apparently came over some time in the late 19th century. Her mother was French Canadian; she had immigrated herself as a little girl, and had worked briefly in the mills before marrying my grandfather. I remember him as an incredibly stubborn, conservative man; a Republican to his toes. As a little boy, when we visited, I was under strict orders not to mention the name of Franklin Roosevelt, as it would set him off. I always did, and it always did. My mother, though in her forties and married, didn't smoke in front of him. And no one drank in front of him. As I remember, he had no use for 1) Negroes 2) all foreigners, 3) Jews, and 4) Catholics. He did, however, make an exception for a second cousin who was Jewish and a millionaire.

My mother went to college. She was accepted at a private college, but when my grandfather brought her up, there wasn't any dormitory space. Never one to waste a trip, my grandfather took her several towns over and enrolled her in the State University. She graduated in 1929, taught school for a year and then married my father, in 1930.

Although I didn't realize it as a small boy growing up, my parents were (and are) a remarkably happily married couple. This must have come about as a near universal surprise to their relatives. My father's family suspected my mother of being a loose woman—a flapper—and gave the family silver to him. Her parents thought my father was beneath her—a college graduate—and her father never forgave them for getting married, taking my mother out of work, and "wasting" her education. On one of my parents' wedding anniversaries her folks gave them a vacuum cleaner; on another they got a dress. There was very little strife in the house. Aside from the usual sibbling squabbles between my sister and myself, I remember growing up with very little tension in the family. While we had little extra money, we neeed little, and my father always expected to inherit something from his parents. They knew they were a cut below the town doctors, but that was what passed for upper class around there. And they were proud they weren't foreign or Negro. Once, despairing that my sister could never seem to find the "right man," my father, in a burst of liberalism, announced that he would be happy if she could even marry "a goddamn Polack if he was neat and clean."

My father never made any money in his small store. In 1948, he bought another larger one—again with the help of his mother's money. He used to take home $50 a week plus food from the business, worked 6 days a week (7 at first) and never had a vacation from 1938 to about 1958, except for a day off now and then to go hunting and fishing. He grew to regret having little education and has always felt inferior around people more educated and better spoken than he. In the middle 1950s he had what was then called a "nervous breakdown," apparently the result of his failing to live up to his middle class aspirations, and saw a psychiatrist for several years, and he always marveled that my mother, a college graduate, married him.

This is a long background to make a couple of points. My roots are in small New England towns, and have been for ten generations or so. And I never could quite figure out what my class background was; some sort of cross between small farmer, a middle class banker/farmer owner, mill worker, storekeeper. I think that it is the combination of class (whatever it is) and rural background that have shaped my experience as an academic.

My father's second store was in a town dominated by a prep school and his first one had been in a college town. Some of my earliest memories are working in his store (actually the earliest are stealing his cigars and candy) and

watching the middle class and especially the academic customers condescend to him. I can remember the tone of voice
and the sweet little smiles. My father took it! In a small store
you don't alienate anybody. I understood that but I was
ashamed for him and (at the time) of him. One of his fondest
memories is of one time when, finally fed up, he told off the
wife of one of the local doctors and asked her to leave. It
worked wonders! She was apple-pie nice ever after.

His relationship with the local academics was a mixture
of fear and respect, combined with contempt. They were
better educated than he; they could speak well at town meetings, and they could make a fool of him. They made more
money, were more respected, and didn't work with their
hands. On the other hand, my father—like generations of
New Englanders before him—was a natural born fixit. He
had a large dose of common sense, grew up on a farm where
things had to be repaired locally, worked in garages, and
generally was the sort who could make things work. One of
his neighbors taught mathematics at a local college. He
once told my father that he wanted to run for a town office
for which you had to be nominated. He then asked if people
would think it strange if he nominated himself. The story
made the rounds of the local folks. "Educated damn fools"
has been my father's summary of college teachers ever
since.

My father wanted very much for me to get the education
which he never had. Accordingly I became a day student at
the local area prep school. This was a shock. I not only saw
my first Negro (at the age of 13), I was also thrown in with
kids from urban backgrounds, many of whom were well-to-
do. Atmosphere there was hearty, aggressive, Christian,
and I did not fit in well. By this time I had imbibed most of
my father's fears. The son of a small-town, poorly educated,
not very prosperous storekeeper, and a day student to boot,
made me feel pretty much apart from the other boys and
from the school and its aims and traditions. I worked my ass
off and got a good education, graduating in the top half of
my class—barely. But I hated the place, and still do.

It never occurred to me not to go to college. I got into the
state university and into a private school. Although it was
much more expensive my parents wanted me to go to a

private school if possible. Accordingly, to foot the bill, my mother went back to teaching at the local high school. My father, apparently, had few illusions about his son: when he dropped me at college he told me that if I worked hard and got C's he would be happy.

After prep school, college was a breeze. I lived off my academic capital for a couple of years, got A's with no work, and was thought brilliant. I got into a fraternity (95% of the other males did too; the other 5% were pariahs) and became as typical a fraternity boy as I could manage. There were some very wealthy people at this school as I discovered, but there were also some from small towns with backgrounds like mine. Some were in my fraternity and some others were among the 5% of pariahs. I became friendly with both.

College opened all sorts of intellectual worlds for me. I had worked hard at prep school, and had ultimately done well, but I had very little intellectual curiosity. In college I read Locke, and John Stuart Mill, and for the first time I got excited by ideas. I took creative writing courses, and some of the non-fraternity people I hung out with were actually intellectual. My first college girl-friend wrote poetry and loved Virgil (but maybe all 17 year old girls do). The second was a transfer student; either the last beatnik or the first hippy and in any event the only one ever to grace the school. She loved literature, wore peasant blouses, and didn't shave her legs. Such behavior indicated something about her morals, or others thought. In a day when college girls didn't, she was nicknamed "Juicy." I was proud of the derived status.

The wealthy students there were the sun-tanned ones after Spring vacation, the ones with sports cars, and they skied a lot. Conversation was of Larchmont, Scarsdale, Shaker Heights, all place I had never heard of, but came to understand were a leg over my town. Little was made of a casual weekend trip to Bermuda. At first I was embarrassed and humbled. When my parents came up for Parent's Weekend of my sophomore year I was terrified that they would expose me. I was, of course, especially ashamed of my father —of his job, his income, that he would make some gaff or other. I exposed them to my friends as little as possible.

Gradually, I managed to come to terms with my background. I distinctly remember sitting around a table in the fraternity with some others with whom I was friendly, and with some of the rich boys, too. The rich ones were happily discussing the prospect of having daddy fly them to Bermuda for vacation. We took this for a while and then patted one on the shoulder and said: "Wouldn't it be easier to have daddy fly Bermuda up here?" He was mortified. I think it was the first time he understood just how oppressive wealthy talk could be.

On the whole, I enjoyed my years in college. Class impinged from time to time, but also I was learning how to deal with it. My decision to go to graduate school was somewhat of a process of elimination. I had joined an Officers' Candidate Program as a junior, but had washed out due to bad eyesight. I did not want to join the business community as most of my friends were doing. And I had really enjoyed my study of history and economics at college. History, I sensed even then, was a dead end. And with economics, I thought, you could do the world some good. I applied to graduate school in economics.

I went to graduate school at two big state universities, getting a Master's degree from one and a Ph.D. from the other. Probably because these were state schools and drew from quite a variety of class backgrounds the issue of class rarely came up during these years. Anyway, after four years, with Ph.D. all finished except for the dissertation, which was mostly finished, I got a job offer from Femed—a small, exclusive New England college for women. It was the best offer that I got and so, with some reservations, I took it.

I have been trying to figure out my relationship with Femed ever since. It is complicated. Class enters in, I think, and I will try to show how. But so do other things. I grew up near Femed: its faculty, in those days, were doubtless among the academics who patronized my father's business. And my father. Thoughts of Thomas Wolfe were in my head as I contemplated a job at Femed. Not many people—faculty or students—have shit on their boots. Anyway, I came to Femed and have been here about 15 years now.

I never quite felt like I belonged to the place, from the very beginning. I think that this has been the result of both class and rural background. I remember interviewing here. I was brought into an office and the two faculty there to interview me turned their backs and discussed the new chair one had bought. After a while, when they got around to me, they were greatly relieved when they discovered that I was a native New Englander, and not from beyond the Hudson, where they still fight Indians and whup niggers. My departmental chair called me in to inform me that male faculty wore a tie and jacket to classes. I was smoking and she never managed to offer me an ashtray. She did inform me that her ancestors had come to the United States in 1630. I said mine had come in 1608—a kind of snobbery I don't like but thought was justified at the time.

Class and background have shaped my relationships with colleagues in several ways, I think. One is in the style of argument. Academics address in verbal, not physical ways. I have seen senior colleagues practice incredible verbal cruelities on junior colleagues. Where I came from this was not done. My parents have always interpreted even a disagreement as potentially threatening. Argument was to be avoided, and nasty argument involving ridicule, satire and even simply hard logic, was impolite. Outside of the home environment in, say, a bar, such argument was not only impolite, it was a way of getting into a brawl. I think in both cases the prohibition on what my colleagues would term "freewheeling debate" stemmed from the perception that it was really aggression. Just like taking a poke at someone. I also remembered the tone of voice that the aggressor usually used—the polite, patient insistence that normal people reserved for dogs, small children and the retarded. It was the same tone in which the better folk had addressed my father. Academics thrive on the sure, or almost sure, knowledge that the addressee won't take a poke at them. That is called academic freedom. I have never quite accepted these rules. My exchanges with colleagues lack that formal, minuet-like quality which I often observe in their debate. I tend to get mad. I have often thought that this probably has something to do with all those times I saw my father "take it" and not act mad because he needed the trade, and because he was vaguely intimidated.

Being an academic has always involved a large amount of guilt for me, and I think it does more for most people with my background. Somehow I wasn't "working" for a living. Working was on a schedule: 8-5, or in my experience, 7:30 to 6, six days a week. Adjusting to an academic schedule means you don't really work. But more important, in my experience, working has always meant a large dose of heavy physical labor. Although my father ran a store most of the years I was growing up, it was small enough that he had to be a jack of all trades. He not only ran it and kept the books and so on, he stocked shelves, cut meat, went to the dump, ran the registers and swept the floor. I worked for him summers while I was a teenager. A normal day involved getting there at 7:15 in the morning and getting home at 6:30 at night, six days a week. Fridays, however, we stayed open until nine. Since he cut the meat, he had to be there, and I remember just how tired he would get. Hell, I remember how tired I would get!

A constant refrain among my colleagues is that they are overworked and underpaid. In my experience the reverse is true. Academic work isn't work, and academic pay is more than I remember anybody around me getting when I was growing up. I have always felt like I won the lottery—a cushy job and fat income compared to what I remember. More than this, what seems to me the insularity of my colleagues' complaint has undercut a large fraction of whatever respect I might otherwise feel for them and the academic community at large. How can such a privileged group, and one so blind to its privileges, ever fathom what is going on in the rest of the world?

I think the concern with work and privilege shapes many, if not most, of my feelings about most of my colleagues at Femed and elsewhere. Do these people really get paid for this? For writing worthless articles during their summer off in Greece, or not writing anything but spouting about the decline of standards, the poor quality of students, the sloppy research done by junior colleagues? The foolish insularity and learned pomposities, the petty academic politics, the courses presented as academic truth are in fact their own prejudices well-dressed in academic jargon. These are what earn a college professors an income in the upper fifth of the population. It is hard for me to hide the contempt I feel for these activities. As a result, I feel detached from most of my colleagues and from the aims and assumptions that apparently guide Femed.

Two other things stand out about my relationship with colleagues. Most of my friends subscribe to liberal or radical politics. During the 1960s many hitched themselves to the back-to-the-land crowd. More recently they subscribe to the small is beautiful group, or are enthusiasts of Barry Commoner. There has always seemed to me to be a large element of urban middle class romantic naivete involved in these movements, and in some cases an arrogant blindness to what rural life is really like. Farming in my limited experience was not romantic! It was awfully hard work for the money. Something to be avoided, or if that was not possible, mitigated, at all costs. I was amazed to discover people who thought potatoes grew on trees suddenly wanting to go back to the land. And I got (and get) very upset when people such as Commoner discuss how much energy is "wasted" on farms. It not only seems to imply that farmers are stupid, it suggests that the critic believes that the use of a haybaler instead of of someone's back is a waste of energy. Again I wonder: how can academics who are so arrogant and ignorant be trusted to shape social policy? And the result is that while I share the liberal politics of certain faculty, I cannot share much of the rest of their world view.

A final point. Part of being rural is to use colorful figures of speech. This is true of both North and South, I think. Perhaps it is a way uneducated people use their imagination; they play with language in different ways than do the educated. I grew up in this environment, and have picked up many of the figures of speech. You don't describe someone as simply happy; "he or she is as happy as a pig in a new suit." As the example indicates many of these are earthy. They are simply a part of speech among many rural people. When you use such metaphors around academics, however, you are likely to be thought either crude or quaint. So there are two choices: change your speech pattern or be viewed as some form of exhibit.

Teaching economics to mostly the rich students of Femed is an interesting activity. It is hard for me to share their belief in their own natural superiority or in the natural inferiority of people who work with their hands or are poor. I once had a student who thought a major social issue was the servant problem. It comes down to a problem of teaching people who are very young from very sheltered and privileged backgrounds about matters that fly in the face of family prejudices. These prejudices, often so smugly and confidently held, amount to an assault of lower middle class, working class, and poor people. They are, accordingly, attacking my own roots, and I find it hard to reason with and be at all sympathetic to such behavior. But that is what I am paid to do.

Students are always polite to faculty where I teach; they are not always polite to clerks downtown. When a student greets me I sometimes wonder what the greeting would be —or indeed if there would be one at all—without my title. So the upshot is feeling slightly like an interloper. Students often invite the faculty over to the dorms for tea or wine and cheese. The dorms reek of old money. And tea was a drink for the English when I was a boy. And I'd rather have beer than wine. But it is always the little things that make you feel out of place.

All of these sentiments and impressions make for some queer results. I have noticed that my contempt for many of my colleagues' pretensions and stupidities has another side —my own unique righteousness and wisdom. So you get into an infinite series of barbershop mirrors: are all my hates just petty little jealousies to make me feel good? And in spite of my contempt for academic pretensions I have certainly made my efforts rooting in the scholarly vineyard. On the one hand I spurn my colleagues' values, but I behave as if I desperately want to be recognized by them. And I guess I do.

I often wonder if I would do it again; and I honestly don't know. Many of my friends romanticize working class jobs; farming, auto repair, carpentry. I don't, and I would not do such work if I could avoid it. From what I have seen, it is a way to work hard, become injured, and stay poor. None of these appeals to me. And there is a whole world of other jobs I know virtually nothing about, so it is hard to compare academic life with what it might really be like to do some other job. So, I might do it again, but who knows, since I backed into it in the first place. Parts of the academic life are rewarding, and I have never believed that a job would be entirely wonderful anyway. As long as you don't hate it, you aren't too bad off. I guess that's a good way to close, because from what I can tell that attitude is itself a result of my origins. Middle class folk expect to have rewarding careers. That was in the pact between God and their families. Other folks have jobs. And if they're lucky, the jobs aren't too bad. Compared with the rest of my family, I'm lucky.

Sam Butler

Would I seek some other kind of work? Hopefully, I am beyond seeking. Location is important to me. Most of America is a poisonous junkyard. I have job skills I could use to live in better places than where I now live, but I am presently constrained from leaving academia because of my desire to pursue knowledge for the social good. That is the only reason I remain within the university. My destiny is in the hands of God

I was born in Boston in the middle of the Great Depression. My father was a laborer, often unemployed, but he spent everyday on the streets looking for work, for he had a large family to support. We were poor.

My mother was of a working class background and spent her youth working in a shoe factory. I had many relatives working in the shoe industry. My mother's family were German and Irish immigrants. My father was a loner whose family roots lay far back in the early history of the state. He was of a puritanical nature.

We remained poor until the outbreak of World War II, when my father found a steady job in the Naval Shipyard. Since, then he has become a more or less prosperous plumber and has entered into the lower ranks of the middle class

Of central importance to my background is a violent, domineering father, who taught the basic survival traits of capitalist society—meanness, bad temper, authority, and violence. The child, seeing the actions of the father and threatened by the adult male, was exposed to a role model of behavior and acquired characteristics needed to survive in the male-dominated capitalistic society. I was fortunate to have a mother who was loving, cheerful, and sweet and taught the importance of social compassion.

I developed an immediate dislike for my father, for he dropped me on the floor when I was less than a year old.

That was perhaps the origin of my taught resentment and resistance to authority. I generally avoided him when he was at home. On occasion my mother would hide my sister and I when my father was due home from work.

The start of my academic career, however, goes back to the "wonderful gift" my father gave me. He had stocked our house with copies of classics and other great books and was an avid reader. He was intelligent and self-educated beyond his high school education. He conveyed to me the virtues of books and reading, for he was calm and content when he read and did not cause trouble around the house. At times, he was even friendly, giving me a nickel or so to run down to the local market to buy the latest pulp mystery or adventure book. Thus at an early age I was exposed to lurid "literature" portraying violence toward women. I was indeed born into the twentieth century. That my father was self-educated was important, for throughout my career I have studied and worked alone and focused upon self-education, gaining more from reading than I did from teachers.

At five years old I had a major accident. I was deliberately tripped by an unreliable friend and gashed my forehead open against the edge of a granite curb. The wound became infected and I nearly died. At ten I was arrested along with another friend for trying to set fire to a pile of leaves. I was fairly innocent and later in life discovered my friend was a pyromaniac. But my father beat me with a set of staghorn antlers, anyway. That experience promptly taught me never to kill deer and to hate cops, and intensified my resistance to authority. On another occasion my father hit me so violently on the head I became more or less permanently half deaf on the right side.

I grew up in a mono-ethnic neighborhood, and because I was of mixed descent, had trouble finding friends. As a youngster, to find friends, I was forced to hike to other parts of town. When I was eleven or twelve, I finally found a good friend named Phil. He was three years my senior, lived in a wealthy section of town, his father was a prominent physician, and his mother was high in social prestige. Phil was being groomed for Harvard, for his father and older brother preceded him. Phil taught me a lot and opened me to the possibility of going to college, for I was his intellectual peer.

As Scouts, we gained a considerable reputation, for we won every contest which was offered. He got accepted to Harvard, but Harvard turned me down twice.

At fourteen I was shipped away to spend the summer working on a poultry farm. It was not a good experience. The following year I received a permanent summer job with the Public School Department, which I retained for eight summers. Those summers I spent working out-of-doors in close contact with school teachers who were supplementing their incomes by working summers. It was good experience; I learned skills, received a good moral education, and made money to allow me to finance my own college education.

At age fifteen I announced to my mother that I was going to college. She explained that I had to get that idea out of my head for the family had no money. I said I would pay my own way. It worked out fine, for my father acquiesced to the idea. At that time, my father was still a laborer, but was taking trade courses and preparing himself for what was to be a successful career as a plumber.

After graduation, I held a job in industry for three years. I married a girl from a bourgeois family. She attended a prestigious, private college and eventually got a job as a teaching adjunct in the university in the town where we lived. We had the chance to intermingle with faculty on a social level, for we lived in a faculty neighborhood and attended functions of the department in which she worked. I decided then to become a professor.

I received a master's degree from the local university, and because I did well, was accepted for the doctoral program at an ivy league university. I had an easy time with doctoral studies and did extremely well. I was accepted as a member of the volleyball club, enjoyed myself socially, and raised a family. But I remained naive about social and political reality.

During graduate school, I was an ivory tower academician and received the appropriate laurels and degree. But I set aside a pile of books on social, political, and economic criticism which I intended to read at some future time. Upon completion of the dissertation, I eagerly turned to these books and promptly became radicalized, destroying my usefulness as a conventional, middle-class scholar. But my career had been set. I spent the years at my first university position engaged in intellectual, cultural, and political radicalism.

Central to my radicalism was a resentment of authority and a constant struggle against it. Academic authority was among the totalitarian systems I resisted, first, because it was authority, and second, because of divergence in fundamental values. Academic authorities with whom I have had the most trouble have all come from higher class backgrounds, have been intolerant of diversity and questioning, and have shown little, if any, understanding, wisdom, or compassion. Academic institutions with their layers of authority and administration, represent the basic hierarchical, totalitarian model used throughout human history to concentrate and maintain power. As such, the structure is a contradiction of democracy. My emotional roots are closely connected to those who struggle against totalitarian systems. I see myself as part of humanity's temporal and spatial struggle against tyranny.

At present, the administration of the university where I am employed is part of a chain of dominance and repression which extends downwards from the local, extremely powerful corporations. The administration openly brags about its connections with "free enterprise." Concepts of truth, knowledge, and justice have long since been sold for corporate dollars. The repressiveness of the administration is well recognized by the faculty, but the faculty members here are wimps and weaklings, too afraid and too apathetic to fight for justice, freedom, and humanity.

My experience with students has always been good, for I approach each student with love and consideration, and I appreciate differences among individuals. I have no problems with students of higher class backgrounds and have become quite friendly with many of them. Basically, my relationships with students is the usual professorial one based upon differences in knowledge rather than upon class distinctions. I do feel, however more sympathetic toward students of lower class backgrounds and would prefer teaching in a university or college which draws heavily from lower class students.

In some aspects, my job has worked for me, for I enjoy

teaching and intellectual pursuits and have been able to use my position to work for social reform. In other respects, however, the job has not worked at all, for the basic values of the profession and other faculty members mark me as an outsider: one who questions, challenges, and attacks the system and structure upon which dominant modes of behavior are based. As a result, I often feel tense, alienated, and uncomfortable with my surroundings. I have also experienced considerable job insecurity and have been dismissed from positions because of value differences.

After being absent from university teaching for a number of years, I remember the horror upon returning to realize that to function as a successful academician it would be necessary to adopt a middle class role. I clearly see how a middle class background is conducive to academic success. Barriers of class can be overcome, but it is more of a struggle because one does not have the "proper" values, attitudes, social training, and respect. The necessity to adopt a middle class role is not only a question of the dominating values of the institution, which have to be at least partly accepted in order to survive, but extends to fundamentals of life such as dress, appearance, lifestyle, and interests.

To me, the middle class requirement is like turning my back upon friends in the ghettos and communes of America. I am willing to make the sacrifice but only in order to maintain an effective position to work for reform. My periods of university employment have been mainly used to work for social change, most commonly sacrificing the rules of the game of academic survival in order to achieve what I considered to be some higher purpose. I use mind and position to struggle against the repressive dominance of the technological-socio-political-economic system, and I'll lose my job in the end. I have the proven ability to publish, but my time is used in the social struggle and in searching for a job to replace the one I am about to lose.

How do I feel about my colleagues? I love them dearly but yet cannot trust them for often many have proven unreliable. Some of my academic friends with the same class origins as I have succeeded in attaining a high degree of middle class stability, while I am still threatened by loss of my job and a return to working class labor. I refuse to use

my talents to work for large corporations which would pay
well for my services.

What surprises me is how vicious some faculty members
can be. A good number of them are also insane. Many lack
moral fiber, others have dangerous gaps in their education,
and many are whores selling their labor skills to perpetuate
horror. Very few faculty members appear to be kind,
although there are some who clearly are. Some hate students, some have difficulty speaking, and others are motivated by greed, lust, and anger.

Have I enjoyed a sense of membership in the community? Not at all; I have always been outside of the
"select" circle. I continuously find my advancement being
blocked for non-academic reasons, mostly the fact that I do
not fit the bourgeois and academic preconceptions of most
faculty and administrators. In terms of the profession I feel
a deep sense of alienation. Most professional literature I
consider to be misleading or worthless and cannot understand why people spend their energy and effort doing it. I
dislike the smugness and arrogance of most members of my
profession, and in general, find them boring people.

When I was new to the profession I had a fine circle of
friends in it, all from the same class background. In our
unity we were strong. But even then, I was a marginal
member with a great desire to break free.

I find professional meetings and conventions irksome.
They take place in corporate convention centers and hotels,
which to me present despicable features of our society—
class and race orientation of menial labor in contrast to the
white, male dominated profession, lavish and tawdry dis-
plays of wealth, plastics and other obnoxious products of
industrial society, poor taste, and the dress, mannerisms
and habits of corporate personnel. I am dismayed to see the
overwhelming numbers of my profession who have sold
themselves to the three-piece business suit, whose work
often shows lack of social awareness or concern, but who
can still walk in the smugness of self-conceit because they
have sold their minds to corporate masters. I have always
wanted to receive professional recognition, but I have
refused to accept the curtailment of academic freedom and
justice which goes along with it. The stark reality of the

present day technological-socio-economic-political system should mean great scope for work for those in the profession. Instead, most of them bring forth a constant dribble of meaningless waste, propaganda in praise of the system, and endless refinements to things which should not be refined at all. I turn my attention to praying for peace.

I am grateful for my education and the chance to work for the social good. I find the university confining with its phosphorescent light, unreliable colleagues and job insecurity. Would I choose another profession? Perhaps not. I am a teacher. I would wish, however, to be three or four times more intelligent, much wiser, spiritually accomplished, and with a better ability to communicate in both the written word and orally. I would love to stand in front of classes all day and teach and talk with perfect, clear enunciation, lucidity of expression, and an infinite reservoir of truth, strength, and joy upon which to draw to illuminate the profundities of great knowledge and wisdom.

It is a question of people versus the "machine." The machine with its club-toting, black-helmeted paramilitary, its greedy power-lusting politicians and leaders, its Huey helicopters, its weapons, and destructive nature, its rape, violence, and destruction of planet earth, and the abyss which lies at the feet of the human race. The machine thrusting itself up in the acne pimples, sore-pus of nuclear reactors, and weapons and all the rest too horrid here to describe. And the university is a niche in the machine with its stockholders, wheeler-dealers, and engineer whores, sold-out liberals, ignorant conservatives, and boards of trustees. The students are so innocent, young, and amenable to education. The university is a flow; students flow through and faculty do too.

Some day I shall return with knowledge. My old image of swooping down out of the hills to ransack the machine with a wild-fanged, hungry pack of wolves, birds, elephants, trees, and snakes, Indian mystics, crazy dope-toting freaks, Commies, Socialists, and Wobblies to recapture production and use it for good is gone. In its place there is wisdom, compassion, and love within each individual—violent father, arrogant faculty—I see a human soul struggling to be free. With some wisdom I return, the way is clear,

I am free: the liberation of the human soul.

It is time to put my boots back on and go out into the world of men, away from ignorant faces of academic whores, stale air, and the dark lights of academic careers.

John Koonings

> I can not see myself ever being a member (of the) academy) with full honors. In fact, it would be terribly difficult for me to accept such membership if so honored. I may have moved physically and economically into a new class, but my psyche is dragging. When non-academics ask me what I do, I experience a strong twinge of embarassment...
>
> I do not work as hard as my father did. I make at least five-times as much money as he ever made in his life. I even own my own home, something he never did. But I must admit that there are moments when I believe that those things have cost me the relationships, the cultural ties, the human interactions which define man most humanly

I do not belong in "The Academy." My perception of the situation is that at best I am an interloper, at worst I am a spoiler. There are places in the institution for two types of persons: those who have prepared for it by attending other institutions which provided them with the proper disdainful and genteel attitiudes and styles, and those who are exceptionally bright. I fit neither category. To say this does not mean that I do not belong in higher education. I do.

I am a product of the state university which cared little for my attitudes and demeanor. And, it was willing to accept my reasonably high level of mediocrity. By doing so, it afforded to me and to my posterity an opportunity for survival in a more carefree, less strenuous manner than my predecessors enjoyed. I formed membership in "The Academy." The knowledge and skill which I acquired were sufficient for me to aid others in the same struggle, a nd that is why I do belong in higher education.

It seems to me that a problem arises here, for just as the university wrought change in my status and nature by allowing me to be part of it, "the Academy" has wrought change in itself by giving broader entry to higher education, and therefore to me. It seems to me that those who constitute "the Academy" do not look favorably upon all those who constitute higher education. It is for this reason that I feel that I am an interloper. And, the more of me there are, the more of me there will be. For that reason I feel I am a spoiler, almost a despoiler.

I am disillusioned. It may be that my disillusionment results from false perceptions; I am not certain. I am certain that my disillusionment is self-caused. When I first began to think I might strive for membership in "the Academy," I viewed it with awe and reverence. I recall that during my interview to enter graduate school I exhibited awe and reverence by repeating frequently that I fervently wished to learn, to reduce my level of ignorance, and that I would do anyhting to be given a chance to fall under the tutelage of men such as the committee members. I am certain those hearing me did not wish to assume such an awesome repsonsibility; nevertheless, they did. I imagined then that I was to be initiated into the priesthood where I would have access to the secrets of the universe.

My first disillusioning experience occurred when I took a course in symbolic logic. I thought that here were the priests of the inner temple. What I discovered were chess-masters. My second disillusioning experience occurred when I finally received my robe and miter and began to function at the level of my colleagues. What I discovered was that, although those who people higher education are better informed, they are neither wiser nor nicer than those people who frequented the bar where my father worked. I can not lay the blame for this disillusionment at the feet of "The Academy." I can lay it at my own feet. My expectations were too high and unjustified.

My only excuse is that I was naive. The environment in which I was raised did little to provide me with an accurate picture of the world and its institutions. My father earned very little money during his working life and the jobs he held offered little stimulation. He tended bar for much of my early youth. During my high school years he drove a laundry delivery truck. As a result, we lived in an area with other "working class" folk. The school I attended reflected my family's status. It offeed little more than discipline, for it was expected than we would reproduce our parents. My step-mother worried a great deal about my being able to get a good job, about paying off the loan company for past Christmases, and about cleanliness. My father seemed neither to worry about anything except his past successes as a manager-trainee with the J.C. Penny company and the fact that the Army turned him down because of a heart murmur. My Welsh grandmother worried a great deal about my soul; but only for a few years.

No one in my neighborhood worried much about education. The social/academic structure of my high school was an almost exact replication of my town. Children from my neighborhood were treated in accordance with the worries or lack of worries of their parents. Those who were not good football or basketball players were "tracked" into vocational or "business education" programs so they could get a job. College was like a mystery. Learning was reserved for the deserving and/or the intelligent.

The family and neighborhood in which I lived were powerless to combat the larger environment, including the school. The people lacked the know-how and the self-esteem. I think the extent of that powerlessness is exhibited in one one way by my mother's comment when at 25 years of age, I told her than I had decided to "go to college." Her response was "Why would you want to do that? You have a good job." It is exhibited in another fashion by the fact that my father never wanted for customers at 6:30 in the morning when he opened the bar. The first shift at the mill two blocks away began at 7:00.

My break with that culture came when I graduated high school and joined the Navy. As a result, I discovered that I could indeed learn and that the world beyond my neighborhood was startlingly different, something for which I was unprepared. During this time I realized that many of the people with whom I had been raised were like stereotypes. I began to believe that I too had been stereotyped and was performing accordingly. Although I did terribly well in two Navy communications schools, most of my career was spent engaged in two "working class" activities, drinking and drinking. However, I did begin to read a bit. During my entire public school career, I had read only one novel, *Hot Rod*. As a business major, I was not required to read anything but the textbooks. The Naval library took me one step further into the new culture, The reading I did there planted a seed which finally took hold, but not until I had returned t civilian life and spent some time in a good job.

When a friend (who is now my wife) began to attend college, I began to wonder if I too might be able to do so. It was an option now only because my Naval career moved me enough to be able to view college as a challenge. I accepted the challenge and won.

I am not certain that my price was/is worth the victory. In the main, I do not share the values of my colleagues, at least as I perceive those values. I have managed to make a certain level of contact with a few persons of similar backgrounds and I think similar attitudes. However, I can not see myself ever being a member with full honors. In fact, I think it would be terribly difficult for me to accept such membership even if so honored. *I may have moved physically and economically into a new class, but my psyche is dragging.* When non-academics ask me what I do, I experience a strong twinge of embarrassment. That embarassment seems to have two sources. The first source is my recognition that I have "moved up." With that comes guilt from the recognition and the admission of the fact. Secondly, the embarrassment comes because I have not yet been able to accept that what I did constitutes a Good Job. My stepmother does indeed offer me up as her son, the college professor, the first in the family ever to go to college, the one who "Granny always said would amount to something." Yet when I go home, no matter how hard I try, I can not go home. The gulf is there, and the praise seems ludricous.

The praise does not seem deserved. There seems to be no basis for it. The culture I came out of was one in which men and women worked long difficult hours for small amounts of money and prestige. Many died young. Many were ignorant. Many were wise. Is what I have done so marvelous that I deserve special social recognition? It seems that to say "Yes" would degrade alot the background from which I have come.

These conflicts, which are a direct result of my meeting the challenge of college, translate into problems in my interactions with students. Many of them come from "well-to-do" backgrounds. They attend college to acquire a passport to a good job. On the one side of my soul is resentment that they appear to move into the chute with such ease. I am therefore quite glib at chastising them for not recognizing their opportunities and for not making the most of them. In essence, I think I am chastising them for not having to.

Because of this, and because of my own insecurity regarding my "qualifications" to be here, I experience much trauma when I must evaluate students. As a result of not thinking I am good enough, I inadvertently demand of them performances comparable to my own, after 16 years and a Ph.D. Yet, I hesitate to judge them, both because I feel I am not qualified, and because I know that they can not meet the inflated standards. Eventually, I blame myself for the whole thing. Had I entered "The Academy" on one of the two grounds mentioned earlier, style or intelligence, I do not think I would experience the same conflict. Those who have been "born to The Academy" are here to preserve it or to expand it and seemingly experience no qualms over black-balling potential members. The intelligent and the fit have an equally clear criterion for judging. It seems then, as a judgement of my progress, that I have alienated myself from my beginnings by moving into a culture which offers me few, if any, binding, sustaining points of contact. I do not work as hard as my father did, though I make at least five times as much money as he ever did. But I must admit that there are moments when I believe that those things have cost me the relationships, the cultural ties, the human interactions which define people most humanly.

There does, however, seem to be one benefit which accrued to me. I can recognize that I am neither particularly content nor welcome in the academic number and I can articulate it. Strangely, those men who were waiting at 6 a.m. for my father to open the bar seemed to sense the same plight in their lives. And, in their own way, they too were able to articulate it.

Conclusions

W hat might we say here, in our concluding note, that
has not already been said by ourselves or by our
contributors? What perspective can we add that is
not already here, what summation might even be possible?
Perhaps none. Yet, we feel the need for a final tying together
of the various strands of this book, especially those woven
midst the struggles and attempts at accommodation described in the past four chapters. Are there common meanings in
those twenty-four stories?

i.

To begin with, it is not possible to predict how many of
our travelers to the professional managerial class would
have made it had it not been for the time of their departure.
As a factor related to the huge expansion of higher education, duly noted, military experience played an especially
big role in opening the world and providing financial support to several of our respondents. O'Malley, Bastian, Koon
ing, Anderson, Brown, and in lesser ways, also Cole and
Bowen, attribute to military experience the opportunity for
self-discovery and financial support. Would they have
found the focus or wherewithall to wend their way to college
and/or graduate school and ultimately to the gates of the
academy without these interventions of war, largess, broad-
ening horizons? Probably not. Beyond military experience,
Nathan Green and John Adamson scratched their way

through graduate school on federal loans; Potter, hardly bookish, was nutured by an expanding state university system that seemed to be looking for homegrown talent. Hence, in about half of our reports, military experience, federal loan programs and the G.I. bill played a major role in making it possible and imaginable for the individual to move on to a career path leading to significant mobility.

Also, noteworthy, many of our respondents reported an early lack of distinction that might have indicated a potential for academic work. Brown, though a good student, concentrated on business and commercial subjects. O'Malley recalls high school as a vague blur. Kooning remembers reading one book in high school, a classic called *Hot Rod*. Anderson enjoyed social life and was indifferent to academic recognition. Cole stayed at home (where he never had friends, an indistinguished loner). Sanger flunked the first grade.

Among those who *do* report early recognition of talent, the picture is inconsistent. A fine example is Finder, who tested well, but did not perform well in school. One of his strongest high school memories is the day he cleaned out the school janitors shooting craps. His career expectations do not seem to have gone beyond working with his father in the fish store. Then, that fateful day comes when he slashes his fingers, rendering him useless as a dismemberer of cod and mackeral. Adamson also tested well, but he was also an underachiever. And so it went in the lives of most of our contributors, becoming professors in spite of backgrounds that in no reported instances provided early encouragement for an academic career path. To be sure, these stories are not ones of simple meritocratic selection of the brightest and most promising aspirants for a place in the sun, though most were surely as bright as youngsters, as adults, most were also simply "extra-hands," called up in an emergency. Most of our contributors also are people who discovered their talents late in life, seized the opportunities offered by friendly circumstances and followed their stars. While we do not wish to diminish their accomplishments in any way, we insist their success in no way affirms the claim that U.S. society is the stuff of the American Dream. Clearly, it was a combination of their talent *and*, most especially, historical circumstances and happenstance that made possible their upward movement. And, our respondents would be unlikely recruits in today's declining academic job market, unless, of course, no one else can be found to join this profession in decline, and workers must again be recruited from the lower ranks.

Let us also recall the origins of these travelers and wonder for a moment if it is imaginable that they could ever feel at home in the U.S. academy. Those who traveled the greatest distance came from bookless homes, bare shacks, workers' hovels, dirt farms. Their fathers were itinerant preachers, low skill workers, farmers, awning salesmen in an age of air conditioning, disabled miners. For those who have traveled less far, those who emerge from the higher reaches of the working class or the lower middle class, some with families mired in a sense of failure, broken dreams, frustrated ambition, we have another set of dilemmas, but similar outcomes. The common triumph took them to the walls of academia, to stand behind lecterns, sit behind polished desks, roam library stacks, talk smart, sip tea. Is it likely many such people ever would feel at home in such places? Professor Potter, as an example, carves out a distinguished career; he is praised as a teacher, respected as a colleague, rises to administrative rank and yet still wonders if he can get through another day without it being "found out" that he really doesn't belong. Professor Brown imagines that he is classless and that he can pass for someone who has "prepped." Professor Puck, God bless him, thinks he "belongs" at his Ivy League University, but no one else does! What, then, did they all do with this out-of-placeness? Let's remember briefly the essays.

ii.

Estrangement and disillusionment with the university are, not surprisingly, the most common difficulties identified by our respondents, no matter what their mode of accommodation or their relative satisfaction with their lives as professors. Estrangement is a variant or combination of the feelings of not belonging, not fitting in, not wanting to fit in or belong, and feeling distances from one's class of origin.

This ensemble of feelings is a crucial component of the phenomenon of internalized class conflict. It should be recalled that such conflict contains a political component which recognizes the antagonistic relationship between the working class and the *PMC*. The conscious recognition of the political component seems diffuse for most of our respondents. What is clear, though, is the sense of not belonging and, more often than not, feeling one degree or another of contempt for those who do "belong."

The sense of not belonging flows smoothly into the other commonly expressed source of distress, disillusionment with the academy. The charges against the university cover a wide range, are well known to the reader by now: the careerism and conformism of colleagues, perverted authority relationships within the academy, the failure of the university to serve sound and laudable academic or social values, are the main ones. For the most part, awareness of the location of the university in the class structure is much in evidence. In fact, many contributors continue to see the university as a progressive institution, or at least one that can be turned to progressive purposes. Yet, the estrangement and disillusionment touch, if they do not fuse, into a common knot of resentment.

For those of our contributors who *accept* the university for what it is or seek acceptance in it, the struggle with being an outsider, disillusioned with university mandarins, is nonetheless visible in some cases. Brown has traveled a great social distance, from grinding early childhood poverty to a highly successful academic career marked by rapid advancement up the ladder of success. Not surprisingly, he has little quarrel with the university and his career in it. Indeed, later in his career he is told he could pass for someone who has "prepped at Choate." He has truly succeeded in overcoming the constraints of his origins, both in form and substance; and, ironically, he would share with those of our contributors, who have ferociously held onto their working class life styles, a general sense of wanting to avoid the animus of middle class professional life. Bowen also enjoyed rapid career advancement. In fact, more than all our contributors, it seems he is neither outsider nor disillusioned. His career moves from advneture to adventure. His tension is more the strain between security, on the one hand, and the excitement of the next career challenge. It seems he has dodged the bullets of the mobility trip entirely, even surviving emotionally the experience of being fired from a job at the top of the academic hierarchy.

Green, no art connoisseur or lover of foreign films, is quite aware of his cultural distance from academic style. Yet, it would seem a small matter. More his concerns are the academic loafers, shirkers, and phonies that clutter his work space. Most significantly, his career is stuck in a second rate school, and he is overworked and underpaid. He continues to believe that if he were to get unstuck and move on and up to better work conditions, the rest of these difficulties would fall easily within the zone of tolerance. Similarly, Biltmore makes no apologies for his presence in academia. He knows—he learned the hard way—academia is not paradise. His criticisms of colleagues and administrators bubble with venom. In his own career, he seems bumped, bruised and battered. But when they get off his back and show him deserved appreciation, he is content to go about his business, advancing progressive causes in the classroom. In sum, these respondents, though they may feel outside, and have had their share of disillusionments, expected and in most cases achieved the satisfactions they looked for in the mobility experience.

For those who accommodate through the discovery of *separate pathways*, it is a different matter. Finder notes that his political consciousness and his intellectual development grow together when he begins college. He meets his political enemies in the fray. His antagonism with academia is sharp. He is an outsider, but it is matter of class struggle and inevitable estrangement. The university is awash with corruption, sychophants and cowards. He makes meaning for himself elsewhere, beyond the walls of the academy, in his writing and research and in his commitment to progressive social change. Though very much outside, he is not particularly disillusioned, since he seemed to recognize the class location of the university early in the game. He has found a resolution in politically purposeful action.

Puck, too, is an outsider. He chose to build walls around himself and run his own college. His contempt for the university and colleagues seems total. Changing the university would involve changing the structure of western civilization. Since he considers this task beyond his capacity, he builds his own college and lets the rest of the university "go to hell with itself." Puck believes he is true to himself and the ideal of the university. He is not the stranger: it is the university that is estranged from itself.

Potter reports strain on both fronts. His sense of belonging is tenuous. In spite of a career of recognition and achievement, culminating at a high level of academic administration, he anticipates "being discovered," humiliated and expelled. On the other side of the dilemma, Potter finds the university a weak shadow of his expectations. Within it, he seeks to enlist support for political issues that concern him and to push decision structures toward democratization and openness. His disillusionment sets him on a path of challenge to the prevailing *status quo*. The weight of feeling outside and the untrackability of the flawed university are heavy upon him, as is the professional style of colleagues. Adamson tries to solidify his position by concentrating on his love for teaching, but feels adrift in much of the world in which he works. A prominent symbol of his alienation is the oar above his dean's desk, an ironic backdrop to any conversation they might have about the search for truth and beauty and justice.

For those looking to *balance* class location, the accommodation that they seek seems more a conscious matter of coming to terms with their past, their roots, and somehow integrating them with current realities of their lives. In some respects, their issues are more focused on finding a balance point between their two historical selves, if not an integration of them. While they have problems with the structure and style of the academy, their attachment to the academy seems more their animating concern.

Wilson's story is especially interesting in this regard. She sought to combine her choice of academic discipline with scholarly interest in her past, in the Pennsylvania Dutch farm tradition. Wisely, she does not imagine that the university is a place where she can find what she is looking

Conclusions 315

for, a niche to give voice to her people and herself. She realizes she must create the niche—and therein tie the ribbons of her life experience together. It seems as though she is one of the lucky ones who can "go home again," if she chooses, for in some ways, she has not yet really left.

Jones seeks to separate his life rather than integrate the antagonistic parts. He constructs his social life in a working class neighborhood; he tries to make it his own. Yet the racism he encounters and the rejection of his political views by friends and neighbors make the fit a bit ragged. By day, he travels off to the university where he seeks to advance progressive ideas. His two worlds do not seem to touch. Sparks fly when they do.

Pappas surveys his journey, assesses his good fortune, but, in spite of working hard to promote a better world, hardly expects meaningful rewards in life from his successful career. He seems to be pulling into family and home, in the tradition of ethnic families of the past, home and family, a fortress. Trent, a young academic, a post-1970 entrant, seems fully emeshed in the strains of class mobility. There is consistency here with her early precosity. She had discovered the "Stranger in Paradise" syndrome early in her career. Her mother, devoted to her daughter's advance to the good life through the use of her gift of intelligence, has become someone with whom it has become difficult to discuss things. There loom the pain of cultural distance and the sting of betrayal. Academic pretense and polite exchanges on the contemporary art scene leave her cold. For now, she looks to "new wave," new associations, breaking out, seeking the grounds for accommodation which might pull it all together. Frost is saddened by the fact that he cannot make real contact with people from his background and suffers their alienation, as well as his own. And, Hall sums it all up, when he says, of his work, "I love it and I hate it!" He has discovered the worst part of all to be the necessity of crushing the dreams of others in order to realize his own.

And lastly there are those who have found *no accommodation*; they either remain on the margin in bitterness or at a level of extremely reduced expectation. Anderson's essay bristles with contempt for bourgeois, academic personal styles, and flames with indignation at the university's failure to live up to minimal expectations. The weight of his anger is heavy on him. O'Malley has tried just about everything to make it work. But, his is the sense of being out of place, ill-equipped and turned off by the academic style of colleagues and the business climate of his work station. His class consciousness is sharp; his attempted accommodations flat. He hangs in, but plots and fantasizes escape to God knows what or where. Butler's somewhat promising career crashes on his awareness of the class location of the university and his recognition of the cost of changing social classes to his sense of politics and personal integrity. The prospect of betrayal looms. He, too, fantasizes, and once, in his most despairing years, they were fantasies of vengeance where he and his brothers rose to smash the toxic order of the university. Brent, like Anderson and O'Malley, has little to hold on to. He is very much an outsider and has little hope that the university can be anything other than a conduit for privileged young people moving on to high places. Yet, he appreciates his job, if not his work life. He is better off than his father. He doesn't want to go back to arduous toil or to the indignities of low status work. Without joy, he stays. It is the barest of accommodations, if accommodation at all. John Koonings's essay concludes the collection. It is touching and insightful. He has traveled a great social distance. The burden of the journey seems to make it impossible for him to feel any sense of full membership. He remains an outsider and now, outside. To some degree, the university survives in his mind as paradise; he is a stranger and he can't go home again. He even wonders a bit if he should ever have left home.

iii.

So, the themes of estrangement or disillusionment, or the two in combination, are dominating motifs of these accounts. Horatio Alger's story appears alongside lost dreams, dashed hopes, despair, disappointment, anger, isolation. Some contributors are adrift, and some are encaged. Some are at the end of this journey; and others at the beginning. Two or three are actually winners of the natural lottery, who combined talent with opportunity and left home to make a better life. Probably none would deny that it has indeed been a better life than the one that might have been had they stayed on the farm, in the mine. We doubt if any would have chosen to be left behind, to deal with low level status, toil or deprivation, accepting the lot of losers.

Further the essays confirm what we knew to begin with: *the myth of upward mobility* is largely a grand lie that expands the occasional rags-to-riches story into a tall tale about how our society distributes its opportunities. Our historical chapter tells us, and our contributors tell us—again and again—the details that belie the myth. And, even those like Brown and Bowen, who make it big and enjoy their success, end up feeling classless, one actually launching onto an entirely different career at age sixty, fired from the job he had worked for all his life.

We have confirmed, too, the limits of the grand analytical mode, marxist or non-marxist, which can help to point us *toward* the truth but cannot tell us once there what we will find *people doing*. Details, details, details! Those are the real elements of an individual life, and, when they are aligned into a story, an autobiography, they remind us with great force that it is human beings who inhabit the neighborhoods of this world, not the conceptual aggrandizements being spun out without end and with abandon by academic theorists. These are no small conclusions, at least to us, for one of *our* problems with the academy has been the difficulty with taking very seriously the ongoing silliness that comprises the "serious"scholarship of many of our colleagues. How sour, indeed, have our feelings been toward those grand conceptions that accomplish the dual task of omitting people *and* justifying and/or ignoring the inequalities of market capitalism at the same time.

The essays, lastly, confirm for us certain truths about the American university. We have found in the stories mostly agreement with our own experience that the campus is not paradise. Primarily, this is true because universities are an integral part of the same class system that denies a fair shake to most of the population: they are a theater where people play out the culture's scripted roles as they struggle for recognition, reward, profit, a preferred place in the smaller or broader pecking order of the profession. Universities are also to a degree responsible for much of the injustice in America because of their role in certifying, accrediting and tracking students. Why would we ever expect *contentment* on the part of faculty there who come from the lower stations? And, how could such academics fail not to harbor resentment against colleagues, the great majority of whose productive work and political stances prove their *utter* disinterest in the fate of those below them in society?

iv.

There seems no more space here for conclusions. We write, at this point, with hope we've been generous hosts to our contributors and treated their trust in us by saying something true about the context in which they made their way upward. We write, also, feeling flush from the learning we have done in the task that the book came to be. And, we close with a final story, one we believe that encompasses all that has meaning for us in the matter. And, it all happened to us on a weekend day, while we were all stirred up together in some part of the papers that became this book.
book.

It was a beautiful autumn day on a well-endowed private university campus in the Northeast, where one of us teaches. It was Parents' Day, and this little piece of paradise was a veritable swarm of well-to-do people, regaled fashionably, progeny in tow. They were making their way down to the football field to watch Saturday's heroes do their thing, part of the usual routines set upon the agenda of such a day on hundreds of colleges and universities around the nation.

In the midst of this splendor, this parade of successful Americans, established and soon to be established, we spied a little band of intruders: before us was a family clad differently. The woman wore a gaudy, flowered print dress. She was overweight, her body looking heavy and worn from the years of some unnameable collection of burdens. The gentleman appeared in a crude plaid shirt and baggy trousers. He looked to us as someone whose body had never been adorned with a blue blazer and crisply-creased, lime-green slacks, clearly the attire of the day at this ritual of American life. This family was out of uniform. Yet, the young person with them, decked in the latest "campus casual," was not perceptibly different from others of his generation winding their way down to the stadium on this memorable autumn day.

At an earlier point in our own lives, we may not even have seen this little interloper family, given our own sense of astonishment that we ourselves were part of the splendor; that had we wanted to, we could have been roaming happily with the propertied and comfortable class of citizens who walked these green lawns with their heirs. How far we had come from our origins to this wonderful world of accomplishment! At last, we were among them! At that earlier point in our lives, had we even noticed the interlopers we might have reflected upon the generosity of open societies, where upward mobility is the payoff for the meritorious and the hard-working.

Yet, at this much later stage of our lives and understanding, what we felt and observed and wondered about was quite different. What was this little band of interlopers actually *feeling* amidst their class superiors? How did the young man feel about the public display of his shitkicker parents? Could he have felt pride that they grew the food that fed this fashionable mob of winners? Where were the others? Were there youngsters there who had convinced their parents not to come? Or were there parents who had chosen not to, fearful of blowing Junior's cover? Perhaps worse yet, did some of the parents make a trip to Wards the week before to acquire an affordable replica of the uniform of the day, hoping to pass by avoiding close scrutiny. We wondered what an interloper in this finery might have replied had someone really at home there—a psychologist and her husband, the owner of a Buick dealership and his wife—inquired: "And, what do you do for a living?" Would the intruders lie? Stammer? Or would the man say only, "I am a worker, or a farmer, a miner, clerk, bus driver, and this is my wife. She works part-time in the kitchen at the local mental hospital."

We wondered, too, about those who *did* belong in this crowd. How had they actually earned the money that gave them advantage over all the others? Had they lied and cheated? Exploited their workers? Were they mean and ornery? Stupid, but lucky? We wondered about all the families in America without recognized accomplishment, whose children didn't turn the corner that day, who stayed close to home or who had gone bad, who had tried but "failed," those for whom no place had been set at the banquet. We even asked each other if it were possible that the little farm family actually felt a sense of belonging; that we had projected upon them all the discontents of the people whose essays were in our book.

We wondered, too, how long it will be before the American dream, like all others, is awakened to; how long it will be before there comes that generation of parents down below who are unwilling to accept the suppression of the full human rights of their own children.

We wondered, finally, the degree to which that collective suppression is a result of the fact that we—and our contributors—had cut and run to join the bosses the very first chance that came along.

Appendix A: Letter Asking for Essays

Dear

We enthusiastically and warmly welcome you to participate in our book, currently underway, and tentatively entitled, "Strangers in Paradise: The Experience of Working Class Academics." You are one of approximately one hundred-fifty academics we know or have been told, were raised in "working class" families. As such a person, we are interested in getting from you a short autobiographical statement about these origins and about your experiences as an academic.

We two were raised in working class families, and, together, we have over thirty-five years of experience as college professors. And, conversations over the past years, where we have often exchanged feelings, attitudes, hopes and dreams about the academy, have led us to believe that our experience there has been substantially different, in many ways, from that of colleagues from different backgrounds. We intend to explore and examine these assumptions in this book.

Attached here is one of the autobiographies that we have already received which exemplifies well the kind of information that would be most useful to us. This essay, written by someone in his forties who teaches political science, is approximately the best length for our purposes, and it is especially useful because it very directly discusses class origin and academic experience. However, we have not attached this essay as the only "model" one might follow. We would hope only that contributors adhere to the following rough guidelines:

Form: Short essay; long letter; tape.

Content: Some comments, however brief, about parents' occupation. More elaborate comments in answer to the following principal questions: 1) How do you feel about your colleagues and about their values? Have you enjoyed a

321

sense of membership in the academy? 2) How has your experience been with students from a higher income family than your own, what has that been like for you? What has it been like to teach students from your own class background? 3) Has your job(s) worked for you? Would you do it again, or would you seek some other kind of work? 4) What has been your experience with academic authority?

Style: It is most important to us that we get the *information*, rather than polished essays, fit for print in a fine journal. Thus, if you are pressed for time, we encourage you to emphasize content rather than style in your response. In some cases, we will quote from the essays, with minor editing, to guarantee clarity. However, *your anonymity will be very carefully protected,* in any case. Neither our readers, nor our other contributors will ever know who has written what part of the quoted material. But we *will* be happy to mention your name in the Preface, if you choose, along with other contributors who make that choice.

Due Date: We would prefer to have these essays as soon as possible; however, we can receive them by August 30 and still meet deadlines we have set for ourselves.

Finally, we would like to urge you to take the time and effort to participate in this book. The American Dream promises much, as all of us know, and often delivers much less. Therefore, those of us who have risen from working class origins to the academy have experienced an especially big leap. It seems important to us, and we hope it will seem that way to you, to learn more about that experience.

Sincerely,

Charles Sackrey, Department of Economics, Bucknell University, Lewisburg, PA 17837.

and

John Ryan, Department of Politics, Ithaca College, Ithaca, NY 14950.

Enclosure

P.S.—Please return your essay and any other thoughts you might have on the subject to either of the co-authors of this letter.